ARCHAEOLOGICAL DISCOVERIES IN THE HOLY LAND

ARCHAEOLOGICAL DISCOVERIES IN THE HOLY LAND

COMPILED BY

THE ARCHAEOLOGICAL INSTITUTE OF AMERICA

Thomas Y. Crowell Company   *New York*

ESTABLISHED 1834

Contents

POST-BIBLICAL PALESTINE

Introduction

Throughout more than a dozen centuries devout, venturesome pilgrims have sought to evoke the past in the land of the Bible. At the holy places they relived historic events and carried off relics to be treasured as revered artifacts. By the nineteenth century scholars began the search for antiquities—inscriptions, sarcophagi, pottery, and the like—a more authentic evidence, and these found their way into Europe's museums. But not until three quarters of a century ago was scientific archaeology introduced into the Holy Land as a surer method of recovering the past of a land significant for what it gave to western culture.

Archaeology had a modest beginning. In 1890 Flinders Petrie recorded for the first time the stratification of a Palestinian artificial mound, or tell, demonstrating that the history buried in the hundreds of tells that dotted the land could be recovered by his painstaking methods of observation and recording. Archaeology enjoyed a steady growth, and by the beginning of World War II its results had become generally accepted as a trustworthy source for the history of biblical times.

The present volume is a record of approximately twenty years, a witness to the flowering of archaeology in the Holy Land. When account is taken of the number of sites dug, the hundreds of people involved in excavations, the books of reports written during that time, it is obvious that these have indeed been active and significant years.

Why has archaeology burgeoned in Israel and Jordan? There have been several circumstances that have made for a quickening of interest. The most obvious stimulus was the totally unexpected appearance of scrolls in the caves near the Dead Sea, a discovery that opened up an entirely new area for exploration and brought sharply into the focus of scholarly attention a segment of history at the beginning of the Christian era, which before had been virtually neglected by archaeologists.

The course of world history has contributed to the expansion of interest in archaeology. Economic prosperity in America and in Europe following the end of the Second World War has made possible the raising of funds to support large excavations and the handsome publication of results. A corps of European scholars, well trained in the history of Palestine, has found a homeland in Israel, where there are an interested public and eager students and amateurs ready to volunteer for field work. Jordan, the other sovereign state of the Holy Land, has encouraged the co-operation of archaeologists from abroad, allowing them a fair share of duplicate artifacts for the education of a wide audience interested in the history and culture of the land of the Bible.

Archaeologists who have dug in recent years have had the advantage of new techniques. Assisted by such specialists as the palaeoethnobotanist, hydrologist, zoologist, anthropologist, and nuclear scientist, they have been able to utilize a variety of new clues to gain a picture of many formerly neglected aspects of ancient life. Who were the people that lived at a site, and where did they come from? What were their crafts, industries, foods, art, religion? Curiosity about water sources, domestic animals, types of cultivated plants has become of increasing concern. The radiocarbon process for measuring the age of samples of carbon has been a particular boon in enabling the excavator to be more certain than ever before about the date of his discoveries, especially those from remote ages. Thanks to recent developments in science, the past two decades of archaeology in the Holy Land have been amazingly productive of information about how man has lived in the past.

The scene of this activity is small: a circle with a radius of eighty-five miles drawn on the map of Palestine encloses all of the excavations described in the following pages. The span of time documented—the vertical dimension—is a long one. From the earliest Neolithic villages at Beidha, which Diana Kirkbride assigns to about 7000 B.C., down to the building of the Hospice of the Knights of St. John at Akko, in the twelfth century of our era, is a stretch of more than eighty centuries.

The authors of these chapters are the excavators themselves—or those involved in primary research—and most of the accounts of discoveries were written while work was in progress or shortly afterward. Thus the reader of these reports has a privileged point of vantage for viewing this widening horizon of history.

Important discoveries of recent times have been made by other than trained archaeologists. The most celebrated nonprofessional is Muhammad edh-Dhib, the Arab boy who, by tossing a stone into a cave in the cliff overlooking the Dead Sea, discovered the first Dead Sea scrolls. This single act of chance touched off a series of reactions: the excavation of the ruins at Qumran below the cave; the combing of the cliffs along the wadis leading down to the Dead Sea in both Jordan and Israel for caves with ancient treasures; and a burst of scholarly work in the study, discussion, and publication of the new materials—activity that may appropriately be termed a new discipline of study. Without Muhammad edh-Dhib the world might have had to wait for generations or even centuries for the scrolls, the Essenes, the Bar Kochbah letters to become known as they are today.

The accidental discovery of an ancient site has often required an immediate response to salvage the remains before they are irreparably destroyed by looters. A veritable flood of ancient jars in the antiquity shops of Old Jerusalem touched off an alarm that eventually resulted in Paul Lapp's discovery of the remarkable cemetery at Bab edh-Dhra', with its estimated 20,000 burials on the eastern shore of the Dead Sea.

In 1955 an ancient wall was uncovered on a hill near Amman, Jordan, as it was being leveled for the construction of a new airport. Salvage operations undertaken promptly by the Department of Antiquities disclosed that the wall belonged to a Middle-Late Bronze Age temple, in which were such rare objects as plaques of gold leaf, cylinder seals, a bronze sword, daggers, and other implements. Spared from the ravages of progress by the administration of a strict antiquities law, the temple was more fully explored in 1966 by excavators who worked amid the Canaanite ruins to the accompaniment of the roar of jets taking off and landing on the runway beside them.

Rumor has had its role in the archaeological discoveries of these past decades. In the fall of 1953 Uri Shoshani brought word to the Israel Department of Antiquities that Bedouin were searching the caves along a ten-mile strip of the mountainous wasteland bordering the western shore of the Dead Sea between Engedi and Masada. A small expedition was dispatched immediately to test the rumor. Two years later another team explored the region and found that there was evidence that the caves had been inhabited in Chalcolithic times and later in the Roman period. The results were important but not spectacular. In 1960, however, word reached Israeli archaeologists that a clandestine search of the caves of the area by Bedouin from Jordan had yielded important manuscripts. Obviously a more systematic survey had to be made of all the wadis leading down to the Dead Sea between Engedi and Masada.

The area was divided into four sectors, each of which was entrusted to a trained archaeologist. From two campaigns carried out with military thoroughness, one lasting ten days in 1960 and another extending over eleven days in 1961, there have come two of the most spectacular discoveries of recent years. P. Bar-Adon tells of one of these, the finding of a hoard of 429 objects in a straw mat in which they had been wrapped for more than five thousand years. The other find was made in the "Cave of Letters," where Y. Yadin had the good fortune to discover not only letters of Bar Kochbah but a rich hoard of possessions—textiles, wood, mats, baskets, bronze, etc.—of Jews who seem to have been supporters

of Bar Kochbah in his struggle against Rome A.D. 132—135. With his customary promptness Yadin has lavishly published this treasure, so well preserved by favorable climatic conditions within the cave, in *The Finds from the Bar Kokhba Period in the Cave of Letters.*

In the fall of 1951 scholars working on the Dead Sea scrolls in Jerusalem, Jordan, were alerted that an important treasure was being discovered when dealers and Bedouin brought some fragments of scrolls for sale. But the sellers refused to disclose the source. Finally, after weeks of anxiety over the damage that was obviously being done to an uncharted archaeological site, Père R. de Vaux succeeded in getting an Arab to agree to take him to the cave from which the fragments were coming. As he and G. Lankester Harding, then director of the Department of Antiquities of Jordan, approached the opening to a cave, fifteen miles southeast of Jerusalem in the Wadi Murabba'at, they counted no fewer than thirty-four clandestine excavators emerging from their dusty work. Half of them were immediately employed to continue the excavation—this time under the direction of legitimate archaeologists with a license from the Department of Antiquities.

The horizon of our knowledge has also been enlarged for the periods before the Bible. Of no less importance than the discoveries that have thrown light on the period of the beginning of the Christian era are those that document man's progress from cave to house, from food gathering to sowing and reaping, and from hunting to animal husbandry. It is noteworthy that the biblical writers were not without a curiosity about the origins of subsistence patterns and the various crafts. Abel, the first to practice animal husbandry; Cain, the farmer; Enoch, who built a city; Tubal-cain, the metal worker—these are mentioned in the Book of Genesis as innovators in the growth of civilization. The very land that inspired these legendary accounts of man's progress toward civilization is today producing significant archaeological evidence for the stages of growth of human culture.

How exciting the emerging evidence is for the rude beginnings of farming, metallurgy, pottery making, weaving, and other skills and crafts may be seen in the articles by Diana Kirkbride on Beidha, Kathleen M. Kenyon on Jericho, and Jean Perrot on his excavations made near Beersheba. Yet there are other sites that have made significant contributions to our knowledge of the earliest periods of Palestinian culture.

For six seasons, extending from 1951 to 1960, M. Stekelis has excavated at Mount Carmel a terrace in front of a cave that overlooks the Wadi Fallah (Nahal Oren). A sequence of three important cultures has been charted, corresponding in order to similar cultures found at Jericho. A walled camp site of the Natufian (Mesolithic) period was superseded in the following period by an oval-shaped house with walls standing to a height of from eight to nineteen inches. Apparently this domestic settlement was permanent, since with it was a cemetery containing fifty skeletons. Lying above this settlement was a later Neolithic village of fourteen rounded houses with floors of beaten earth and occasionally with paving of pebbles. Arrowheads appear here for the first time. With the invention of the bow a major technological advance had been made. Potential energy could now be stored until the precise moment when it was needed. One man with a bow and a quiver of arrows replaced a large group of men, each with his spear. Such a sequence of deposits at Wadi Fallah records the slow transition from the cave as a shelter to the fortified and protected camp, and then to the stage of community housing with individual units for the smaller groups.

Yet another step in the progress of man in Palestine has been disclosed at the open-air site of 'Ein Mallaha ('Eynan), overlooking Lake Huleh, which Jean Perrot has excavated for five seasons from 1955 to 1961. The village seems to have the distinction of being the first permanent settlement apart from caves yet known. The houses are round and built of stone walls, which in one place stand to a height of about three feet. Pestles and grinders evidence the use of grain for food. Here, as Perrot suggests, may have been the "first experiments at the domestication of cereals." All three layers of houses found at 'Ein Mallaha, with a rich culture that makes use of decorative art on stone vessels, seem to belong to a period, scarcely documented before, lying at the very beginning of village settlements.

The findings from these two excavations of Mesolithic and Neolithic remains, together with the data from Jericho and Beidha, can now be placed in the framework of what had come to light earlier from Garstang's excavations at Jericho, Garrod's work at Mount Carmel, Neuville's explorations and excavations near Bethlehem in the Judaean desert, and occasional sites in Transjordan and elsewhere. The resulting picture shows clearly that Palestine, with its wide diversity of climate, is a crucial area for documenting the long process of the rise of civilization and cities. One can see the small beginnings which later, after millennia of time, were to become the established patterns known so well from the periods after writing took up the story of man's progress and preserved it.

The excavation of cities mentioned in the Bible has been the major concern and has involved the greatest expenditure of effort during these past decades. Interest in biblical history has been the magnet that has drawn excavators to such sites as Jericho, Hazor, Arad, Jaffa, Shechem, Ashdod, and Gibeon. Some, like Jericho, Hazor, and Shechem, had been partly excavated earlier; others were virgin sites.

The general reader may find himself curious about a number of things taken for granted by the field archaeologist eager to tell about what he has discovered and how it relates to other findings. Why did he pick the site? What was he looking for? How did he plan and finance the project? What tools did he use? And what general procedures did he follow? The answers to these questions differ from site to site, but some specific illustrations may be appropriate.

Most excavations are undertaken because there is a problem to be solved. In 1956 G. Ernest Wright was attracted to Shechem, a site that had been turned by former excavators into a maze of exposed rocks and holes—an extraordinary archaeological puzzle. He saw it as an ideal training ground for young biblical scholars, who in addition to field experience could find there a site rich in literary tradition. "Surely," he argued, "if this maze could be made to make sense, then nothing would appear insurmountable." Kathleen M. Kenyon was challenged to reopen work at Jericho by a threefold objective: to excavate tombs, to clear important Neolithic remains discovered by Garstang, and to "obtain additional evidence on the date of the fall of the latest Bronze Age city, presumably to be associated with the Israelite invasion under Joshua. . . ." The site of el-Jib presented a topographical problem: was it or was it not the site of ancient Gibeon, most famous as the place where the sun stood still? Excavations at Ashdod ought to throw light upon the Philistines, a people important in biblical history.

Given a problem and a site that may help to answer it, how does one proceed? First money and manpower are required. Few excavators have been as ready to publish their financial accounts as has Kathleen M. Kenyon, who has listed to the penny her expenditures from 1952 to 1958 at Jericho. Seven seasons cost $84,610, or an average of $12,087 for a season of about three months of work involving a staff of about two dozen people. The money came from forty-three universities, societies, and museums, and from some individuals. Other expeditions have cost more; some, less.

The size of the scientific staff varies considerably. Diana Kirkbride conducted the first three campaigns at Beidha single-handed; not until 1963 did she have additional staff, which in that year numbered six people. As representative of a large archaeological project, the campaign of three months that Yadin carried out at Hazor in 1955 may be taken as typical. A staff of thirty-eight, including field directors, recorders, architects, photographers, surveyors, draughtsmen, pottery restorers, and students were housed in a kibbutz and at a nearby army camp. For offices there were available three prefabricated bungalows and a shed. A light railway, field telephones, and two staff cars were used to solve the problems of communication. While an average of 110 laborers did the heavy work on the tell for eight hours a day, the staff kept to the spartan schedule of work from 5 A.M. to 10 P.M., with only a few short breaks for meals and rest. Generally a staff is composed of technically knowledgeable people with some interested professors and students, who after the work is finished are scattered widely over the world to teach or continue research on some aspect of the results of the expedition.

The equipment of the archaeologist, if one were to believe the cartoonist, consists of a spade or pick carried by a bespectacled figure wearing shorts and a pith helmet. A more realistic picture is that of a supervisor approaching early in the morning a plot five by five meters square and carrying a dusty bag. Inside the bag there would be a curious assortment of equipment: a trowel; a notebook with lined millimeter paper; labels and string for attaching the tag to the basket for the day's accumulation of potsherds; nails; cord; a level; a 20-meter cloth tape and a 2-meter steel tape, for measuring and drawing to scale the vertical section of the plot he is digging; a brush and a knife, for cleaning and lifting small finds; and occasional special equipment for dealing with unusual conditions. The archaeologist may have come on foot from a nearby camp of tents, or commuted by Land Rover from more permanent quarters at some distance. He may even have descended into his cave site on a cliff by a rope ladder, as did the archaeologists working in the Cave of the Treasure.

The inventory of laborer's tools is more limited: the pick; the hoe by which dirt is pulled into a basket; sometimes the shovel; and the wheelbarrow. More skilled workmen use the broom, the brush, the small pick, the trowel, and the sieve. In general they move the dirt slowly and in small quantities so they may have a chance to discover small objects of value.

The achievements of the latest period of archaeological work in Palestine have been made possible because of painstaking work and publications of earlier archaeologists. They established the method and fixed the guidelines of stratigraphy and typology. The confidence with which modern excavators write of the dates of their discoveries has been made possible by a vast accumulation of data extracted from stratified deposits in the formative years of the science.

Long before the beginning of what might be termed scientific archaeology in Palestine there was no lack of interest in the antiquities of the Holy Land. They were collected and studied seriously—particularly those bearing ancient inscriptions. The Mesha stela (found in 1868), with an account of the war between Moab and Israel, and the Siloam inscription (1880) were two of the most important discoveries for the study of the Bible. Neither was made by a planned expedition; like the finding of the Dead Sea scrolls, they were purely the result of chance.

When Petrie cut a trench into Tell el-Hesi, a mound in southern Palestine to which he had been sent by his sponsor, the Palestine Exploration Fund, he kept careful record of the artifacts from each stratum, noting especially such small but significant things as potsherds. He observed that changes had taken place in the forms into which the potter had molded the plastic clay. Variation in style in the making of such everyday but fragile utensils as pottery gave him a key for dating the various levels of accumulated debris in which the pottery was found. Thus, pottery sealed within the strata of a tell, in the order in which it had been built up through the centuries, provided a sure basis for dating—a method, although refined and augmented by new evidence, that has not been superseded to this day. Petrie was the first to treat a tell with the respect it deserved as a unique source for the history of the successive settlements upon it.

Even the word "tell" reaches back to the time when cities were rebuilt upon former ones. The conservative practice is described in a couplet from the poetic oracles in the Book of Jeremiah:

The city shall be rebuilt upon its tell,
And the palace shall stand where it used
to be.   (30:18)

Throughout more than twenty-five centuries the name has clung to the artificial mounds built up by the destruction and rebuilding of cities near some defended pass, strategic trade route, or important water source. The landscape of Palestine is dotted with them. Nelson Glueck charted over two hundred tells in the Jordan Valley between the Yarmuk and the Jabbok rivers, a distance of thirty miles. Some are high—Tell es-Sa'idiyeh towers 138 feet over the surrounding plain; others are discernible by a rise of only a few feet. All of them have on their tops and sides bits of broken pottery, the key for determining the periods in which they were occupied.

With the introduction of Petrie's method, the tells of the Holy Land became the sources for history and not merely hunting places for antiquities. F. J. Bliss continued the excavation of Tell el-Hesi and found no less than eight city levels, each with its own distinctive culture. R. A. S. Macalister chose the biblical city of Gezer, where he excavated from 1902 to 1909; he promptly published three volumes of useful evidence. Samaria, a city prominent in the history of the Kingdom of Israel, was excavated for Harvard University by George A. Reisner from 1908 to 1910. German and Austrian archaeologists began to explore the covered remains of such well-known biblical cities as Taanach (1901–04), Megiddo (1903–05), and Jericho (1907–09). Limited funds were sufficient only for trenching these mounds—a fortunate circumstance, since to Gezer, Samaria, Taanach, Megiddo, and Jericho a later generation of archaeologists was to return with improved methods for checking earlier results. The outbreak of World War I, however, brought an abrupt end to the period that marked the beginning of archaeology in Palestine.

Between the two World Wars archaeology advanced as a science. There were refinements in techniques, particularly in the dating of pottery, as many major excavations were made. Megiddo was the most ambitious project. Strategically located at an important pass in the mountain range, this ancient Armageddon was again the scene of

excavations from 1925 to 1939—this time with adequate funds given by John D. Rockefeller through the University of Chicago. A complex of stable-like buildings, attributed by the excavators to the time of Solomon, ivory carved with exquisite artistry, an elaborately engineered water system, and no less than twenty strata in which the history of the site was carried back into the Chalcolithic period—these discoveries provided a wealth of new data and significant contacts with biblical history.

Almost as ambitious was the work of the University of Pennsylvania at Beth-shan from 1921 to 1933. Four impressive Canaanite temples were uncovered and a record was made of eighteen different levels of habitation reaching back to around 4000 B.C. The British had the good fortune of finding in 1935 and 1938 a total of twenty-one ostraca —letters written in Hebrew in the time of Jeremiah—at Tell ed-Duweir, ancient Lachish. Less spectacular but scientifically significant was the work of W. F. Albright at Tell Beit Mirsim from 1926 to 1932. With patience and a genius for stratigraphy Albright found a sequence of well-stratified layers extending from about 2200 to 586 B.C. The results have become a kind of paradigm for subsequent archaeological work in Palestine.

Not content with the earlier probes at Jericho, Samaria, and Beth Shemesh, new teams worked these sites with notable success. During the period between the wars a new site, Tell en-Nasbeh, was completely excavated by W. F. Badè and the results were published in two useful volumes.

With the outbreak of World War II and the beginning of the troubles in Palestine, field work again ceased. Yet this very lack of opportunities provided the occasion for new syntheses of data and for the publication of reports of former excavations. Thus, at the end of the war and the cessation of troubles in Palestine, the time was ripe for a new start. The achievements of two decades chronicled in this volume could not have been made without the labors of those who began and carried on the science of archaeology in the Holy Land.

Archaeological research—particularly in an area such as Palestine, where it is possible to relate the findings from a tell with writing handed down from the past—does not move forward in a straight line. Hypotheses about the meaning of new findings must be subject to test. New data can invalidate old theories; and it can also supply the missing link in the chain of understanding of some long-buried enigma. The recovery of evidence is not the whole of biblical archaeology; there is the study of evidence, which attempts to form an intelligible and significant segment of history.

While the discoveries of two decades were being made, the process of re-evaluating earlier finds was carried on. The claim that Solomon constructed the famous stables at Megiddo, cited so frequently in popular accounts of archaeology, has been seriously challenged by Yadin, who would now place these remarkable buildings in the century following Solomon's time. The tumbled walls at Jericho, attributed by the excavator of the 1930s to the time of Joshua, are now dated to a time many centuries before the Conquest of Palestine. And what was once thought to have been Solomon's smelter at Ezion-geber appears to the excavator to have been a storehouse or granary.

When one considers how much archaeological work has been accomplished in the past seventy-five years he may wonder about future possibilities. Is it likely that radically new information will turn up? Or has archaeology reached the point of diminishing returns? In 1944 the Government of Palestine published in its official *Gazette* a list of 2,862 archaeological sites on the west bank alone; many have been found since. Only a few more than a hundred of these have been trenched or partly excavated; possibly another hundred have yielded minor bits of information; and only one, Tell en-Nasbeh, has been completely stripped of its strata. Obviously the major sources for the history of the Holy Land have not yet been touched.

If past experience is any reliable guide, a cautious projection into the future should include the probability of surprises and the steady growth of reliable data for a reconstruction of history as new sites are dug by techniques constantly refined and improved. Given peace in the land, a supply of well-trained archaeologists, and adequate financial support, the horizon of our understanding of the past should continue to expand.

JAMES B. PRITCHARD

ARCHAEOLOGICAL PERIODS OF THE HOLY LAND

Kebaran Stage (food-gathering)	To 9th millennium B.C.
Natufian (incipient food-producing)	9th to early 7th millennium B.C.
Pre-Pottery Neolithic	Early 7th to late 6th millennium B.C.
Pottery Neolithic	Late 6th to end of 5th millennium B.C.
"Chalcolithic"	End of 5th to end of 4th millennium B.C.

Early Bronze I	About 3100–2850 B.C.
Early Bronze II	About 2900–2600 B.C.
Early Bronze IIIA	About 2650–2500 B.C.
Early Bronze IIIB	About 2550–2350 B.C.
Early Bronze IIIC	About 2400–2250 B.C.
Early Bronze IV	About 2200–2000 B.C.

Middle Bronze I	Before 2000 to before 1800 B.C.
Middle Bronze IIA	About 1700 B.C.
Middle Bronze IIB	About 1600 and early 1500 B.C.
Middle Bronze IIC	About 1575–1500 B.C.

Late Bronze I	About 1500–1400 B.C.
Late Bronze IIA	About 1400–1300 B.C.
Late Bronze IIB	About 1300–1200 B.C.

Iron I or Early Iron	About 1200–900 B.C.
Iron II or Middle Iron	About 900–587 B.C.
Persian or Late Iron	587–330 B.C.

Hellenistic	330–63 B.C.
Roman	63 B.C.—A.D. 330
Byzantine	A.D. 330–638

NOTE: The terminology for the periods and the dates assigned to them vary considerably, especially for the periods before Late Bronze. The listing given above for the earliest periods through Middle Bronze II is taken from William F. Albright, "Some Remarks on the Archaeological Chronology of Palestine before about 1500 B.C.," *Chronologies in Old World Archaeology*, edited by Robert W. Ehrich, 1965, pp. 47–57.

'Ein Mallaha

Hazor

SYRIA

Akko

SEA
OF
GALILEE

Haifa

Wadi Fallah

Beth She'arim
Nazareth

Megiddo

Taanach

Beth
Shan

MEDITERRANEAN SEA

Samaria

Shechem

JORDAN R.

Jaffa

JORDAN

AMMAN

Mezad Hashavyahu
Gezer

Tell en-Nasbeh

Khirbat al-Mafjar
Jericho

Ashdod

Gibeon

JERUSALEM

Khirbet
Qumran

Teleilat el-Ghassul

Beth Shemesh

Ramat
Rahel

'Ain Feshkha

Marisa

Wadi Murabba'at

DEAD
SEA

Tell el-Hesi

Lachish

Hebron

Dhiban

Gaza

Tell Nagila

Nahal Hever

Engedi

Tell Jemmeh

Masada

Tell Beit Mirsim

Tell Far'ah

Beersheba

Arad

Tell Far'ah

Tell Abu Matar
Tell es-Safadi

Bab edh Dhra'

Auja el-Hafir

Sbeita

ISRAEL

Beidha

Petra

SCALE
14 MILES TO THE INCH

0   14   28

Ezion-Geber

GULF
OF
AQABA

BEFORE THE BIBLE

Safadi during the sixth season of excavations. The division of the site into numbered squares measuring 5 x 5 meters facilitates the exact location of each find. The shafts giving access to the subterranean dwellings are visible.

The Dawn of History
in Southern Palestine

by JEAN PERROT

Beersheba lies in the center of an extensive semidesert area which stretches from the Gaza coast to the Dead Sea and the Araba Valley. This is a vast plain of reddish, gently rolling earth cut by riverbeds (wadis), which the short and violent winter rains can fill with raging torrents. Almost overnight the parched browns and grays of the desert change to a tender green and the earth is carpeted with flowers.

Embarking upon the reclamation of this difficult region, the Israelis have encountered at every step the traces of their predecessors: the Nabataean merchants who, shortly before the beginning of our era, founded the caravan cities such as Petra and 'Abda; the Israelites who, under King Solomon and his successors, the kings of Judah, built fortresses in the Negev to control the road to Ophir and protect their exploitation of the copper mines in the Arabah; and, still earlier, the Amorites, the contemporaries of Abraham and Hammurabi. Throughout the millennia, history seems to repeat itself; the Negev has been inhabited only intermittently by a sedentary population. At various times, social, economic or political pressure forced the farmer into the Negev, where he had to

exert all his ingenuity to overcome unfavorable conditions. But whenever this pressure disappeared, the settlers withdrew, leaving only nomads to roam the land. Between the waves of population flowing into the Negev there were centuries of oblivion, when the sands of the desert covered the ruins of civilization.

In the spring of 1951, a young man from Kibbutz Mishmar Hanegev, near Beersheba, led me to the banks of a wadi where he had found scattered sherds of coarse pottery and flint flakes. Upon examination and comparison of these artifacts with already dated Palestinian material, it was evident that they were remains of a settlement going to the fourth millennium B.C.—a period of which nothing had been known in southern Palestine.

Our investigations began in June of the same year at Abu Irqayq, on the bank of Wadi Zumeili. Surface surveys carried out in this region by amateurs had already pinpointed about fifty sites along many of the wadis of the northern Negev. All the sites were located in similar areas. In the immediate vicinity of Beersheba, where the underground water table is easily accessible, the

Photographs Mission Archéologique Française en Israël

sites were clustered closely together. We undertook the complete excavation of two of these—one near Bir Abu Matar and the other near Bir es-Safadi. Our efforts have been richly rewarded and we have a fairly good idea of the material culture and daily life of the first inhabitants of the Negev, who lived fifteen hundred years before Abraham, in the second half of the fourth millennium B.C.

We uncovered almost intact their peculiar villages, not, as normally expected, on the surface of the hills but completely underground, dug, sometimes to a depth of twenty feet or more, into the alluvial loam forming the upper part of the wadi terrace. The nature of the soil favors this kind of subterranean dwelling, which offers excellent protection against the sweltering heat of

Gallery connecting the rooms of a subterranean dwelling.

the day, the chill of the night and the wind-borne sand. It is unlikely that these villages were built in this fashion for reasons of security—the absence of any weapons or fortifications bears witness to a peaceful life such as Palestine has enjoyed only rarely during its history. The earliest dwellings were large rectangular rooms opening on a horizontal gallery on the slope of the terrace. Their shape was not well suited to the soft soil and they crumbled rapidly. Soon the inhabitants preferred to build rows of smaller, rounded or egg-shaped underground rooms, connected by tunnels and entered through vertical shafts sunk into the end rooms of each row. Footholds cut into the walls of the shafts facilitated descent and ascent. The shafts also assured the ventilation of these dark little rooms, where fires were kindled on small hearths, and which were lit by primitive lamps.

Several times, perhaps as a result of prolonged droughts, the subterranean villages of Beersheba were temporarily abandoned. The galleries were walled up, the shafts blocked and all visible traces of dwellings smoothed away, so that whatever the people could not carry away with them remained well hidden in the underground houses. Sometimes the inhabitants stayed away longer than they expected, or did not return at all, and thus left us to find some of their houses complete with furniture and domestic installations: basins, hearths, and bell-shaped grain pits covered by flat stones.

When the subterranean rooms eventually caved in, the people preferred to build round or oval houses in the hollows thus formed on the surface. Built of mud brick on stone foundations, these houses were roofed, at surface level, with beaten earth supported by wooden beams. They are an interesting intermediate stage between the subterranean dwellings and the rectangular houses, also of mud brick on stone foundations, which

Group of basalt vessels, one with hollowed-out foot; these are always found in groups of three. The rim is decorated on the inside with incised hatched triangles; the number of triangles is generally a multiple of seven.

still later were built right on the surface. To this last phase at Safadi belongs a large structure which must have served as a public building, although we do not know for what purpose.

The economic organization of the village corresponds to an already high degree of development. Owing to the stability of the natural environment—the presence of a peculiar species of land snails suffices to prove that the climate of that time was the same as today—its economic life can be reconstructed with remarkable accuracy. At this stage hunting is no longer of much importance, while agriculture and cattle raising provide almost the entire food supply. In normally rainy years, the wadis of the Negev preserve sufficient moisture to allow extensive cereal cultivation wherever the soil is fertile. In addition to agricultural tools of stone and bone—picks, hoes, and sickles— we found in the storage pits of Abu Matar and Safadi remains of wheat, barley, and lentils. The domestic animals were mainly sheep and goats; the dog, the pig, and the donkey were known, as well as a dwarf ox, a working animal adapted to local conditions. Handicrafts were well developed, and each village seems to have specialized to a

certain degree in a particular craft—pottery-making, weaving, basket-making, the manufacture of objects of stone, bone, and ivory. The first specialized craftsmen appear at Abu Matar, where remains of copper smelting and manufacturing were found.

The presence of a copper industry at Beersheba before 3000 B.C. is even more surprising when it is remembered that copper ores are not found in the immediate vicinity. The smiths of Beersheba had to travel more than sixty miles to the rich copper-ore deposits of Wadi Feinan, southeast of the Dead Sea. The fragments of malachite which they brought back were pulverized on flint anvils and, after reduction with charcoal, smelted in earthen furnaces; primitive bellows were probably used for obtaining the necessary high temperatures. After being refined in crucibles, the metal was poured into molds for making mace heads, implements, and jewelry.

In addition to being clever craftsmen, the people of Beersheba were artists of no mean ability. Their sense of beauty found expression even in the most ordinary objects. The graceful pottery vessels are often decorated with red-painted geometric motifs. More costly vessels, made of basalt, include beauti-

Bone pin with head shaped like a female figurine. Height 2¾ inches.

Head of an ivory figurine representing a woman; the hair is gathered on the top of the head and falls down the back in a "pony tail." The coiffure is crowned with an animal(?). Height about 3½ inches.

Copper awl with bone handle. Length about seven inches.

ful bowls and stands with hollowed-out foot. Rectangular palettes of polished marble were used for crushing black, red, and green face paints. Ornaments are very numerous—stone and ivory bracelets, beads of frit and shell, pendants of mother-of-pearl, bone, and turquoise. Two ivory pins with decorated heads, one representing a bird and the other a human figure, show an artistic sense which is fully revealed in a series of remarkable ivory figurines. Ivory carving seems to have been of particular importance among the crafts practiced at Bir Safadi. We had the good luck to uncover an ivory carver's workshop, complete with workbench, tool—a copper awl still in its bone handle—and raw material, an elephant tusk. Elephants are known to have existed in Syria as late as the eighth century B.C.; however, the possibility cannot be excluded that the ivory was imported, perhaps from Africa, together with the large shells from which beads and other ornaments were made. Our figurines are not unlike the early Predynastic sculptures of Upper Egypt, but the style of the Beersheba ivories is different and they are generally superior in execution. The figurines apparently represent a worshiper standing in ritual nakedness before a divinity; they bear witness to religious concepts which also find expression in schematic representations of humans, animals, and sexual symbols, probably connected with a fertility cult. Curious assemblages of pebbles—found on the floors of the dwellings, and always grouped in multiples of seven—may perhaps point to ancestor worship. These pebbles are marked in red paint with various signs—crosses, darts, squares, pictographs.

Who were these people and whence did they come? The skeletons unearthed at Beersheba belong to two different racial groups, the Proto-Mediterranean, known to have been established in Palestine since earliest times, and the Armenoid (Anatolian), which

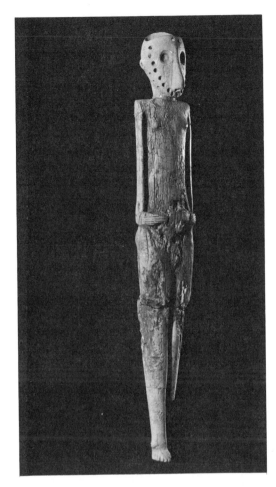

Ivory figurine, thirteen inches high, representing a naked man with hands at the waist holding up a loin cloth (broken). Hair and beard were attached by threading through the holes in the haws and around the head.

is known at this time only in the Sumerian cemetery at Kish, and which here makes its first appearance in Palestine. Of the four individuals belonging to the first group, three —a man and two women—had simply been thrown into a disused grain silo after the man had died a violent death. The fourth skeleton, that of a woman, was found in another silo, lying contracted on its side. The burial customs of the Armenoid group—represented by six skeletons—were different: the long bones were collected after the flesh had wasted away, and were placed against the wall of the funerary chamber, with the skull on top. The main physical characteristics of the Armenoids—a short, broad skull, a long straight nose in line with the forehead, and abundant hair—seem to be exactly reproduced in the ivory figurines. An interesting relationship between race and culture may be glimpsed here, and it might perhaps be suggested that an Armenoid group played a primary role in introducing into Palestine this new element which we call the Beersheba culture.

The Beersheba cultural complex is indeed distinctive. Entirely different from that of the indigenous settled population, it bears the mark of its nomadic origin. The excavations at Beersheba have shown the existence of continuous relations with the Transjordan plateau, from where hard stone (particularly basalt) and copper ore were brought. Metallurgical crafts as practiced at Beersheba could develop only within reach of the rich copper deposits of Wadi Feinan. These and other considerations, which require confirmation by investigation east of the Dead Sea, as well as more general anthropological factors, suggest the eastern border of the Transjordan plateau as the dwelling place of the Beersheba people just before they came to Palestine.

It would seem that, toward the middle of the fourth millennium B.C., certain population groups east of the Jordan River which were already well on the way to sedentary life began migrating westward. We do not know the reasons for this migration, which may have taken place around the entire periphery of the Syrian Desert. Palestine seems to have been invaded peacefully both north and south of the Dead Sea. The newcomers gradually established themselves in the northern Negev and in those parts of the country which, like the Jordan Valley and the coastal plain, were less favorable to settlement than the central hill country and consequently less densely inhabited by the indigenous population. There they found living conditions and natural surroundings not very different from those they had left.

The disappearance of the Beersheba people a few centuries later was apparently just as sudden as their arrival. The poor soil and marginal conditions of this region must have set a limit to the growth of the population and inhibited the normal development of the culture. Unable to grow, it must have lost vitality and faded rapidly. Perhaps these difficulties, together with a change in general conditions, led to a return to nomadic life. In the present state of our knowledge we can only offer conjectures. It is certain, however, that before the beginning of the Bronze Age in Palestine, even before the first historic dynasties established themselves in the valleys of the Nile and the Euphrates, the Negev once again was deserted.

Beidha: An Early Neolithic Village in Jordan

by DIANA KIRKBRIDE

Set in a wide wadi, or valley, flanked by sandstone cliffs and backed by the high lime-stone ridge of Jebel Shara' (the biblical Mount Seir), is the site of a village which flourished about nine thousand years ago, at a time when stone tools were used but pottery was not yet being made. (The period is known as the Aceramic Neolithic.) This site, now called Beidha, lies about an hour's walk through the mountains to the north of Petra. The site was later terraced for agriculture by the Nabataeans and a deep torrent bed has eroded some of it, but no permanent habitations have been built there since the Neolithic people abandoned their village. The nearest perennial water supply then, as now, is a small spring called Diba-diba, some 200 meters above the wadi on the steep slopes of Jebel Shara'. By present-day standards Beidha is remote, over two hours' walk from the nearest point a vehicle can reach, but about nine thousand years ago it was one of a number of small settlements situated within walking distance of each other on the protected contour terrace which also houses Petra.

This terrace, at Beidha about 6 kilometers wide, is 1,000 meters above sea level and some 400 meters below the high plateau of the Arabian Desert on the east, from which it is screened by the ridge of Jebel Shara'; on the west it terminates abruptly at the precipitous drop to the Wadi Araba. Jebel Shara' not only induces rain-bearing clouds to release some of their moisture on the protected shelf of land but it has a series of springs that issue from its upper reaches, following an impermeable stratum in the calcareous deposits. Even after millennia of despoliation by man and his animals, these ridges still bear remnants of the ancient oak-pistachio-juniper forests, which in Neolithic times were inhabited by animals such as aurochs, wild boar, and probably leopard as well. Thus Jebel Shara' may have been something of a natural division delimiting the itinerant inhabitants of the plateau from the settlers on the shelf below.

As a result of six campaigns up to 1965, Beidha affords the largest uninterrupted exposure of Early Neolithic habitation yet excavated; it also supplies an architectural record in stone construction which is at present unique for this early period. So far, six main building levels have been differentiated, comprising four different types of

9

*Site of Beidha in its splendid setting. Originally the village
spread across the area now eroded by the gully at left.*

architecture; in addition, each main level has its own individual phases. The houses are all semisubterranean and were entered by three descending stone steps. This building practice has made stratigraphical recording of the ruins particularly complicated; instead of leveling off a disused house and then building up, the ancient inhabitants of Beidha first dug down, thereby frequently obliterating the plan of the lower buildings and levels.

The top level (I) has been almost entirely eroded and destroyed by terracing for Nabataean agriculture; its over-all plan cannot be traced. One collapsed building and scattered remains of wall foundations suggest that the houses were small, of a simple rectangular ground plan, and had plastered floors.

In Levels II and III the village was built up on practically identical plans. In both

levels there was, on the same site, a large house on the edge of the village nearest to the rock face, and to this were attached enclosures and pens, presumably for safekeeping of the herds by night.

The large house in Level II has a single room, 9 x 7 meters. The walls (still almost a meter high) and the floor are plastered with a strong lime plaster that has been relaid and recoated many times; some of the flooring layers have a red-painted band extending about twenty-five centimeters inward from the walls and continuing up them, presumably to form a dado. A similar band outlines all the main features of the room: a circular hearth, a deep stone-lined pit, and a large, roughly squared polished block of stone plastered against the wall just inside the entrance. Plastered floors and walls colored in similar fashion were found in the pre-pottery level at Hacilar in southwest Anatolia and at Jericho. Two walls of this large house mark the perimeter of the village at this point and period; beyond them only rubbish dumps have been traced. The house entrance opens onto a protected court, beyond which lies a further enclosure. During a later period this enclosure contained small stone pens and irregular curving walls which may have served to protect domesticated goats and perhaps decoy birds. This large house stood for a very long time and was rebuilt, refloored and redecorated repeatedly without its plan being materially altered. It was at all times the only structure of its kind within the portion of the village that has been preserved.

To the south and west of the large house and beyond the courtyards the area was densely built up with so-called corridor houses. These are long rectangles with the entrance at one end; each has a central corridor a meter wide and six small rooms (1 x 1.5 m.) divided by the corridor into three opposing pairs, like stalls in a stable. The rooms are separated by strongly built stone baulks, some wider than the rooms themselves. No plaster has been found on the walls, but sometimes the floors are plastered. Artifacts, tools, and raw materials found in these buildings strongly suggest that they were workshops rather than dwellings, a hypothesis which is given additional weight by the fact that no domestic hearths have been found in any of them.

The function of the wide stone baulks separating the small rooms cannot be de-

General view of the excavations. Main house of early Level II is in center, and beyond it corridor workshops of Levels II and III. Buildings of earlier levels may be seen on extreme left and in front of main house.

Close-up of main house of early Level II, showing plaster floor, entrance steps, large stone set against wall, and hearth with sill. In foreground, right, part of a Level V round house; beneath it a small Level VI segmented hut.

cided with certainty, but it seems most probable that they were interior buttresses upholding a lightly built upper story. In this case there would have been a large room of about thirty square meters, ample space for a family to live above the workshops below. Although in some cases standing remains of walls run to a height of almost two meters, there is as yet no evidence for a second story, but the nature of the fill found above the occupation levels in the workshops bears out the theory to some extent. Substantial pieces of plaster (many colored red), flints, stone and bone implements, and beads are found, and sometimes heavier pieces of equipment such as querns show evidence of having fallen from above.

The fact that these workshop buildings

Worktable in the bead and bone-tool maker's workshop, Level III. Ribs, long bones, and shoulder blades of animals are lying about, ready to be fashioned into tools.

are of a plan completely different from that of the big main house, to which they seem connected by layout and stratigraphy, suggests that the latter may have been the communal meeting and eating place for the adjacent workers, even if they did not sleep there. However this may be, it seems that the big houses are the only buildings in Levels II and III supplied with large domestic hearths.

The corridor buildings provide the bulk of the finds of these two periods, and with each season new evidence is added to substantiate their identification as workshops. Besides flints they contained objects that suggest a certain degree of specialization in the crafts. Presumably each building belonged to a certain family. One unit may show evidence for the practice of a specific craft or crafts, while the contents of others are more general.

One workshop obviously belonged to a specialist in beads and bone tools. In it we found stone, bone, and shell beads at every stage of preparation; some stone beads were found with the grinding process incomplete, others with the perforation just begun, while most were finished, ground, polished, and pierced for suspension. There were mother-of-pearl, cowrie, mollusc and bivalve shells, some pierced and one with the boring incomplete. Bone beads also occurred at every stage of the making. One long, slender tibia lying beside a slab table had the shaft divided by carved grooves into nineteen fairly equal sections. Nearby were separated slices or rings, rough and unworked, as well as the finished product, shaped, smoothed, and polished; a complete bracelet of such bone beads was found in another house.

The bone tools also provided a fine cross-section of the maker's art: beautifully polished spatulas, slender points, and long weaving implements. The latter were made of worked ribs of aurochs. In addition we found the tools used in the manufacture of these articles, and blocks of haematite and pumice probably used to shape and polish them. The craftsman worked on flat stone slabs that lay on the floor. His raw material, ribs and long bones of animals, was found in the corridor as well as in the room.

Several other set-pieces of this kind were encountered in Levels II and III: one small room held a large slab on which lay the frontals of a skull, probably of an ibex, with a magnificent pair of sweeping horn cores, while another complete pair was near the table; nearby lay the frontals of a third skull, but with the horns cut off, and in a corner was heaped a selection of ground stone tools. Another workshop showed a mixture of horn and bone working, with ground stone tools and beads as well. Still others contained a preponderance of ground stone implements, grinders, pestles, and axes. Querns were abundant in all levels, and when worn out they were frequently used as building material.

One of the corridor buildings seems to have been more like a butcher shop; one small room was filled with animal bones (some jointed) and horned heads; the room opposite, across the corridor, was filled with heavy stone implements, grinders, hammerstones, heavy choppers, and chunks of flint raw material. The contents of these houses give a fascinating glimpse of life in the village nearly nine thousand years ago.

Level IV consistently shows a form of architecture diverging from Levels II and III. It displays the finest building techniques of any period at Beidha. Completely circular houses exist alongside rectangular ones with gently curving walls and rounded corners. One large house had post-holes within its walls, a link with earlier levels. All the houses found so far are free-standing and single-roomed. They are semisubterranean, and each has a yard outside. For the most part walls and floors are plastered, and in some houses there are small circular fireplaces with raised sills. It is now clear that Levels II and III represent an architectural tradition foreign to the indigenous architectural evolution shown in earlier levels (IV–VI).

Not only is the architecture of Level IV different, but so is the building technique. Instead of small, roughly square boulders, the walls were made chiefly of hard, flat slabs of mud stone. These petrified clays are deposited in narrow strata within the Cambrian sandstone, and when used as building material they form walls of real beauty.

There is no evidence for specialization of crafts in the Level IV houses found so far, although one small building containing three

Exterior wall of a Level IV house made of flat slabs of petrified clay, showing characteristic gentle curve.

querns must have been set aside for grinding and pulping.

Level V was much damaged by later building activities. As we shall see, there is strong evidence for architectural evolution from Level VI, which betrays increasing confidence in the building materials and also perhaps an alteration in the communal life of the village. Instead of being built in clusters for the mutual support not only of the buildings but also of the families dwelling there, the structures are now free-standing and single-roomed. On the one hand we

Segmented house of Level VI with anteroom and part of a neighboring house. Note wall slots for posts.

still have several examples of the post-houses characteristic of Level VI, reflecting a conservative element; on the other we have houses ranging from round through rather freehand curvilinear plans, some with no sign of wall posts, others with just a few that can have served no structural purpose.

The structures, almost devoid of contents, were composed of one continuous circular wall broken only by the entrance. Rather thick and sometimes resting on a foundation of larger slabs, the wall was plastered, as was the floor. These houses are similar to those of the Pre-Pottery Neolithic A at the site of Jericho.

Level VI contains the earliest Neolithic houses yet found and they are unique. Arranged in separate clusters like cells in a honeycomb, these semisubterranean structures are essentially circular in plan. However, Level VI appears to represent the initial Neolithic settlement, and here again a different architectural tradition is met with. Although of circular aspect, the dwellings are composed of short, straight segments of walls with angular, unboned joints. They give the impression that the builders had the intention of making round houses long before they had mastered the technique necessary for doing so in stone; only by the time of Level V was this lack of experience finally overcome.

The individual rooms within a cluster were erected around an inner skeleton of posts and beams. Stout posts dug into the floor at regular intervals were united by beams to a strong central post. A wide stone wall was then erected around this scaffolding, with short segments of its interior face holding the post on each side. The interior wall face thus bears vertical wall slots at regular intervals where the posts had stood. Usually floor and wall were plastered, as were the ceilings, while above the beams brush or reeds were laid at right angles; the

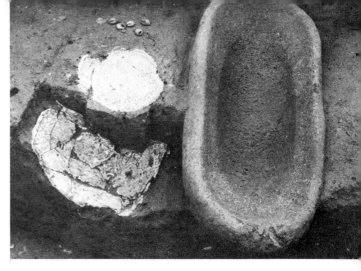

whole supported a thick clay roof which was probably given a fresh coat of mud annually.

The rooms within a cluster share party walls, and they intercommunicate internally through anterooms and short corridors, while stone steps regulate the differences in the floor levels of the individual rooms. It seems that each cluster of post-houses had an encircling wall, beyond which lay the courtyards with hearths. Three separate clusters have so far been located.

One house was destroyed by a fierce fire, and the resultant baking and solidifying of the mass of clay, mortar, and plaster from roof and walls supplied a magnificent series of plant impressions. In addition, a heap of carbonized pistachio nuts, which may originally have amounted to some five gallons, was found on the floor in perfect condition. They seem to have been lying in a basket; the resin released from the nuts by the heat has preserved imprints of the weave in a thin skin of tar.

This house, too, supplies evidence not only that the inhabitants of the earliest Neolithic level at Beidha made lifelike animal figurines but, more important, that they were experimenting with modeling small

Figure of ibex modeled in clay, found in burned house of Level VI.

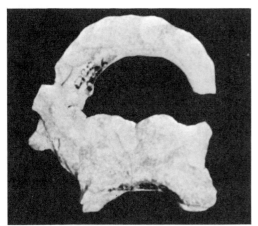

Two baskets coated with lime lying beside a small oval granite trough and pebble polishers.

receptables in clay. From this house—and baked hard in its destruction—came a section of a small, very primitive clay bowl as well as a lively representation of an ibex and modeled aurochs' horns. The only other figurine found at Beidha is a tiny unbaked squatting "mother goddess" exhibiting the characteristic steatopygous features of the period. The breasts are modeled, but there are no arms; the head is missing. This little sculpture was found in an unburnt workshop of Level II. Beidha does not offer evidence of intentional firing of clay.

The crafts seem to show a certain degree of specialization even at this early date. One room contained heavy implements, grinders, polishers, axes, and querns, in addition to a large basket coated with bitumen and an almost equally large wooden bowl marked only by a circular shadow on the floor. A neighboring apartment held a preponderance of bone tools, many lumps of coloring material, various stone implements, and a large stone bowl. Next door, the room seems to have been devoted to more delicate crafts. It contained an oval wooden box holding 114 choice flint arrowheads and points tightly wrapped in some material now decayed to a white powdery substance. Nearby lay two baskets coated with lime plaster and a fragment of a bitumen basket, with a small

Carefully buried headless adult skeleton.

oval granite trough beside them; numerous polishers, small axheads, and various abrasive stones as well as highly polished bone tools lay scattered about.

These houses must be replicas in stone of huts made of more perishable materials, probably with brush and clay filling the gaps between the wall posts. Somewhere in the stratified sand that underlies part of the Neolithic village we may find traces of these prototypes.

Burial practices at Beidha were of the somewhat macabre type made familiar at other sites such as Hacilar, Çatal Hüyük, and Jericho. Decapitation of the dead and secondary burial beneath the house floors seem to have been the lot of the majority of adults found, while infants and small children were usually buried under the floors in an undisturbed state. As yet only about six adults have been found, as against twenty

children, so probably while infant mortality was very high there may also have been a cemetery outside the village, so far undiscovered, to accommodate all but a few favored adults.

A third dimension can now be added to the material remains of Early Neolithic Beidha. Dr. Hans Helbaek, palaeoethnobotanist; Dr. Dexter Perkins Jr., zoologist, and Robert L. Raikes, hydrologist, visited the expedition and have worked over the evidence in their specialized fields.

The inhabitants of Beidha cultivated hulled, two-row barley as their chief crop; lacking the physiological changes that in the long run occur with domestication, it was in reality the wild barley, *Hordeum spontaneum*. They also grew emmer wheat, although not quite on the same scale as barley. To augment their cultivated crops they gathered pistachio nuts, acorns, and the seeds of various leguminous plants, among other wild species. Evidence, not yet conclusive, points to the herding of domesticated goats, while the aurochs, bezoar (considered to be the ancestor of the domesticated goat) ibex, gazelle, wild boar, hare, jackal, and members of the horse family all lived in the vicinity and were hunted for their meat, skin, and bones. Although no remains have yet been found, it is probable that leopard also was present in the region as it is today.

Beidha, then, is one of the very early Neolithic settlements which have been found in the general area of the Near East. They are all based on an economy comprising cultivation of cereals, collection of wild plants, and herding of goat, sheep, or pig, in addition to hunting. For the most part these villages, including Beidha, are situated in or next to areas where the wild prototypes of domesticated plants and animals are indigenous.

Beidha was also favored by easy access to a great variety of useful minerals. Limestone, sandstone, and granite form the local environment, with basalt fields a short day's walk away; flint pebbles abound in the wadis surrounding the site, and another, though less valuable, raw material is found in the strata of tabular flint in the limestone of the upper slopes of Jebel Shara'. Haematite, red and yellow ocher, malachite and mica are encountered in the mountains lining the Wadi Araba just below the site as well as in the local stream beds. Although no traces of prehistoric workings are left, salt was another commodity available in the immediate vicinity of Beidha; present-day Bedouin still extract it with water from crushed sandstone fetched from certain rock strata and isolate it by evaporation.

Long-range trade is evidenced by the occurrence of certain materials which cannot possibly originate within this mountainous desert environment. We have found obsidian which can have come only from Anatolia, slowly transmitted to the various settlements by itinerant tribes. These wanderers must also have carried pumice and shell from the Mediterranean and Red seas to Beidha and its neighbors. The basis for this barter cannot be established in detail at the present stage of our knowledge of the general area in this remote period, but there is no doubt that minerals such as haematite, malachite, and ochers would be in demand in other settlements.

While removing the floor of a Level VI post-house we exposed the top of an underlying mud-brick wall; the interior face, curved and lined with mud plaster, lay just inside the stone wall of the post-house. The small portion of occupation debris available produced purely Mesolithic (Natufian) artifacts. Now we have mud-brick walls below the Neolithic village in three separate areas, and the highest Natufian level is cut into by the lowest Neolithic one. There should be at least two meters of architectural deposit that was not revealed in the prelimi-

nary soundings. Probably the Neolithic newcomers to Beidha were attracted by the sight of a small tell with denuded mud-brick walls on the summit, surrounded by inviting arable land, and settled in the same place.

One point can be noted about the original Natufian settlers. They were foreigners who came from an alluvial environment, bringing a tradition of building in mud brick to a region where stone abounds and the local sandy silt is totally unsuitable as a basis for bricks. Although the discovery of a Natufian settlement at Beidha is of the utmost importance, more work is still necessary on the unique earliest Neolithic levels before we can turn to this interesting and unexpected development.

Shadows on the ground are rough bricks, or cores, which formed the wall of a Mesolithic (Natufian) house. Above are the walls of a Level VI Neolithic house. Natufian flints came from the deposit between.

Mesolithic structure, possibly a sanctuary. A platform of natural clay (removed over the rest of the area) is bounded by stone walls, of which two are exposed, and the angle of a third is visible running into the far balk. In the wall on the left are two stone sockets, and a third socketed stone is broken beside them. The holes in the surface of the clay platform were cut down from higher levels.

Jericho:
Oldest Walled Town

by KATHLEEN M. KENYON

Much of the Jordan Valley is an arid wilderness, but where there is water, the soil is very fertile, and the tropical climate encourages luxuriant growth. At first view of the brilliant green vegetation of the oasis of Jericho, standing out from the dazzling whiteness of the rest of the Jordan Valley, it is easy to understand why the site was important for thousands of years. Jericho was the site of one of the earliest villages in which nomadic man settled down and made those experiments in agriculture which mark the introduction of the Neolithic Age. It is from the early settled peasant communities like Jericho that man began to progress toward civilization. Progress was, however, dependent on the discovery that wild grains could be cultivated and wild animals domesticated to insure a permanent food supply.

Jericho, in the great rift of the Jordan Valley, nine miles north of the Dead Sea, and some 800 feet below sea level, is certainly a site in which conditions were favorable. The copious perennial spring at the foot of the mound that marks the ancient city assured the early settlers that their town could be truly permanent.

Jericho has been excavated on a number of occasions, beginning as long ago as 1867. A recent campaign consisted of six seasons' work between 1952 and 1957 by the British School of Archaeology in Jerusalem, in collaboration, in some seasons, with the American School of Oriental Research and the Royal Ontario Museum.

The excavations established a sequence of occupation that began in the Mesolithic period, ca. 8000 B.C., and continued, though probably with some interruptions, until the end of the Middle Bronze Age, ca. 1560 B.C. Brief revivals took place in the Late Bronze Age and in Iron Age II, but the importance of the original Jericho, which lies beside the modern village of Ain-es-Sultan, ends with the Middle Bronze Age. For the period from the fourth millennium onward the history and culture of the town are similar to that of many other Palestinian towns. When the remains of the successive Neolithic stages were first discovered, Jericho provided the only known evidence of a large-scale settled community dating back to the seventh and eighth millennia B.C. Since then, other sites have produced evidence for periods approaching the same dates. Jericho remains unique

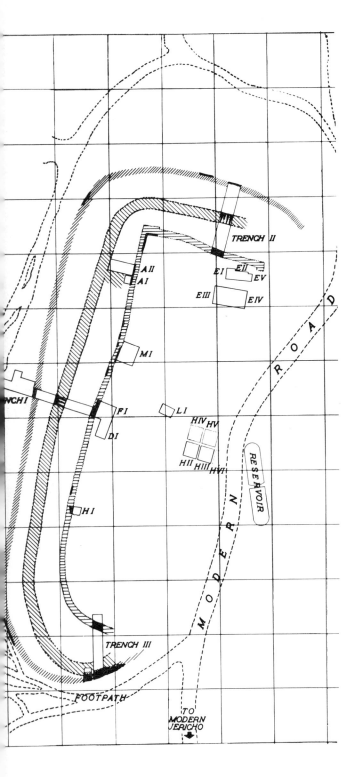

TRENCH II

A II
A I
E I
E II
E V
E III
E IV

ROAD

M I

R
O
A
D

NCH I
F I
L I
H IV
H V
D I
H II
H III
H VI

RESERVOIR

M
O
D
E
R
N

H I

TRENCH III

FOOTPATH

TO
MODERN
JERICHO

as the only site that has produced a complete sequence of development from nomadic beginnings to full urbanization.

The excavation of the total fifty feet of depth of the whole tell, covering at its stage of maximum extension about ten acres, has naturally been carried out only in a limited area. Nevertheless, bedrock was reached in five sites, widely spaced from the extreme north to the extreme south of the tell. It is likely, therefore, that representative evidence of the sequence of events has been recovered. Evidence of the earliest occupation came from a single site, Squares E I, II, and V, toward the northeast end. On bedrock was found a curious structure which, from the associated finds, was certainly Mesolithic, of a culture allied to the Natufian of Mount Carmel. It consisted of a rectangle in which the natural clay, removed over the rest of the area, had been retained and revetted by stone walls in which three stone sockets had been set. The structure was certainly not a domestic one, and the most probable interpretation is that it was a sanctuary erected by Mesolithic hunters visiting Jericho, beside the spring, in recognition of its secular importance. The structure was ultimately destroyed by fire, for which a radiocarbon analysis gives a date of ca. 7800 B.C.

It is to be presumed that the men who erected it were nomadic like the rest of the Natufians, but at Jericho some of their descendants settled down—and thus took the

Plan of Jericho. The Pre-Pottery Neolithic A town wall was identified in Trench II on the north, Trench I on the west, and Trench III on the south. The Early Bronze Age walls follow the innermost line shown. The outer lines are those of the plastered scarp of the second stage of the Middle Bronze Age defenses and the stone revetment at the foot of the final phase of these defenses.

first step toward civilization. The evidence for this comes from Site M. There, the first thirteen feet of deposit above bedrock were built up by an innumerable succession of tramped earth surfaces, visible in section but barely traceable in plan, each ending against a slight hump. The humps must represent the bases of the superstructure of shelters of wood, skin, and mud, shelters suitable for a people constantly on the move. But the deep accumulation of such remains shows that their occupants had developed a close attachment to the same spot. At first they may have returned seasonally, but eventually they settled permanently because in due course the slight shelters were translated into solid structures. These were round like their predecessors but with solid walls of bricks, plano-convex with a hogback outline, and provided with a porch leading down into the slightly sunken interior. The houses appear above the deposit already described.

The structural sequence is coherent. More important, so is the cultural. The flint and bone industries found in the Mesolithic structure are the ancestors of those in the thirteen feet of incipient settlement, which can best be described as Proto-Neolithic, and the industries of this deposit are the ancestors of those found in the round houses of the fully developed Pre-Pottery Neolithic A stage.

Like the Mesolithic, the Proto-Neolithic evidence was found in one area only, but once solid houses were developed, the spread was rapid. These houses appear on bedrock from north to south of the tell. More striking still, soon after the houses had extended to cover an area of about ten acres, the settlement was enclosed by massive defenses. In Trench II on the north and Trench III on the south these are ill preserved, but in Trench I on the west they are preserved in what must be near their original dimensions. The stone-built wall survives to a height of

Typical house of Pre-Pottery Neolithic A period. The houses were round in plan, slightly sunk below the exterior level. On the far side is a stepped entrance, presumably a porch. The steps were sometimes of timber. The typical plano-convex bricks are visible in the foreground. The houses may consist of a single room, or two or three round rooms may be grouped together. In the courtyards outside were fireplaces, grinding stones, and other installations.

Great stone tower of the Pre-Pottery Neolithic A defenses. On the right-hand side is the top of the final stage of the town wall with which it was associated. The earliest town wall belonging to the first stage of the tower is visible immediately to the left of the later wall. This early wall was abolished when an outer skin was added to the original tower. In the foreground, on the left, are portions of a succession of structures, water tanks or storage areas, built against the tower. These were succeeded by houses (removed before the photograph was taken).

20 feet, with outside it a rock-cut ditch 27 feet wide and 9 feet deep. Behind the wall was a circular stone tower, surviving to a height of thirty feet. The tower was provided with an internal staircase giving access to the tower from the interior of the town.

The illustrations show the enormous impressiveness of these defenses. They had a long life, for there were four structural stages, including three complete rebuildings of the town wall. After the final structural stage, levels of occupation continued to accumulate until they had nearly reached the surviving top of the tower. At this point a destruction of one of the houses by fire provided material for a radiocarbon test, which gave a date of 6800 B.C. A date of 7000 B.C. for the first stage of defenses is thus an absolute minimum.

Such remarkable structures at this early date means there was a developed communal organization capable of undertaking massive public works. The inhabitants of Jericho in 7000 B.C. were not a mere agglomeration of families: they could co-operate for a common purpose. This progress may be connected with the developing means of supplying a group large enough to occupy close-packed houses on a site covering ten acres within a comparatively brief interval. It was at most a thousand years from the time when their ancestors were basically food gatherers. The environment of Jericho—abundant water, rich alluvial soil, a tropical climate—would be favorable for experiments in agriculture. But in its natural state the effect of the spring would have been comparatively local. To water the large area which the wasteful methods of primitive agriculture and stock-breeding would require could have been done only with irrigation. An irrigation system needs control, and from this may have developed the community organization of which the defenses give evidence.

This Pre-Pottery Neolithic A culture was undoubtedly indigenous to Jericho and shows all the stages of transition from a nomadic to a settled economy. The process was a lengthy one. In all areas excavated, layer after layer of the typical round houses succeed one another. In the later stages, the defenses apparently were allowed to decay and the houses spread beyond them down the slopes.

Jericho of the Pre-Pottery Neolithic A stage came to an abrupt end. Above the remains of the first phase appears an entirely new type of occupation. A period of erosion intervenes between the two, with buildings on the edge of the mound denuded, and rain-water gullies cutting down to a considerable depth in more than one place. It is, however, impossible to estimate whether the erosion resulted from a succession of heavy storms in a single winter, or whether it stretched over decades. One thing is certain:

thereafter a new people appeared, with a fully developed culture and an architectural style of its own.

The new houses were far more sophisticated than their predecessors, with a whole sequence of rectangular rooms grouped around a courtyard, in a plan which was remarkably stereotyped from one end of the tell to the other. A special feature was the polished plaster floors, with the plaster carried up the face of the walls, which were of mud bricks but of a form completely new—elongated, with a herringbone pattern of thumb imprints. The whole material equipment was new. The flint industry is of the type usually, though inaccurately, called Tahunian; the rich bone industry of the preceding stage disappears, and even the querns are of a new type.

Unlike the Pre-Pottery Neolithic A culture, Pre-Pottery Neolithic B was not indigenous. It is probably related to the Neolithic

Part of a house of Pre-Pottery Neolithic B. The plan, with a range of rectangular rooms connected by wide doorways, is typical. In the foreground are smaller storage rooms. The floors and walls are plastered, with a highly burnished finish.

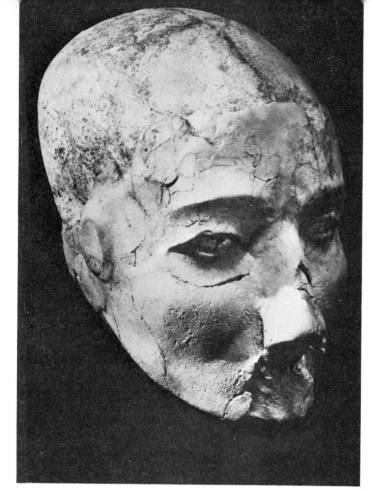

Portrait head of Pre-Pottery Neolithic B. The features are molded in plaster over a human skull, including in this case the mandible. The top of the skull is left bare, and there may originally have been a wig or a headdress. This is the finest head found.

Three portrait heads. Ten were found altogether. All except one were provided with eyes made of sections of bivalve shells; the tenth had eyes of cowrie shells. The individuality of expression is well illustrated here. These heads, unlike the other illustrated, did not have the mandible included, and the chins are molded over the upper teeth.

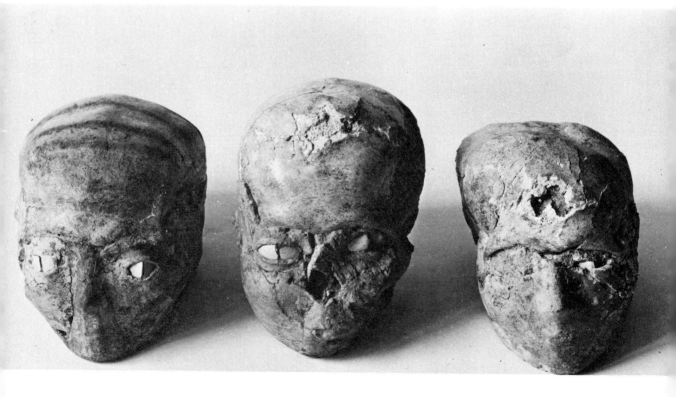

of Anatolia, where the remains of Çatal Hüyük have many similar features. The relation is that of a shared ancestor, and further research may find such an ancestral culture in Syria. The new people probably appeared at Jericho about the middle of the seventh millennium, and their culture may have lasted until nearly the middle of the sixth millennium.

Pre-Pottery Neolithic B Jericho was populous and well organized. What is probably a succession of town walls has been identified on the west side. To the north and south, the town extended beyond the limits of the earlier one. The most remarkable product of Pre-Pottery Neolithic B is undoubtedly the series of portrait heads molded in clay over human skulls. Numerous burials were found beneath the floors of houses, and from many of the skeletons the cranium had been removed. At least some of these crania, in one case with the mandible as well, were preserved and given the appearance of their owners during their lifetime. These plastered skulls must be interpreted as a form of ancestor worship, and thanks to them remarkable light has been thrown on the artistic development of ca. 5800 B.C.

Pre-Pottery Neolithic B also came to an abrupt end. It remained resolutely independent of all pottery utensils. When pottery appears, it is in pits cut into the ruins of the pre-pottery town. These remains were eroded, but the time scale of erosion is difficult to establish and so far there are no absolute dates for the Pottery Neolithic cultures. The pits proved to be the sites of huts, whose stratification indicates a long sequence of re-cuttings, gradual fillings-up followed by a sequence of new pits. Pottery was abundant, consisting largely of very coarse straw-wiped vessels, but with a few finer bowls and jugs decorated with chevrons of red on a cream slip, to which the name Pottery Neolithic A was given at Jericho.

At a later stage normal buildings appear, with walls of bun-shaped, plano-convex bricks. This stage is marked by the appearance of new pottery, usually covered with a matt red slip, with decoration in bands of herringbone incisions, jar rims of the type called bow rims, splay-ended handles; this has been called Pottery Neolithic B. Though there was doubt on this point for some time, it is now clear that the two types of pottery do represent two separate stages. The whole stage is definitely retrogressive. The inhabitants were simple villagers living in huts, and their occupation may have been to a certain degree seasonal, indicating that they were pastoralists rather than agriculturalists.

The dates of both the beginning and the end of the Pottery Neolithic stage at Jericho are uncertain. At a guess, the first appearance must have been about 4500 B.C., and the final stages must have lasted into the fourth millennium. Pottery of both types has been found on other sites. None of these help to date Pottery Neolithic A, but Pottery Neolithic B has some contacts with the Ghassulian culture, and the latter can be shown to overlap with the arrival of the groups known at Jericho as Proto-Urban, for which there is a radiocarbon dating ca. 3300 B.C. at Jericho.

At Jericho there may have been another gap at the end of the Pottery Neolithic stage, since there are no contacts between the earlier group and the Proto-Urban people. The appearance of the latter marks the beginning of a new epoch in many respects. The Jericho evidence suggests that in the last third of the fourth millennium groups of newcomers were reaching Palestine and that their amalgamation provided the basic stock from which sprang the population of the Early Bronze Age. The most striking new feature is the practice of burying in rock-cut tombs. No burials of either Pottery Neolithic group have been found. The new-

comers were responsible for the earliest of the century-long succession of tombs cut in the slopes surrounding the site. The remains of several hundred individuals were found in single tombs, and it is clear that the bones were stacked in the tombs after the flesh had decayed. With the skeletal remains were many pottery vessels, and their characteristics suggest that two successive groups arrived and subsequently merged. The newcomers seemed to have lived on the town site in houses that were either round or had rooms with apsidal ends, but the full evidence from the various sites has not yet been correlated.

The Early Bronze Age at Jericho seems to emerge from the Proto-Urban, though there may be an additional cultural element. This is a fully urban stage, for the greater part of the town was enclosed by mud-brick walls. The complex of the structures in all excavated areas suggests a thriving population, and the many rebuildings of the town walls, sometimes in new positions, show how necessary it was to keep the defenses in repair, either against the occupants of neighboring Palestinian towns or against invaders from the east.

In one area, seventeen successive stages in the town walls can be identified. The seventeenth was destroyed by a raging fire, and its destruction marks the end of the Early Bronze Age town, probably ca. 2300 B.C. The catastrophe was the work of nomadic invaders who can be identified as the Amorites, and the succeeding period can best be described as Intermediate Early Bronze—Middle Bronze. For a long time the newcomers only camped on the site, and when they ultimately built houses, these were of flimsy

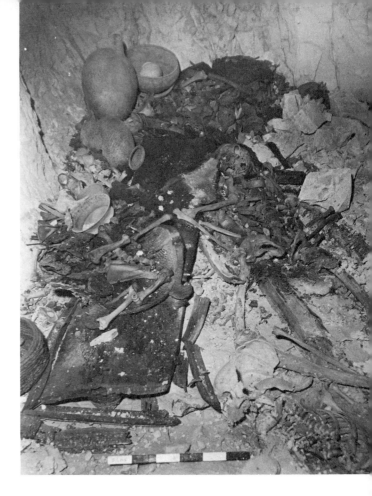

House of Middle Bronze Age Jericho. On the left is a street which in the background has a series of stone-cobbled steps ascending the hill; in the foreground the drain beneath it has been exposed. On the right are shops and storerooms, while the living quarters would have been on an upper story. The houses were destroyed by fire; the section in the background shows streaks of burnt material washed down over the destroyed walls during the period of abandonment following the destruction c. 1560 B.C. Above these streaks a line of stones represents the foundations of a wall—all that remains of the Late Bronze occupation—just below the modern surface.

Tomb of the Middle Bronze Age. The skeleton of the principal burial lies on a wooden bed. Beside it is a wooden table with a wooden platter loaded with joints of meat. Around the wall are jars that had contained liquid, vessels for eating and drinking, and a basket with toilet equipment. At the rear are the remains of earlier burials pushed back to make room for the final ones, which included another adult, an adolescent, and a child.

construction. They never built a town wall. The greater part of the evidence about them comes from tombs, and the different tombs and offerings show that the social structure was tribal, and they emphasize the nomadic character of the population. About 1900 B.C. there was another complete break. New groups once more brought an urban civilization, and the pottery and other material make it clear that the newcomers of the Middle Bronze Age were closely linked with the population of the Canaanite towns of coastal Syria.

Once again Jericho was a fortified town. The evidence for this is restricted to a small area on the east side, for most of the Middle Bronze Age strata were removed in subsequent denudation phases. The early defenses consisted of mud-brick walls, similar to those of the Early Bronze Age. These were suc-

ceeded by something very different. The full stratigraphical data are still to be worked out, but it seems likely that the change came in the second half of the eighteenth century B.C. The new defenses consist of a steeply sloping bank, revetted at its foot by a stone facing, with the town wall standing on its summit. This type of defense can be traced from Carchemish on the Euphrates to Tell el-Yahudiyeh near Cairo, and can clearly be associated with the Hyksos, warrior bands who dominated Syria and Egypt in the eighteenth and seventeenth centuries B.C.

Some of the best evidence of the material cultures of the Middle Bronze Age at Jericho comes from the tombs. Burial was by interment in rock-cut tombs, with a succession of burials taking place in each tomb; they were, in fact, family vaults. Each individual was buried with the possessions he would require in the after-life—food, furniture, and personal toilet equipment—but curiously enough no provision at all was made for spiritual needs. The environment of the Jericho tombs was uniquely suited to the survival of organic matter, and in those tombs, which suffered no later disturbances, evidence has survived about the wooden furniture, certainly about the contemporary houses, the basket work, the textiles and food, all of which make an invaluable contribution to the knowledge of the period.

The latest Middle Bronze Age houses were destroyed by fire. In all probability the destruction can be associated with the expulsion of the Hyksos from Egypt; it may have been the work of the Egyptians themselves between ca. 1580 and 1560 B.C., or that of the groups expelled from Egypt. It is at any rate clear that at Jericho there is no evidence of the sixteenth-century occupation that is found, for instance, at Megiddo and Tell el-Ajjul. Corresponding to this gap in material remains are layers of wash on the tell. The first evidence of reoccupation, from finds on the tell and in the tombs, belongs to the second half of the fourteenth century B.C., with a terminal date of 1325 B.C. If the destruction of Jericho is to be associated with an invasion under Joshua, this is the date that archaeology suggests.

The remains of this fourteenth-century occupation were almost entirely destroyed by erosion. Overlying these erosion levels are buildings of the seventh century B.C. The end of this occupation comes presumably with the Babylonian destruction. Thereafter, the tell ceases to be the nucleus of Jericho, and successive centers of the town of this same name are to be found within the oasis.

The Cave of the Treasure

by PESSAH BAR-ADON

The region of the Dead Sea, one of the most arid areas of the world, has in recent years been one of the most fertile from the archaeologist's point of view. There seems no end to the marvelous discoveries that are made in caves hidden in the cliffs, which escaped notice until the accidental discovery of the first Dead Sea scrolls suggested that these almost inaccessible hideouts would be worth investigating.

A full-scale exploration of a great number of caves was staged in 1960 and 1961 by Hebrew University, the Department of Antiquities, and the Israel Exploration Society, assisted by the Israeli Defense Forces and numerous volunteers. The expedition, which explored the caves in wadis of the Judaean desert, was divided into four groups, each assigned to a specific area. The leaders of the groups were N. Avigad, Y. Aharoni, Y. Yadin, and the author. The co-ordinator of all four groups was J. Aviram. My sector included the southern bank of Nahal Hever, Nahal Holed, Nahal Asahel, and Nahal Mishmar (nahal = valley). The first week was spent in surveying dozens of caves along the edge of cliffs which rose to a height of 200 meters, climbing and being lowered into the caves by a single rope. Work in the caves was extremely difficult because of the ever-present clouds of dust. Even the use of

masks was ineffective. Finally we decided to excavate a cave in Nahal Mishmar which had been inhabited and which we were sure had not been visited by Bedouin.

The approach to the cave was extremely difficult and hazardous; entrance was gained by means of a rope ladder. It seems clear that in ancient times access to this cave as well as to others nearby was somewhat easier than it is today, for traces of a trail are still visible along the cliff. However, it can never have been very easy to enter the cave, and this meant that the inhabitants could not be taken by surprise. In order to overcome them it would have been necessary for an enemy to conduct a siege, cutting off their supplies of food and water. Two springs rise from the side of the cliff more than six hundred feet below the cave, but even if they yielded water at the time when the caves were occupied they can hardly have been of much use except during peaceful periods. For even in ancient times the descent must have been very difficult, and anyone climbing down the face of the cliff would have been conspicuous. In winter, water may have been obtained from rock pools in the vicinity, which would have been filled with rainwater, or by flood waters pouring down the Judaean mountains.

The Cave of the Treasure—the name we

W. Braun—D. Harris

The treasure in situ *in the cave. The preliminary sorting is begun.*

Straw sieve found in the cave, 38 cm. in diameter. The inside was worn from use, while the outside was well-preserved.

Helene Bieberkraut

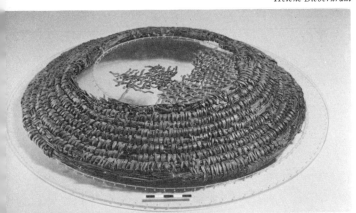

gave it—is a natural cave situated near the top of a cliff which rises 984 feet above the level of the Dead Sea. The cave has two main chambers, each about 39 x 46 feet in area and from 5 to 11½ feet in height. There are also some crevices, which have not yet been entirely explored. The ceilings of both chambers were coated with soot, but on one there were large patches of unblackened stone where parts of the ceiling had fallen, presumably after the inhabitants had left the cave. A floor of beaten earth and straw extends over both chambers, and on these uppermost floors were found fragments of papyri inscribed in Greek and Hebrew, as well as ostraca (potsherds) with Hebrew inscriptions.

In the first chamber there were two hearths, one square, the other circular. Both contained ashes, broken cooking pots, and blackened remains of food. In the second chamber, on a somewhat lower level also of beaten earth, there were traces of other fires. This level probably represents the occupation of Jewish fugitives at the time of the destruction of the Second Temple in the year 70.

From these layers came many remains of the Roman period—lamps, glassware, leather objects, and fabrics. The evidence seems to show that the cave was inhabited by ordinary people who had been forced to leave their homes and seek refuge. The valuable possessions they brought with them indicate that they made this move with relative deliberation, but there are signs that the cave was finally abandoned in a hurry.

The floors of beaten earth covered an earlier level of debris dating from the Chalcolithic period (fourth millennium B.C.). There was no occupation in the intervening three thousand years. Chalcolithic remains include fireplaces and household utensils, mainly pottery but also a unique basket sieve. There were also pieces of straw matting, straw trays, parts of a basket, and a woven rope. Among the pots were a small bowl that had been used as a lamp, as is shown by marks of soot on the rim, part of a churn, and various kinds of jars. A clay figure of a sheep was found, and many animal bones were uncovered: sheep, goats, a mole, a rabbit, various birds, and many sea shells. A large quantity of grain was discovered, including uncarbonized spikelets of wheat and barley, making it possible to determine the species and even the variety. The wheat was found to be emmer, and this was the first time it had been discovered in an excavation in Palestine. Also for the first time in this region was found einkorn wheat, the most primitive of the cultivated wheat species.

But the great surprise came on the eighth day of our work in the cave, in the 1961 campaign. In the north wall of the cave a sloping stone was found to be covering a natural niche. Through cracks at its edge could be seen the glint of metal. At once we set about clearing away the loose earth all around the stone until it was entirely exposed. We had to stop work when darkness came, but early the next morning we started to uncover the great hoard that the niche contained. At the moment when the treasure was revealed there was an awed silence—and then in an instant the narrow space in the cave was filled with an outburst of rejoicing.

All the objects—of which there proved to be 429—were wrapped in a straw mat. It took us three hours to remove them. Almost all are of metal; six are of haematite, six of ivory, and one of stone. While some of the objects can be named and their function is understood, others are of completely un-

Elaborate wand, or standard, decorated with ibex heads. Height 27.5 cm.

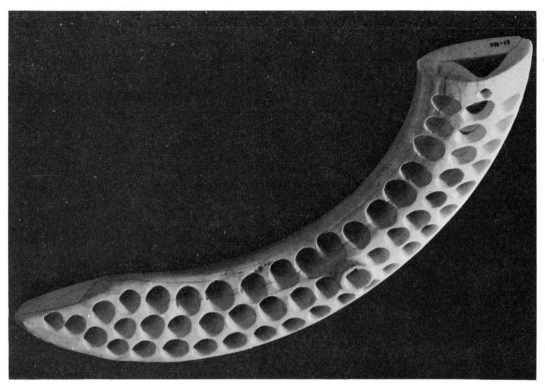

known types, not previously discovered else-where. We therefore devised names for them, according to their resemblance to known objects. There are about 240 metal "mace heads" of various sizes and shapes, some with incised and relief decoration. Six mace heads are of haematite—rounded, flat-tened, and egg-shaped—similar to others found elsewhere in the Palestinian area. The one stone mace head is of rounded form, much like others found in the Near East.

There are about twenty metal chisels and axes, such as have been found on other Chalcolithic sites in Palestine and also in Egypt, Syria, Anatolia, and Mesopotamia. About eighty metal "wands," or standards, some hollow and some solid, of varying shapes and ornamentation, were included in the treasure.

Five objects made of hippopotamus tusks, each perforated with many holes, have one fragmentary parallel from Beersheba. There is also a unique box made of elephant tusk, elongated and slightly concave in form.

Ten metal "crowns" were found (9 to 19.5 cm. in height). One is a hollow cylin-drical object with flattened, protruding rims and concave sides in which there is an aperture about five centimeters square (barely visible in the photograph). At the top of either side of this opening is a cylin-drical boss, and on the lower rim there is a boss-shaped foot and two perforations where others were to be attached. Above one side of the aperture is a spool-shaped object on a stem, and a broken projection shows that there was one on the other side to correspond with it. On the outside the crown is decorated with an incised design

Object made from a hippopotamus tusk, from Chalcolithic level.

Two views of a hollow wand terminating in a human head. Height 13.2 cm.

Metal "crown" with elaborate ornamentation: two gates, two birds, and a pillarlike object above an opening in the side that is barely visible in the mirror view of the object, at the right.

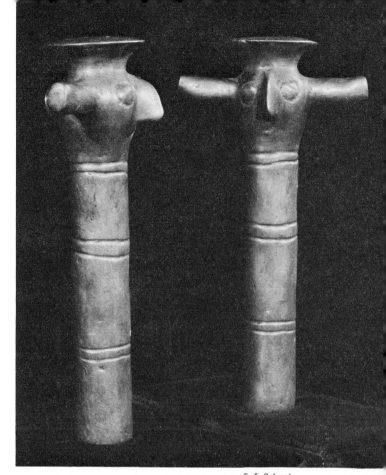

S. J. Schweig

S. J. Schweig

consisting of three horizontal broken lines with herringbone pattern between. Fixed on the upper rim are two objects resembling gates, each decorated with small bosses and with a pair of horns protruding from the top. Between these are two rather crude figures of birds.

Another crown has a representation of a human face with a prominent nose and well-defined eyes. A human face also appears on one of the standards. Both are like those on Chalcolithic stone ossuaries found at several sites in Palestine. There is also a striking resemblance between the decoration on the first crown and that painted on ossuaries and on implements of the same period. From the evidence of the ossuaries as well as from that of a fresco found at Teleilat Ghassul (see *Israel Exploration Journal* 12 [1962] 224-225) it seems most likely that the decoration of the first crown represents a temple. Many of the other objects in the hoard were doubtless of religious significance.

Intensive work is now being done in analyzing the metal of the objects and in identifying its source. It has been found that it is copper with a high percentage of arsenic. The cloth, wood, matting, and other organic matter are being studied at the Institute of Fibres and Forest Products Research of the Ministry of Commerce and Industry, in Jerusalem. In addition, Carbon 14 tests are being made.

The discovery of these objects of excellent workmanship raises questions, such as the identity of their makers, the purpose for which they were made, the method of using them, and so forth. When these questions have been answered we shall know a great deal more about the Chalcolithic Age and its people. At this early stage of research it seems that the connections of the culture represented in the cave point toward the north. If the objects we have found really are ritual appurtenances from a temple in the region, then we will want to know what made the owners of the treasure hide it, what prevented them recovering it, and, more generally, what caused the sudden destruction of many settlements in Palestine at the end of the Chalcolithic period.

The Cemetery at Bab edh-Dhra', Jordan

by PAUL W. LAPP

In the late 1950s a trickle of Early Bronze pots began to appear in the antiquities shops of Jerusalem, in the Hashemite Kingdom of Jordan. They appeared to range from Early Bronze I to III B, that is, they spanned the entire period from the latter part of the fourth millennium B.C. to near the end of the third. They were reported to have come from the Hebron area and even from Qumran. From 1960 to 1965 the trickle became a stream, then a flood. Now the pots glut the market.

Early in 1964 came a report which made it clear that a major source of the pots was a cemetery just south of the large fortified site at Bab edh-Dhra', near the eastern shore of the Dead Sea facing the Lisan. On October 26, 1964, Siegfried Mittmann of the German Evangelical Institute and I went to investigate the area. We returned with some sixty more or less complete pots, taken from the surface where they had been carelessly strewn. We informed colleagues of our findings and a small two-week campaign was planned to begin in March 1965.

On March 13 a large truck left with our gear at 5:30 A.M., while we left at 6:45 A.M., taking the Mojib road to Kerak and the fairly good road from Kerak to Ghor el-Mazra', at the edge of the Lisan. We began setting up camp on an unused roadbed at the point where the new road turns south for Ghor es-Safi.

The usual beginning-of-dig problems were quickly settled. There was an ample supply of workmen in a neighboring encampment; there was a good spring for our water supply a few kilometers off; the cemetery was on government land. Our chief problem was to locate tombs as efficiently as possible. We made arrangements for the services of a local expert for the next day and hoped for the best.

In the morning we hired thirty-five men, eight for each of four supervisors, a guard, a camp boy, and a water man. The supervisors divided their men into two four-man search teams, and we began to test. On the first day we found chiefly quantities of potsherds, and it became apparent that we were digging in a large camp site and were outside the cemetery area. Dr. Mittmann's group, just beyond the confines of the settlement, almost immediately struck a mudbrick wall. This proved to belong to a large charnel house, and for the entire campaign

Dr. Mittmann was occupied in clearing this building.

That evening we had a session with another local expert, who told us that he knew of tombs which had yielded a truckload of pottery. The next morning he did his best to show his ability as a diviner. His formula was simple: to find large, smooth black stones with faces emerging at the surface. This formula worked very well, and we soon discovered the truth—the cemetery had been so intensively used that we were almost bound to hit something wherever we dug. We estimated that if the rest of the cemetery was like the area we worked, it would have contained a minimum of twenty thousand shaft tombs!

By the third day we had located enough tombs to more than occupy us for the projected two-week campaign, and we decided that it should be extended for an additional two weeks. During the last half of the campaign we had to exercise rigid discipline to keep from starting new tombs which could not be finished. Even so, the night before our departure saw us like a band of tomb robbers removing 347 pots from just inside the doorway of one more charnel house.

Bab edh-Dhra' was discovered in 1924 by W. F. Albright. Twenty years later he published a short article (*Bulletin of the American Schools of Oriental Research* 95 [1944] 3-11) on some of the potsherds he had collected from in and around the fortress and from a cairn burial. His conclusion was: "The latest possible date for any Bab edh-Dhra' pottery is thus the 21st century B.C., and its maximum scope is 23rd-21st century B.C. I am inclined, moreover, to date most of it about the 22nd century B.C." This dating still seems entirely sound for the city's surface sherds and the cairn burial involved.

We found three distinct kinds of burials in the cemetery—cairn burials, charnel houses, and shaft tombs. The cairn burial (the lat-

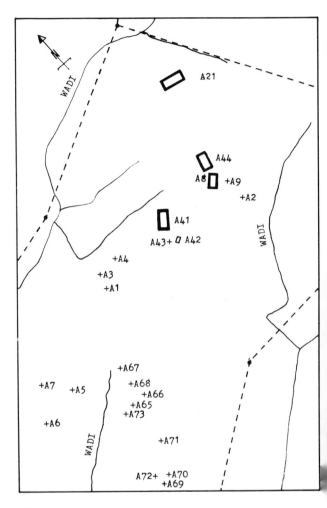

Plan of tombs excavated at eastern end of cemetery.

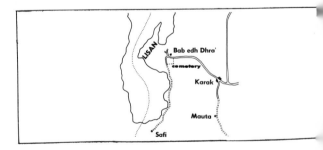

est type) consists of a shallow pit in which was placed a single articulated skeleton together with some pots and, in one case, a dagger as well. The pit was then filled with stones which formed a heap above the original surface. There may be variants of this type, but not many of the cairns—which were few and widely scattered—were excavated. The pottery represents a complete break with that of the fortified town and the charnel houses, and is to be assigned to the Intermediate Bronze Age. It apparently belongs to the people who destroyed the Early Bronze town and camped in the vicinity during the last quarter of the third millennium.

From our limited evidence it seems that during the period of the fortified town burials were largely in charnel houses. We excavated four of these completely, as well as parts of two others. They were rectangular mud-brick buildings without interior partitions. Poles were found in pieces of fallen roofing. The buildings varied in size from about 11.50 x 5.50 meters to 7 x 5 meters. Each had an entryway in one of the broad sides, as in Early Bronze temples and houses. The entrances commonly had a very large threshold slab. There is evidence that they were sealed by mud-brick walls forming a "forecourt" of something under 1.50 x 2 meters. In one case, where the entrance was flanked by two rather well-dressed orthostats, each over a meter in height, the threshold was packed with skulls. Parts of the wooden door frame and wooden nails were preserved.

The floors were usually cobbled, but in one instance a smaller building had a tramped earth floor. The buildings contained piles of mixed bones and pots. Some piles contained chiefly long bones, others only skulls with a few long bones, still others a wide variety of bones; some contained only miniature pots, others only large pots, while still others included both large and small. We also found

Cairn burial. Single flexed burial placed on a mat with small pot above feet. The head lay just below the surface and 12 cm. above floor of shaft-tomb chamber, which is partly disturbed.

Charnel house A21. Rectangular mud-brick building (roughly 11.5 x 5.5 m.) with stone-paved entryway, large threshold slab, and cobbled floor. Several piles of pots mixed with bones had been removed before photography.

Crescent-shaped battle-ax, probably of copper (length ca. 30 cm.) from a charnel house (A44) bone group consisting mostly of long bones and skulls.

three copper daggers, each with four rivets, a crescent-shaped copper battle-ax, stone plaques and mace heads, and quantities of beads. Signs of burning were found in some of the buildings, but in only one did the burning extend over a large part of the interior. In two others there were considerable traces of burning in the vicinity of the doorway, which involved large quantities of cloth as well as of wood associated with the entryway. In these two last cases it is clear that the burning occurred just before the building was sealed, for there is no evidence of later destruction.

The pots from the buildings are contemporary with the sherds from the walled city. There seem to be indications that some of the buildings were sealed before others. The latest was probably not sealed earlier than the twenty-third century B.C. This date may also be suggested for Jericho Tomb A 114 (B) with its similar battle-ax, lamp, and pots (K. Kenyon, *Jericho I* [1960], 175-179). In this light the city represents a late outpost of the Early Bronze city-state tradition, and its charnel houses display a new and fascinating facet of this civilization.

The third and earliest type of burial was in shaft tombs. We cleared some nineteen shafts and their thirty-five related chambers. All of these contained tomb groups of the same type, with the exception of two (A 4 and A 43) which were also distinguished by

specially constructed entryways consisting of well-shaped, slab-lined sides supporting a slab roof.

Tomb A 4 belongs clearly to the twenty-fourth century B.C., along with Jericho Tombs A and F 2. It contained exquisite red-burnished jugs and lattice-painted juglets with pierced lugs, both of which are also prominent in the charnel houses. This tomb, besides containing the articulated burial of a child laid upon an articulated adult skeleton, was also one of the few which provided clear evidence of dismembered burials. The contents were in a state of complete disarray, but the well-sealed entryway and rich contents show clearly that the tomb had not been robbed.

The other shaft tomb with a stone-lined entryway (A 43) contained a ceramic group as yet unparalleled at edh-Dhra'. While some of the forms are duplicated in the charnel houses and others in the earlier shaft tombs, only this tomb contained pottery with painted bands of parallel strokes, such as are traditionally assigned to Early Bronze I. The finding of this Proto-Urban ware together with lattice-painted juglets typical of Early Bronze II suggests that Proto-Urban pottery may be at least partly contemporary with the main ceramic tradition of the Early Bronze Age. Other vessels in this shaft tomb, such as "red-cross" bowls, have parallels in Syria, Anatolia, and the Aegean area. This tomb lay directly below a charnel house, and its shaft cut into that of one of the earlier shaft tombs. Thus stratigraphically it lies between them and typologically it has strong links with both. Its plan is similar to that of A 4, but the arrangement of the contents follows the earlier tombs with a central pile of disarticulated bones. The painted tradition is the obvious predecessor of the lattice tradition, which, in fact, is found on the same vase. If this group of tombs is assigned a date near the beginning of the third millennium, more than five hundred years are left for the accumulation of the numerous charnel houses.

The rest of the shaft tombs were unusually consistent in their contents, but there were almost always one or two unique features to keep our interest from flagging as we tediously chipped away with penknife and brush at the hard-packed silt deposit which filled most of the chambers. The usual pattern is a circular shaft appearing below 50 cm. to one meter of surface wash. Blocking slabs at the base of the shaft cover the entrances of from one to five chambers. There is a 50-cm. step down to the floor of the dome-shaped chamber. In the center of the typical chamber was a heap of bones lying on a mat, with the long bones of several adults and perhaps a child neatly laid on the pile. To one side was a line of skulls or skull fragments. Surrounding these and lining the walls were from ten to seventy-five pots, usually nested and stacked. One or two stone cups were common, but never more. Then there were the unusual features. One tomb had two beautiful stone mace heads. Another had two vases of the type called *kernos*. Another had a square chamber with a flat roof only 47 cm. high. In still another was a woven mat with what must have been an exquisite pattern. Other tombs had pots which contained hundreds of beads. In one there was a clear impression of cloth on a long bone. In another tomb the marks of the tools used to carve out the chamber were beautifully preserved. Several had bones scattered through the tomb and pots heaped up on them. One contained two articulated burials together with the usual disarticulated deposit. Most fascinating was the discovery, during the tedious job of clearing out and recording the bone pile, of the first female figurine of unbaked clay, a prototype of the Late Bronze type with exaggerated pierced ears. Three

Charnel house entryway, looking outward at pile of skulls and bones packed between orthostats of entrance. Thin mud-brick wall surrounds, and probably sealed, the stone-paved entrance. Above the bone pile were large quantities of cloth, mostly burned, but some still well enough preserved to resist tearing.

Same entryway after removal of bone group. Two steps lead down to clay floor. Heaps of pots flank entry; copper dagger lies between (to right of scale). There were also over a thousand beads and several stone plaques.

Shaft-tomb chamber (A 69) shown after removal of limestone chips which fell into chamber when slab blocking entryway was removed. Left to right: stone cup, row of skulls, bone pile, pots, and remains of a wooden staff (center background). There was no evidence that the pots had ever contained anything.

Find the figurine! Center of photo is figurine of unbaked clay embedded in a shaft-tomb bone pile. Note the large doubly pierced ears, beaked nose, raised stump arms, female breasts, base with slightly stumpy feet.

bone piles produced seven of these figurines.

The most exciting experience of the dig came with the removal of a blocking stone from the first perfectly sealed chamber we discovered. Despite dislocation by roof fall and silting we were fairly sure of the original tomb plans, but here was a chamber with each pot and bone just as it had been left over forty-five hundred years ago. The serrated marks of the flint tool with which the chamber had been cut were preserved over the entire domed surface. The lines of the mat on which the bone pile had been laid were clear, and beneath were cracks in the floor which had dried out before the mat was laid. Twenty-five pots were neatly stacked and nested, and it was clear that they had never contained food or liquid; in fact, they had never been used and most of them did not even need dusting. There was a neat line of skulls: three adults, one child, and one infant. The long bones of adults and children were carefully placed on top of the pile of bones.

In the light of this evidence and the overlapping of Early Bronze I and II typology in tomb A 43, I would assign these tombs to the late fourth and the early third millennia B.C. The same pots are represented in the camp-site layers we encountered on our first day of excavation. These belonged to people who camped at the site before the fortified city was built. For how long is difficult to say, but certainly the creation of a cemetery of twenty thousand tombs took considerable time.

As we look over the masses of pottery we have found, we cannot help thinking that the people who produced a three-million-pot cemetery were as much slaves to pots as are archaeologists!

A Canaanite-Hyksos
City at Tell Nagila

by RUTH AMIRAN AND A. EITAN

On the inner coastal plain of southern Israel, about twenty miles north of Beersheba and nineteen east of Gaza, is situated the mound known as Tell Nagila. Covering an area of about ten acres and rising six-seven meters above the surrounding area, Tell Nagila is in the shape of a rectangle with rounded corners. It is founded on a low, natural hill overlooking the left bank of the river called Nahal Shiqma. Tell el-Hesi lies on the same river. The first excavations in this area were carried out by Flinders Petrie, the great pioneer of Near Eastern archaeology, between 1890 and 1935. Tell el-Hesi, in fact, was the first mound ever excavated in Palestine. In this region, near the important bridgehead of the coastal road, at the southern gateway leading to Canaan and to one of its major ports, there was much political and military contact between Canaan and Egypt.

The area is dotted with similar mounds, only a few of which have been tested by the archaeologist's spade. Some have been identified with ancient cities. Tell Far'ah is thought by W. F. Albright to be Sharuhen, known from biblical and Egyptian sources to have been captured after three years of

siege by Ahmose, the first ruler of the XVIIIth Dynasty. Benjamin Mazar has suggested that Tell Jemmeh may have been Yursa, described in Egyptian sources as a town which rebelled immediately after the campaign of Ahmose. It will be of interest to learn how our tell fits into this picture.

Four areas have been excavated on the tell itself, as well as one area and two tombs south of it. Fourteen strata have been distinguished, representing the history of the town from the Chalcolithic to the Mameluke period. It was not continuously occupied, however, during this long span of time. The extent of the Chalcolithic settlement is still unknown. Above it there must have been a considerable settlement during the Early Bronze II-III periods, and a small tomb (DT 1) south of the tell belongs to it. A gap of six or seven hundred years followed, before the city of the Middle Bronze II B-C period came into being under the Hyksos, who ruled both in Egypt and in Canaan. This city seems to have had the main—if not the only—period of prosperity in the history of Nagila. The tell owes its shape and the accumulation upon it mostly to this period. The Late Bronze Age seems to have

*View of Tell Nagila looking southwest. The
northern slope and the northeast corner, with
Area F, are shown.*

*Plan of the tell indicating areas excavated.
Area A: city center; Area B: gateway to
Umayyad khan; Areas C and F: fortifications;
Areas E and G: unfortified settlements;
Area D: tombs.*

had a sparsely built settlement. Another gap
in the history of the tell occurs in the following period (Iron Age I). During Iron
Age II unfortified settlements existed both
on the mound and on two natural slopes
south of it (Areas E, G). On the tell are
only a few architectural remains, mainly of
silos. On the hills and slopes south of the
tell toward the river, part of a village was
excavated, which proved to contain rich
finds of the seventh century B.C. Only scanty
remains represent the Hellenistic, Roman,
and Byzantine periods. Then followed that
long gap in the occupation of the site before
a large rectangular caravanserai (about 2½
acres in extent), was built on the western
part of the tell; this was the last occupation.
In spite of this long history the accumulation of debris does not exceed 3–4 meters in
thickness, at least not in the center of the
tell, where virgin soil has been reached.

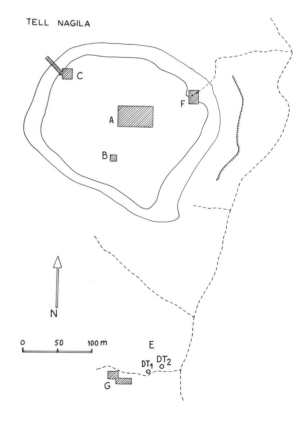

TELL NAGILA

0   50   100 m

N

E

DT₁ DT 2

G

Our excavations give us a detailed picture of the extensive city of the Canaanite-Hyksos period. We uncovered a living quarter and part of a public building in the center of the city (Area A), an elaborate fortification system around it (Areas C and F), and a rich tomb (DT 2) south of the site (Area E). At this period the settlement was not confined to the walled city but spread to the north and south as well as on the eastern slope above the river. Information about the houses has come from the center of the tell. Four or possibly five strata covering the two hundred years of this period came to light. The three upper strata are similar in plan and in character, but not enough is known as yet to describe the two lowest levels.

The changes from one stratum to the next are slight and do not affect the plan and orientation of the houses: walls are reused, sometimes repaired, and floors are raised; sometimes new walls are added and others removed. The plan of the excavated section shows parts of four blocks of houses opening onto two parallel streets. There may have been streets or lanes at right angles to these. The streets are about 1.50 m. wide, paved with pebbles and potsherds laid in beaten whitish clay.

The houses, built close together, always have common or connecting walls, either a side or back wall common to two rows of dwellings or a front wall connecting adjoining houses. In some cases a few steps lead down from the street into the house. Generally rectangular in shape, the houses seem to be composed of one or two small rooms opening onto a courtyard. The size of a room is generally 2 x 3 m., while a courtyard aver-

Area A, plan showing the various strata. Stratum VIII: MB II B; Stratum VII: MB C; Stratum VI: LB; Strata IV-III: Iron II A-B; Stratum I: A.D. 1100–1500.

Area A, street and houses of the Hyksos city looking south; in background appear northeast corner and part of north wall of the Mameluke khan.

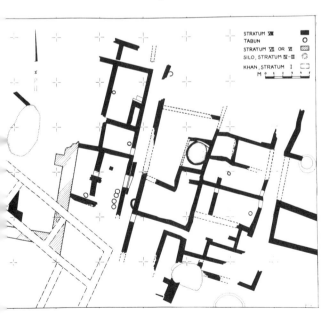

ages 3 x 5 m. One side of the courtyard is sometimes roofed, as indicated by column bases found in a few courts. The columns must have been made of wood, which has long since decayed. These roofed sheds are often paved with flagstones, but generally the floors are of beaten earth. Both stone and sun-dried bricks were used as building material. Usually the lower part of the walls are built of rough field stones, while the upper structures are of brick. The foundations generally extend two or three courses below the floors. The thickness of the walls varies between 40 and 60 cms. The walls, plastered with mud, are not always straight and are mostly of poor workmanship, suggesting that there were no second stories except perhaps for the light sheds on the roofs. It may be assumed that this area is representative of the general town plan, which seems to be oriented to conform with the rectangular shape of the whole settlement.

Built-in furniture includes clay ovens, with openings on the top and on the side, benches of clay or stone, small rounded depressions in the floors lined with pebbles to hold vessels, and rounded silos either lined with stones and plastered or simply mud-plastered. Of the movable furnishings only those made of imperishable materials have been preserved. Pottery is the commonest of these, along with flint implements and grinding stones. Much rarer are objects of luxury type such as faïence and alabaster bottles, ostrich eggshells used as vessels, bone inlays from wooden toilet boxes, in the shape of stylized birds and human figures, scarabs, and a cylinder seal. Very few bronze implements were found—which may be accidental. There were jars and jugs for storing both liquids and dry foodstuffs, juglets used as dippers, cooking pots, dishes and bowls, some red-slipped and burnished, as well as a pair of grinding stones. One vessel, a simple jar, has a painted decoration

Y. Lehman

Seven scarabs found in Tomb DT 2.
1: Hathor; 2: goat, back originally inlaid;
3, 4, 5: scroll designs; 6, 7: meaningless signs
on the faces, lotus and sign on backs.

Micha P.

Group of vessels found in a courtyard in
Area A. Among these are a cooking pot, various
bowls and dishes, juglets, and storage jars.

*Red-slipped and burnished vessel in the shape
of a bull, from Area A. Height 16.5 cm.*

on its shoulder consisting of straight and wavy lines, red and bluish-black, on a white background, a style typical of this period.

In the immediate vicinity of these houses there came to light parts of two large buildings possibly having some public function. These are constructed on a larger scale and their walls are much thicker (1.50 m.), which may indicate that there was a second story.

A clay vessel in the shape of a bull comes from one of these public buildings. The body, which is hollow and has an opening on top of the back, is wheel-made, while the legs are solid, with divided hoofs. The dewlap is prominently shown. The vessel is red-slipped and burnished; the eyes are painted black. This vessel is reminiscent of others common in the Hittite Middle Bronze repertory.

Among the finds of special importance is a potsherd with a fragmentary inscription. Incised deeply before firing, the signs are in two horizontal lines, apparently to be read from right to left. Of the first line only one fragmentary sign is preserved. An important feature is the dot in the second line separating two words, neither of which is complete. Although the reading is uncertain, it is clear that the inscription is in the alphabetic Proto-Canaanite script. This sherd seems to bear one of the earliest Proto-Canaanite inscriptions and thus adds an important contribution to the existing corpus.

We have learned a great deal about the fortifications of this city from a section cut in the northwest slope (Area C). This type of fortification uncovered here is usually designated as "Hyksos *terre pisée* glacis." It is an elaborate construction composed of an earth embankment, a brick wall, earth thrown against the brick wall, and a moat at the foot of the slope. It was an enormous task to build such a fortification. First, the embankment of earth was piled up, encircling the area of the city; then a sun-dried brick wall 2.30–2.50 m. broad was erected on the inner slope of the embankment; finally large quantities of earth and crushed chalk were thrown and beaten against the wall and over the whole slope, creating an even, hard surface. In section this *terre pisée* shows alternating layers of the various kinds of fill used. At the foot of the hill a moat was dug. The glacis extends down to the inner rim of the moat. The brick wall, which is preserved to a height of about three meters, served on the outside as a supporting wall for the *terre pisée*, but on the inside was a normal upright wall, originally higher than it now stands. The level inside the wall is about 1.50 m. lower than the top of the glacis outside.

The location of one cemetery seems to be indicated by the finding of a tomb (DT 2) of the Middle Bronze period, cut in the soft chalk on a slope south of the tell. (The Early Bronze Age tomb was also found in this area.) The tomb is shallow and composed of three small chambers in a row, with an entrance to the southernmost chamber, and passages from one to another. This tomb, although cut in the rock, must have had an outer wall of stone or brick. The roof was partly the living rock and partly of the usual roofing material (brush and earth) supported by the wall. There were about forty-five skeletons, the bones in disorder, but the skulls assembled carefully along the walls and in the corners. About 150 pottery vessels of various types include many juglets and dipper juglets, bowls and jugs and jars. Inside two of the jars were dipper juglets, which suggests that they were originally suspended within the jars from a small stick laid across the mouth. Among the vessels were a single black juglet with punctured dots, of the so-called Tell el-Yahudiyeh ware, and a unique bowl decorated with incisions on its shoulder and rim. Forty-eight

Micha P.

General view of Middle Bronze Age tomb DT 2, as found.

scarabs of various local styles were found, which show fine workmanship. One alabaster bottle and one of faïence were found in the tomb, as well as some toggle pins, three bronze swords, and the shell of an ostrich egg. A jug of red-on-black ware imported from Cyprus was among the finds. This and the alabaster and faïence bottles, which must have been imported from Egypt, corroborate the well-known fact that there was commercial contact in this period among Canaan, Egypt, and Cyprus.

One of the most interesting objects is a krater of bichrome ware found while clearing the side of a gully cut by the rains into the northeast slope of the tell (Area F). It was in pieces, lying on a stone pavement that seems to belong to the Late Bronze I settlement, according to the stratigraphy. The krater, with two shoulder handles, is a shape typical of this ware, in which the vessels have geometric and figure designs in red and black. On one side there is a single figure, a humped bull tied to a rope with a nose ring; the other side has two figures, an "ibex" and a bird. The bull may be considered a *pars pro toto* representation of a sacrificial scene, as for example in the wall painting at Mari (A. Parrot, *Mission archéologique de Mari, vol. II, Le palais, peintures murales* [Paris 1958] 20, figure 18). This implies that there is more than mere

Micha P.

Bichrome krater (two-handled deep bowl) of Late Bronze I. Height 31 cm.

decorative purpose in the figurative element of the bichrome style, and eventually we may hope for light on the function of the vessel. The "ibex" has a birdlike, smiling face, too long a neck and too short legs, while the bull and the bird are more naturalistic. Can the "ibex" have symbolic significance, or is it just the result of the artist's imagination? This, as well as many other questions raised by our excavations, is yet to be answered.

Our intention, when we resume work in Tell Nagila, is to concentrate on specific points which should complement the picture obtained during our two seasons of work. These include additional information on the fortifications, on town planning, on the houses and the large public building, as well as the character of the settlement at the beginning of the Late Bronze Age. Nagila is certain to contribute to understanding the problems of the end of the Hyksos regime in southern Canaan.

Rock Engravings in the Central Negev

by EMMANUEL ANATI

Since the middle of the past century the Negev, the southern desert of the Land of Israel, has been a fertile field for archaeological research. Its connection with the wanderings of the Children of Israel in the desert, together with the extremely interesting remains of colonization and agriculture in the Roman and Byzantine periods, has made it the pivot of attention for archaeologists such as Robinson, Palmer, Vincent, Abel, Lawrence, Woolley, Alt, Glueck, and many others. Much has already been discovered there; nevertheless vast areas remain as yet unexplored and even unvisited by the trained observer, and consequently every visit brings unexpected surprises.

The rock engravings, or petroglyphs, with which we are concerned had been noticed previously by various travelers, and until quite recently had been considered by most observers to be the work of modern Bedouins. Some of them are, in fact, modern, as we shall later see, but side by side with them ancient engravings are to be found. The distinction between the various types was first made possible by the accidental discovery by an expedition of the Hebrew University's Department of Geography of ancient inscriptions accompanying some of these engravings. A further survey enabled the author to discover a focal point where the petroglyphs were found in great quantities, accompanied by as many as sixty new inscriptions.

The inscriptions were written principally in Thamudean, Nabataean, Greek, and Early Arabic. We could discern that both the Thamudean and Nabataean inscriptions were always related to a particular kind of engraving, Greek to another, and Early Arabic to a third type. Moreover, many of the rocks bear engravings of various periods superimposed, each period having a different shade of patination. The observation of these details on more than five hundred rocks permitted us to distinguish seven different styles. The latest one is modern, the sixth is always connected with Early Arabic inscriptions, the fifth with a few Greek inscriptions, the fourth with Thamudean and Nabataean inscriptions. The other three styles are not accompanied by any inscriptions whatsoever. While the four later styles are to be found in profusion, these three earlier ones are scarce, and therefore create chronological problems.

Photographs Department of Antiquities, State of Israel

Wall engravings in the cave at Wadi Ramliyeh, representing a man and a horned animal. These are the oldest engravings found in the region (Style I).

A tool in situ. *The tools, of local flint, were generally left on or near the engravings.*

We assign to Style I some engravings on the wall of a cave in Wadi Ramliyeh. These differ from all the open-air engravings in technique and size; a schematized man is probably represented, and the upper part of an animal with big round horns. They are very deeply engraved and their full length is about two meters. We have no clues whatsoever as to the precise date of these engravings, but we believe that they compare in technique to some early engravings at Kilwa in southern Transjordan, tentatively dated by Rhotert to the Stone Age. All the other engravings are much smaller, the figures varying from five to forty centimeters.

Style II is characterized by emphasis on space value and a tendency to rounded, simplified forms. Details are omitted; no eyes appear and often the animals' legs and horns are indicated by one stroke for each pair. On one rock, engravings of Style IV, which possess here a patina of a much lighter shade, were superimposed on others attributed to Style II. This permits us to conclude that Style II is considerably earlier than Style IV, which has been assigned to Hellenistic-Roman times. Petroglyphs similar to those of Style II have been found in southern Transjordan and in central Arabia, but as they have not been definitely dated, they cannot contribute much toward determining a chronological framework for our finds.

Style III is more realistic. Human representations appear as well as hunting scenes. In contrast with the previous and subsequent stages, this one is full of life and movement. Such details as eyes, and beards of antelopes, now appear. We have no clue

A drawing of the two stylized horned animals belonging to Style II.

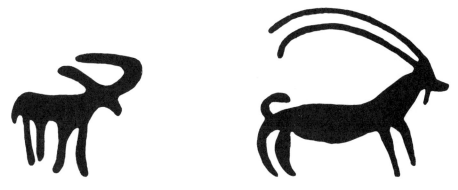

A realistic antelope and a horned animal belonging to Style III.

A hunting scene belonging to Style III. The life and movement that appear in this style are in complete contrast with the previous and following styles.

Dog running after an antelope, a subject very common in several periods. This engraving belongs to Style IV. The same subject is used with a completely different approach in Style III.

The engraved impression of a hand. This subject is typical of the Nabataean period.

to the framework to which this style belongs.

Style IV is schematized and linear. The drawings have no volume; they are static repetitions. With the help of the Thamudean and Nabataean inscriptions that accompany them, their date can be determined as within the period from the third century B.C. to the third century of our era. From this time until the Middle Ages, we find very few changes. The same stylized antelopes appear again and again until late in the Arabic period. Styles IV, V, and VI differ from each other in some details, but the general approach remains much the same.

Style V is a return to realism and movement. It shows that a new wave of life had penetrated into the region. Generally the drawings remain linear, but sometimes the

Engravings of Style VII (the modern style) superimposed on others of Style IV. The different shades of patination can clearly be seen in the photograph.

spaces are filled in. Occasionally objects are defined by a contour line only. Together with antelopes similar to those of Style IV, we find a great number of camels and horses and also scenes of battle, of horse racing, and of caravans. In Styles I-IV we witness the expression in art form of a pastoral and hunting life, but, as the culture developed, new elements such as commerce and war were added to the subject matter, showing the gradual infiltration into primitive rural life of a more sophisticated civilization. Clearly this change was a consequence of the appearance of Roman and Byzantine armies in the area. Style V must belong to the period between the third and seventh centuries of our era.

Style VI returns to the linear and static characteristics, showing how the withdrawal of Byzantine influence caused a return to

Long-horned antelopes belonging to Style V.

A warrior on horseback, armed with a spear, Style V.

A stylized man belonging to Style VI.

the former way of life. The drawings are even more stylized than those of Style IV and they tend to be abstract and ornamental. This style is always accompanied by Early Arabic inscriptions, thus dating it from the seventh century all through the first centuries of the Moslem era.

The Bedouins have continued to engrave these same rocks until this very day, but they have become illiterate and their drawings usually consist of tribal marks and other signs.

By examining the various styles we obtain a surprisingly clear outline of the historical background of the region. This art form, with which we are acquainted in the Sahara, has left its traces in almost all the desert regions of North Africa and the Middle East, from Algeria in the west to eastern Arabia and Mesopotamia in the east. The discoveries described here belong to the same general pattern, and we hope that they may provide a link between the petroglyphs of Asia and Africa.

BIBLICAL CITIES
AND TEMPLES

A view of the Canaanite "Holy of Holies" as it appeared at an advanced stage of excavation. The lion orthostat block can now be seen.

The Rise and Fall of Hazor

by YIGAEL YADIN

Strange as it may seem, practically nothing was known about the Canaanite and Israelite cultures of Galilee until we began excavations at the site of ancient Hazor. Hitherto, the bay of Haifa on the west and the Sea of Galilee on the east were the northern limits of archaeological activity in Palestine relating to those periods. This fact alone was sufficient reason for excavating at Tell el-Qedah, a large mound nearly nine miles north of the Sea of Galilee and five miles southwest of Lake Huleh; but our attention was attracted to the site for two other important reasons: first, its shape, size, and location; second, its probable identification as the city of Hazor.

The mound lies at the foot of the eastern ridge of the Upper Galilee mountain range, in one of the most strategic areas of ancient Palestine—dominating the highway from Egypt to Mesopotamia, Syria, and Anatolia.

The site comprises two distinct areas: the tell and a large rectangular plateau. The tell is a bottle-shaped mound more than six hundred yards long, its "neck" to the west and its "base" to the east, with an average width of about two hundred yards. It is unusually large—more than twenty-five acres in area. Its steep slopes rise from the surrounding wadis (river beds) to a height of about forty yards. The large rectangular plateau, nearly three quarters of a mile long, with an average width of 750 yards, lies immediately north of the mound. It, too, rises from three wadis and ravines on the north, east, and south sides, and its steep slopes are strengthened by the addition of glacis, or supporting walls. The western side of the plateau was especially protected by a large wall of beaten earth that still rises to a height of about fifteen yards. At its base this wall is about one hundred yards thick. Outside it and parallel to it is a large moat. The whole area is thus a well-fortified enclosure. This type of site, large in area and fortified by beaten earth wall, glacis, and moat, is quite rare. Only Carchemish and Qatna are comparable in character and in size. This fact led the late archaeologist John Garstang (who first identified Tell el-Qedah as ancient Hazor) to suggest that the "camp enclosure was large enough to accommodate in emergency 30,000 men with a corresponding number of horses and chariots."

In early times Hazor was undoubtedly a city of high importance. Apart from numerous biblical references, it is one of the few Palestinian cities of antiquity mentioned in pre-biblical literary documents from Egypt, Palestine, and Mesopotamia. Hazor is even mentioned in the Egyptian Execration

Photographs by J. Schweik and A. Volk

57

Texts of the nineteenth century B.C. These texts list potential enemies in the distant provinces of the Egyptian empire. Two recently published cuneiform letters from the important archives of Mari—modern Tell Hariri on the Middle Euphrates—written about 1700 B.C., inform the king of Mari that messengers from various cities in Mesopotamia are on their way to Hazor. Another letter tells the king that a caravan has arrived from Hazor and Qatna, accompanied by Babylonian envoys. In still another letter (as yet unpublished) Hazor seems to be referred to as a horse-breeding center.

Hazor is later mentioned among the cities conquered by the Pharaohs Thutmose III, Amenhotep II, and Seti I. An interesting allusion to Hazor is found in the famous Papyrus Anastasi I (thirteenth century B.C.). Hori, a royal official, challenges Amen-em-opet, the scribe, to answer a number of military and topographical questions.

Perhaps the most important references to Hazor are in the famous Amarna letters from vassal rulers to Egyptian kings. In four letters Hazor is the subject of the correspondence. In two letters the kings of Tyre and Astaroth, respectively, complain that Abdi-Tarshi, king of Hazor, had rebelled against the Pharaoh and captured several of their cities. The other two letters are from the king of Hazor, denying the charges.

But it is in the Bible that Hazor really comes into its own as a key city of strategic importance, according to the book of Joshua and the Deborah narrative in Judges. The victory of Joshua by the "waters of Merom" marks a decisive phase in the conquest of northern Canaan: "And Joshua at that time turned back, and took Hazor and smote the king thereof with the sword: for Hazor beforetime was the head of all those kingdoms . . . and he burnt Hazor with fire"

Air view of Hazor, showing the six areas excavated during 1955 and 1956.

(Joshua 11:10, 11). Later, during the period of the Judges, it was against Jabin, another king of Hazor, that the Israelites had to fight. "And the Lord sold them into the hand of Jabin king of Canaan, that reigned in Hazor, the captain of whose host was Sisera, which dwelt in Harosheth of the Gentiles" (Judges 4:2). And they went to battle under the inspiration of Deborah and the command of Barak, "And the hand of the children of Israel prospered, and prevailed against Jabin the king of Canaan, until they had destroyed Jabin, king of Canaan" (Judges 4:24). This battle, which took place in "Taanach by the waters of Megiddo" (Judges 5:19), marks the beginning of the final phase of the subjugation of the Canaanites.

Two later biblical passages mention Hazor. Solomon rebuilt Hazor and Megiddo and Gezer (I Kings 9:15), the three strategic cities dominating the plains of Huleh, Jezreel, and Ayalon (modern Latrun), making them royal cities, apparently garrisons for his hosts of chariots. The last we hear of Hazor in the Bible concerns its capture in 732 B.C. by Tiglath Pileser III, king of Assyria.

The latest historical reference to Hazor is in I Maccabees (11:67), where we are told that Jonathan the Hasmonean fought against Demetrius (147 B.C.) "in the plain of Hazor."

Professor Garstang was prompted to make his soundings in Hazor (in 1928) by his desire to fix the date of the Exodus and the occupation of the country by Joshua. Unfortunately, apart from a brief description in his famous book *Joshua, Judges*, the results were never published in detail. Garstang's main conclusion was that during the fifteenth century B.C.—the period in which he believed the story of Joshua began—the camp enclosure "was apparently occupied only by temporary structures." He con-

cluded, moreover, that during the fourteenth and thirteenth centuries Hazor's days as an important city were past—while most scholars held that it was precisely during this period that the main phase of the Exodus and the conquest of Canaan occurred. Garstang based his opinion on "the complete absence of Mycenaean specimens," for Mycenaean pottery appears in this part of the world only after about 1400 B.C. and disappears at the end of the thirteen century.

A row of nine monolithic pillars discovered by Garstang in a very narrow trench, which he dug in the center of the mound, was the starting point for the excavation of Area A. Garstang thought that the pillars were part of a stable of the Solomonic period, but this proved incorrect. It is now known that these pillars, as well as a similar, parallel row, were originally part of a large public building of the time of Ahab (874–852 B.C.). Above the original floor level (Stratum V) were four subsequent architectural phases, in all of which the pillars were reused in a variety of ways. Strata III and II embodied them within their walls or demolished those which interfered with their architectural plans. Stratum I used the tops of the pillars as part of the floors. This stratum, nearest the surface, contained the remains of a town of the late eighth and early seventh centuries B.C.—a modest settlement built on the ruins of a city (Stratum II) which had clearly been destroyed by fire. Many beautiful basalt and pottery vessels found intact suggest that the population fled in haste and did not return. The date of the destruction, ascertained through the pottery, was the second half of the eighth century B.C. We therefore assume that this was the city known to have been destroyed by Tiglath Pileser III in 732 B.C.

We found that the public building in its

Ivory cosmetic palette found in the house of Makbiram. On the front is a stylized Tree of Life in relief; on the back is the head of a woman. Two small birds are carved on the narrow sides, on each side of the woman's face. Length 4¾ inches.

original form had two periods of occupation, the first (Stratum V) in the reign of Ahab and the second (Stratum IV) during the times of his successors. It may have served as a storehouse of the type mentioned in II Chronicles 16:4: "And Benhadad . . . sent the captains of his armies against . . . all the store cities of Naphtali."

In the city of the third stratum, which contained typical ninth and eighth century pottery, we found the first Hebrew inscriptions discovered in Galilee from the period of the kings of Israel. The buildings of Stratum III belonged to wealthy merchants of the time of King Jeroboam II (786–746 B.C.), and in one of these were two jar fragments bearing inscriptions in the old Hebrew script, one incised, the other painted. The first inscription reads **LMKBRM**, "belonging to Makbiram." This Hebrew name is hitherto unknown. The second inscription, unfortunately incomplete, might be read as:

YRB'A (= Jeroboam?)
BN'ELM (= the son of Elmatan or Elimelekh)

In the same house (which we called the house of Makbiram) we also found a beautiful ivory cosmetic palette. The walls of this house had been heavily damaged by an earthquake. Could it have been the earthquake referred to in the Book of Amos: "The words of Amos . . . which he saw concerning Israel . . . in the days of Jeroboam the son of Joash king of Israel, two years before the earthquake"?

Below the large building there are at least three more Iron Age strata. All eight strata are included within a period of about five hundred years and supply important pottery material datable within a narrow time range.

East of the large building we discovered,

in Stratum VII, a well-constructed city wall with casemates, probably built by King Solomon. The fact that the wall crossed the center of the mound from north to south suggests that Solomon built a garrison city on only part of it (I Kings 9:15). This wall was later abandoned when the city expanded eastward, and the casemates were turned into workshops and living quarters. In one casemate we found about twenty jars, covered by the fallen roof, which had contained wine or oil.

To establish the relationship between Stratum VII and the latest Canaanite city (thirteenth century B.C.) we cut a deep trench east of the casemated wall. This showed that between the Solomonic and the Late Bronze cities there was at least one other stratum belonging to the first centuries of the Early Iron Age, that is, between 1200 and 930.

The most strongly fortified point was at the western tip of the mound. It was here (Area B) that we discovered a series of citadels, the latest belonging to the Hellenistic period and the oldest to the Assyrian, later reconstructed, during the fifth or fourth century B.C. The Assyrian fort was in the form of a square. It consisted of a central open court flanked on north and south by oblong halls, with a row of small rooms all around. The later reconstruction of the building included the erection in the northern hall of a partition wall containing

The fort of the Assyrian occupation which was restored during the Persian period; in the center is the south hall which, together with a similar hall on the north, flanked the central court.

many niches and several crude mangers. This suggests that the fort then served a small cavalry garrison.

Although this fort was well preserved, we decided to remove it in the hope of uncovering the citadel of the Israelite period. We were amply rewarded for our decision: below the later building was a most imposing citadel composed of two parts. In the south was the fort proper, and north of it an annex containing living quarters. The plan of the fort is simple: a square with a row of square rooms on the north and south sides, and two long, narrow halls in the center. The fort has very solid walls (up to six feet thick) which occupy about forty per cent of its total area, and very deep foundations, in some places extending to about nine feet below the floor. The corners of the building are formed by imposing ashlar blocks, some almost five feet long. But the most interesting feature of this area is the evidence of the terrific destruction which befell it. All the rooms were covered with a layer of ashes about three feet thick; the stones were all black, and numerous charred planks and fragments of plaster from the ceiling were scattered all over. The eastern side—the direction from which the fort was attacked—had been destroyed to such an extent that at some places only the foundations remained. What living evidence of the destruction described so vividly by the Psalmist (137:7): "Rase it, rase it, even to the foundation thereof"!

The type of pottery found on the floors indicated quite plainly that this was the destruction wrought by Tiglath Pileser III—a tragic illustration of the laconic biblical description of this event (II Kings 15:29): "In the days of Pekah king of Israel came Tiglath Pileser, king of Assyria, and took Ijon, and Abel-beth-maacah, and Janoah, and Kedesh, and Hazor, and Gilead, and Galilee, all the land of Naphtali, and carried them captive to Assyria." A brief inscription on one of the wine jars discovered in the citadel adds an intimate touch: LPQH, "for Pekah." The kind of wine was indicated, too: SMDR, that is, *semadar*. This word, which occurs three times in the Song of Songs, has been translated as "tender grape." "The fig tree putteth forth her green figs, and the vines with the *tender grapes* give a (good) smell" (2:13).

Among the many interesting objects found in this area is a small ivory box of Samarian style with delicate carving representing (at the left) a cherub and (at the right) a figure kneeling before the Tree of Life. Also here was found an incense ladle of local marble bearing a beautifully carved hand on the underside, the fingers grasping the bowl. These discoveries were from the last phase of occupation, during the reign of King Pekah. We found ample evidence, however, that the citadel was first built much earlier, probably in the time of Ahab.

In the southwest corner of the large rectangular enclosure on the plateau, close to the beaten-earth wall, we excavated Area C. Here we had the threefold objective of verifying the nature of what Garstang called the "camp area," ascertaining the date of its last occupation, and determining just how the earth wall had been constructed.

The discoveries here were startling. Three feet below the surface we found the remains of a well-built city, with houses and a system of water channels. And much to our surprise, we found the floors of these houses littered with Mycenaean pottery and with vessels of local make, all dating to the last phases of the Late Bronze Age—the thirteenth century B.C.! In other words, here was definite proof that the last city in this enclosure met its end at the time considered by most scholars as the period of Joshua's conquest. There is not yet proof that the city was destroyed by Joshua; such an assumption must be tested by excavation. But certainly one of the obstacles to the theory that Joshua conquered Hazor was Garstang's belief, based on the absence of Mycenaean pottery, that the city had been destroyed about 1400. This difficulty has been removed.

To establish the date of the earliest occupation of the enclosure, we removed Stratum I (the latest city) in the area excavated the previous year. Below it appeared another city (Stratum II), dating to the fourteenth century B.C., approximately the Amarna period. Removing this, we reached still another city (Stratum III)—after a gap corresponding to Late Bronze I (fifteenth century B.C.)—which appears to be built on virgin soil, and thus must be the oldest. This city, from the last phase of the Middle Bronze Age (late eighteenth to early sixteenth century B.C.), had been destroyed by fire, probably by one of the New Kingdom Pharaohs, Amenhotep II or, more

probably, Thutmose III. A pathetic sight appeared below the floors of its houses—scores of infant burials in jars. Each jar contained a skeleton and one or two juglets; in some cases the jars contained two infants. This method of burial is known from other contemporary sites, but the great number of burials in each room—some obviously deposited at the same time—might indicate an epidemic.

The most important discovery of all occurred within the last fortnight of the 1955 campaign. Two small Canaanite temples of the Late Bronze period, one on top of the other, were found at the foot of the beaten-earth rampart. In a central niche, high above the floor, we found the "Holy of Holies." Here was a basalt statue of a male deity seated on a throne, holding a cup. A row of stone stelae stood to the left of the figure. Seven of the stelae are plain, but one bears a simple, effective design: two hands stretched upward, as if in prayer, toward a

The "Holy of Holies" of the Canaanite temple, as first discovered. At left is a seated deity, beside him a row of stelae, with the offering table in front. The orthostat block with a lion carved in relief was found below the stela lying at the extreme right.

Basalt statue of the deity from the Canaanite sanctuary. He is seated on a throne and holds a cup. Height 17¾ inches.

sun disc within a crescent. To the left of the stelae we found a basalt orthostat block bearing the figure of a lion in relief on the front and side. This sanctuary group is unique in Palestine, and in many respects also in the entire Near East. Although Hittite influence is clearly visible, the sculpture is Canaanite in execution and detail. The many vessels found nearby point to a date in the thirteenth century B.C. Here we have a most striking example of Canaanite art, of which so little has been known up to now.

In 1956 we continued to dig in this area and were well rewarded. Near the sanctuary was disclosed another room, full of stelae thrown down in disorder and lying in heaps. Was this a storeroom or had the stelae been cast there by the conquerors? This we do not yet know. While clearing this section we discovered a remarkably intricate system of stone walls and buttresses supporting the lower slopes of the earth wall—some dating to the Middle Bronze period when the wall was built, and some to the Late Bronze period, in the final phases of occupation.

We also enlarged our excavation to the north. Here were storerooms full of big jars as well as potters' workshops, all probably connected with the sanctuary. In one of the potters' shops we discovered a complete potter's wheel (made of two basalt blocks) still in place, with one of the last objects the potter made before he had to flee—an unusual cult mask. In his storeroom we discovered about forty complete vessels: chalices, bowls, lamps, and little jugs.

But the greatest prize was still to come. In the storeroom, hidden below a heap of bowls and placed in a specially prepared jar, we found a cult standard—a bronze plaque, with a tang for fastening it to a pole. The face of the standard, which is plated with silver, bears an image of the snake goddess holding a snake in each hand; above is her emblem—a crescent and a conventionalized snake. This standard, obviously one of the treasures of the sanctuary, was probably carried in the cult procession.

During 1955 two other sections within the rectangular enclosure (Areas D and E) were excavated. Our aim was to determine whether the situation in Area C was characteristic of the whole enclosure, and indeed it was. In both areas we found the same features: the latest buildings, of the thirteenth century B.C., were built upon older settlements, the earliest dating to the Hyksos period (eighteenth century). Many cisterns were discovered, some as deep as thirty feet. These had been used later as burial chambers or as silos, and they yielded a rich harvest of pottery and scarabs. The most important single object found in Area D was a small fragment of a jar bearing two letters: 'LT in the Proto-Sinaitic alphabet—the alphabet from which were evolved the old Hebrew script and later the Latin alphabet. This is the first time that this script has been found in Galilee and the date of the jar (thirteenth century B.C.) is close to that of a similar fragment, found some years ago at Lachish by the late J. L. Starkey, which bears an inscription ending with the word 'LT = Goddess.

In 1956 a fourth area (F) was excavated within the enclosure of the Canaanite city, a few hundred yards east of Area D. Our starting point here was a large stone block protruding from the ground. This turned out to be a huge altar, weighing about five tons. It was obvious that in the last phase of occupation an attempt had been made to pull the altar down. After clearing away the surrounding earth we could see that in the latest phase (Stratum I) an open canal led to the altar, which stood in the middle of an open court flanked on two sides by a series of large rooms. In these we found many large stone jars, some fine Mycenaean pottery, a stand for incense vessels, a basalt slab, presumably an offering table, and a seated figure of basalt. At the north side of the court was a platform of small rough stones; this probably served as a "high place," or *Bammah*, for the cult. A stand for incense was found on it and a beautiful alabaster vessel lay just south of it, in a built niche.

Clay cult mask found in the potter's shop near the Canaanite sanctuary. Note the holes for fastening it to the face. Height 6 inches.

The cult standard. This unusual object is made of bronze, the front plated with silver. In the center is represented the snake goddess holding a snake in each hand. Above her head are a crescent and a conventionalized snake; the latter appears again at the bottom of the standard. This is the first object of the kind found in Palestine. Height 6 inches.

Fragment of a jar bearing two painted letters in the Proto-Sinaitic script. Found in Area D; thirteenth century B.C.

The whole area was obviously a holy place. The temple may have stood south of the altar, with storerooms and living quarters to the north and south. An interesting feature of this area is an intricate complex of underground water channels, sometimes as high as three feet, built of large stones and covered with huge slabs. These channels, which run east-west and south-north, probably belong to an earlier stratum (III) —the last phase of the Middle Bronze. The builders of the Stratum II altar (fourteenth century B.C.) reused them by joining to them a small channel system that emanated from below the altar. The earlier system belonged to a large building complex (with walls about six feet thick) of which not enough remains to restore its plan or to ascertain its exact function. We assume that it was part of a fortified *temenos* (sacred enclosure).

In 1956 the greatest surprise came as usual in the last fortnight of excavation, when we struck an opening in the rock about fifteen feet below the foundation of Stratum III. This opening, which had been closed with huge boulders, led into a tunnel hewn out of the rock, about thirty-six feet long and six feet high. When we explored it we felt that it might have been hewn only yesterday—so well was it preserved. But when we reached the chamber to which the tunnel led we found that debris from the fallen ceiling blocked the outlet. It was dangerous to proceed, but the temptation was too great, so we decided to dig a vertical shaft from above, and at a depth of twenty-four feet we reached the room. By the end of the season we had succeeded in clearing only about eighteen feet through the length of the room and there was still no end to it. In the meantime another tunnel with many offshoots, about thirty yards long, was discovered nearby, and again it was too dangerous to clear it in a hurry. What was the purpose of these tunnels?

To summarize briefly what we have learned of Hazor's history from our first two season's work, we know now that the Canaanite city extended over the whole site, that it must have had a population of thirty or forty thousand, and that it was destroyed in the second half of the thirteenth century B.C. On the mound proper cities continued to be built, destroyed, and rebuilt throughout the Israelite period, until the last Israelite city (Stratum II) met its end in the year 732 B.C. Following its destruction by the Assyrians Hazor was no longer a great city, and after a short occupation in the Assyrian period (Stratum I) the mound was abandoned except for a fort at its west end during the Persian and Hellenistic periods.

The results, on the whole, are of the greatest importance and show how apt was the biblical description of Hazor as the capital of Canaan and the stronghold of Israel in the north.

Excavations at the Oasis of Engedi

by BENJAMIN MAZAR

One of the most interesting sites on the western shore of the Dead Sea is the Oasis of Engedi. Famed in ancient times as a flourishing settlement, it was at various periods an administrative and economic center, and particularly a place for growing exceptionally fine spices and dates. The Hebrew name 'Ein-gedi (in the Greek and Latin sources, Engaddi, in Arabic 'Ein Jidi), never forgotten over the generations, is actually the name of the perennial spring, the principal life source of the oasis, which flows from a height of two hundred meters (670 feet) above the Dead Sea. We find this name as early as the cycle of stories about David (I Samuel 23: 29–24:7). The wasteland along the western shore of the Dead Sea, which was then a grazing ground for shepherds and a refuge for political delinquents, was called the Engedi desert; and the "Engedi strongholds," where David and his men hid from King Saul, apparently were enclosed camps at the almost inaccessible tops of the mountain crags. However, we have no proof that there was a permanent settlement in the oasis as early as the tenth century B.C. From the archaeological evidence it can be concluded that a permanent settlement, which is mentioned several times in the Bible (e.g., Joshua 15:62), was not established until the seventh century B.C. The literary sources and the archaeological evidence conjoin to form an intelligible picture of the history of Engedi, starting with the last phase of the Kingdom of Judah (end of Iron Age II) and going on until the Byzantine period.

Archaeological interest in Engedi started in April 1949, when a small expedition headed by the author, with the participation of the late Professor A. Reifenberg and Dr. Trude Dothan, began a systematic survey in the oasis. Most attention was commanded by Tell el-Jurn, an elongated, narrow hillock rising above the valley in the northwest part of the oasis. From the trial digging it became clear that because of its strategic position the settlement on Tell el-Jurn played an important role in the history of Engedi, especially in the Iron II period as well as in Hellenistic and Roman-Byzantine times. The most interesting discovery was a structure of stone blocks on the western slope of the hill, which proved to be a solid Hellenistic tower.

The investigation of building remains, ter-

67

races along the mountain slopes, and aqueducts leading from the spring to reservoirs in the valley demonstrated that in ancient times, particularly in the Hellenistic and Roman-Byzantine periods, the inhabitants of Engedi had developed an efficient irrigation system and advanced techniques for collecting water. The obvious conclusion may be drawn that abundance of water and climatic conditions conducive to tropical vegetation made it possible to carry on the cultivation of rare spices, Engedi's famous products. The development of the agricultural settlement was certainly dependent upon a central authority which dealt with the upkeep of the terraces, aqueducts, and reservoirs and also with the security of the population by means of a network of strongholds and watchtowers placed at strategic points. On the other hand, whenever the government weakened and the local authority became lax, the settlement declined and at times even ceased to exist.

Following the initial survey and the trial digging of 1949 came other surveys, at first directed by Dr. Y. Aharoni and afterward by J. Naveh. These brought out interesting details about the defense network of the oasis and its water supply, and also revealed remains of the Chalcolithic period.

Following these surveys, two excavation campaigns were conducted at Engedi, in 1961 and in 1962. Both were sponsored by the Hebrew University and the Israel Exploration Society, and were led by Mr. I. Dunayevski, Dr. Trude Dothan, and myself, with the assistance of graduate students of the Archaeology Department of the Hebrew University. Our principal work was done at

The southern part of the oasis of Engedi, seen from the west. In the center is the mound which is now known as Tell el-Jurn, and in the background is the Dead Sea.

Jean Perrot

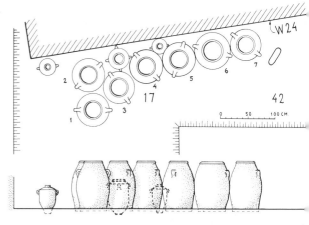

S. J. Schweig

A house situated on a terrace on the northern slope of Tell el-Jurn. Period V (ca. 625–580 B.C.).

The drawing shows the placement of a series of "barrels" (large clay pithoi) in the courtyard of a building on a terrace on the southern slope of Tell el-Jurn. Period V.

Various types of pottery vessels which were discovered in the buildings and courtyards of Period V, along the southern slope of Tell el-Jurn.

S. J. Schweig

Tell el-Jurn, but we also uncovered a Chalcolithic building complex on the terrace above the spring as well as two structures near the spring: an Iron II watchtower and a lime kiln of the Roman-Byzantine period.

Tell el-Jurn is a small hill whose top, though elongated, is very narrow (about 25 meters, or 80 feet); the hill was by nature easy to defend, but the narrow top made it inconvenient for a large settlement. It was essential, therefore, when the settlement began to spread out, to construct terraces on its slopes on which buildings could be erected. As a result of our excavations we were able to establish a chronological sequence and to determine five occupational periods, each representing a definite historical period:

V: End of the Kingdom of Judah, approximately 625–580 B.C.

IV: The Persian period, fifth-fourth centuries B.C.

III: The Hellenistic period, third-second centuries B.C.

II: The period from Alexander Jannaeus to Herod the Great, 103–37 B.C.

I: The Roman-Byzantine period, third-fifth centuries A.D.

The most important result of the excavations at Tell el-Jurn was the discovery of the flourishing settlement of Period V, which represents the time of Josiah, King of Judah, and his successors until the destruction of the Judaean kingdom and the abandonment of southern Palestine. This settlement was built on the top of the hill and on the terraces along its slopes down to the bottom, and it was surrounded by a sloping rampart whose exact character is not yet fully understood. The buildings and their courtyards, as far as they have been uncovered on the terraces along the northern and southern slopes are remarkable both for the wealth of finds and for their unusual char-

acter. Especially worthy of note is the series of large "barrels" of coarse clay, up to a meter in height, which stand in groups in the courtyards. With these barrels was an abundance of pottery and also various basalt utensils and implements of bronze, iron, and bone, as well as lumps of asphalt from the Dead Sea. Among the pottery the most notable vessels are jars, decanters, little jugs for perfume, cooking pots, bowls, and lamps, the great majority characteristic of the latest stage of Iron II in Judaea (late seventh and early sixth centuries B.C.). There are also several rare types. Altogether the finds in the courtyards, which were uncovered under a layer of ash, appear to have served for special industrial needs, probable the perfume industry. Not only does the arrangement of the vessels seem to fit in with everything we know about the preparation of perfume and cosmetics in ancient times but literary sources inform us that Engedi was one of the centers of perfume production on the shores of the Dead Sea and in the southern Jordan Valley. Particularly instructive is the information on the production of a perfume called *Opobalsamon* in Greek sources and *Aparsamon* in Hebrew and Aramaic sources (apparently *Comiphora opobalsamum*), produced only in this region and considered in ancient times to be one of the most expensive and desirable perfumes. It thus seems that it was the cultivation of balm which brought economic importance to the oasis on the banks of the Dead Sea, including the agricultural complexes of Qumran—'Ein Feshkha, Engedi, and Zoar (Ghor es-Safi, south of the Dead Sea). Josephus, Pliny, and others, as well as the Talmud, testify that Engedi was one of the most important places for the cultivation of balm. A Talmudic source even alludes to an old tradition, that the "poorest of the land," whom Nebukadnezzar's general left as "vine-dressers" (Hebrew *kormim*) in Judaea (Jeremiah 52:16) after the destruction of Jerusalem (586 B.C.), are indeed the "balm-gatherers from Engedi to Ramta" (in the southern Jordan Valley).

We may therefore suppose that during the reign of Josiah Engedi became a royal estate, its inhabitants employed in the growing and manufacture of balm. The workshops of the perfumers, who were apparently organized in a guild, after the model of the linen, metal, and pottery manufacturers in Judah, were located in the fortified settlement of Tell el-Jurn. It is quite possible that after the destruction of Jerusalem the Babylonian government attempted to continue the production of balm for its own advantage. But this continued for a short time only, perhaps only until the last campaign of Nebukadnezzar to Palestine, in 582–1 B.C. Incidentally, we found on a ribbed jar handle, unearthed in the ashes of Period V, a seal impression which includes a double-winged symbol (slightly different from the "winged scroll" in the late royal seal impression from Judah) and a short inscription. The four Hebrew characters may be read *lmrt* ("belonging to mrt" or "nrt"). Professor S. Yeivin has suggested the reading *lmr'* (the upper part of the last letter being damaged), which may possibly be the official Aramaic title *mare'* = "lord," "sovereign"; and this then presumably refers to Nebukadnezzar.

In the building of Period V were found some objects of special interests, including Hebrew epigraphic material. One is a stamp bearing the name *Tobshalom* and alongside the script geometric designs, one of them resembling the plan of the building in which it was found. In the same building, under the floor of one of the two rooms, was found a pot covered with an oil lamp, and in this was a hoard of silver ingots of various shapes which must have served as a form of currency. In another place

was found a small quadrilateral seal with the Hebrew inscription: *'Uriyahu* (son of) *'Azaryahu*. Also of particular interest are three stone weights with the sign representing the royal shekel (approximately 11.40 grams), accompanied by the numbers 1, 4, and 8, respectively. Dome-shaped weights of this type have come to light at various sites in Judaea; they all belong to the last phase of the Kingdom of Judah. From this period there are also an Egyptian scarab and a few alabaster juglets, some imported pottery vessels, including Cypro-Phoenician examples, as well as a comparatively substantial amount of women's jewelry such as rings, earrings, and beads. All these finds testify to the growth of Engedi by the end of the Kingdom of Judah and her connections with the capital and farther centers.

This ancient settlement on Tell el-Jurn was completely destroyed and abandoned after a conflagration. In its place a new settlement (Period IV) was built, probably in the second half of the fifth century B.C. Like its predecessor, this settlement extended along the top of the tell and on the terraces along its slopes, and was surrounded by a narrow wall. On the terraces were discovered a few remains of structures and plastered installations which might have been for industrial use. There is no doubt that Engedi at this time belonged to the province of Judah; it is proved, incidentally, by two jar handles which bear the well-known seal impression *Yhd* (*Yehud* = "Judah").

After the destruction of this settlement by the Nabataeans, and its subsequent abandonment, a fortress (Period III) was erected on the top of Tell el-Jurn. It comprised two parts: the western section surrounded by a stone wall about 1.40 m. thick, with a quadrangular tower at the western end; and the eastern section, stretched out over a larger area and surrounded by a thicker wall

(1.70–2.00 m.), with a quadrangular tower on the south. This fortress was probably built during the Ptolemaic period. We have testimony of a settlement in Engedi at this time in the *Ecclesiasticus* of Ben-Sira (early second century B.C.), which mentions the famous dates of this oasis. We do not know when this fortress (whose purpose was apparently to guard the royal estate) was destroyed, but we suppose that the destruction took place in the reign of John Hyrcanus the Hasmonean (134–104 B.C.), who conquered Idumaea, including the western shore of the Dead Sea, and probably annexed Engedi to the Hasmonean estates.

The next occupational period (II) is essentially that of John Hyrcanus' son Alexander Jannaeus (103–76 B.C.). This was certainly the most important period in the

S. J. Schweig

Seal with Hebrew inscription: 'Uriyahu (son of) 'Azaryahu. Period V.

Stone weights found in buildings of Period V. The inscriptions read, left to right: 1 shekel, 4 shekels, 8 shekels.

S. J. Schweig

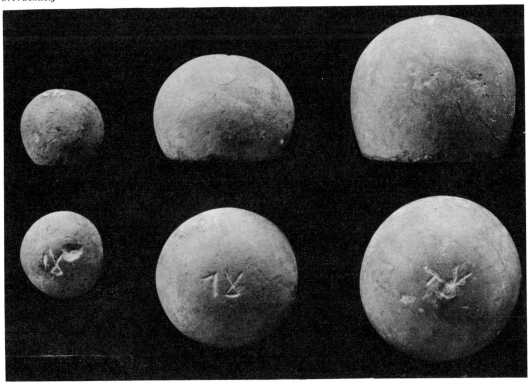

growth and development of Engedi, parallel to that noted at Qumran. Judging from the many coins gathered in the vicinity of Tell el-Jurn and over the whole oasis, as well as from finds in tombs recently investigated by Professor N. Avigad at Wadi Sudeir (Nahal David), north of the oasis, Engedi reached the peak of its development in the days of Alexander Jannaeus. It appears that the Hasmonean king gave special attention to the economic development of the Dead Sea region; and it is quite possible that with the annexation of Moab, east of the Dead Sea, to the Judaean kingdom, there was then communication by means of ships sailing across the Dead Sea. It also appears that at this time Engedi became the chief township of an administrative unit in Judaea, and this apparently accounts for the inclusion of Engedi in Josephus' list of toparchies (*Wars* III. 3.8).

This is the period also of the strong fortress surrounded by a wall of large stones two meters thick, which continues along the heights of the slopes of Tell el-Jurn, strengthened by an elaborate rectangular tower outside the wall of the fortress, at the western end of the tell. That this fortress is principally from the days of Jannaeus is proved by his coins and by pottery. As for the town itself, it clearly extended over the wide areas of the oasis.

We cannot determine the precise date of the destruction of the fortress nor of the decline which set in at Engedi. But in view of the fact that no remains from the days of Herod the Great were uncovered at Tell el-Jurn, nor any coins from his time in the oasis, we may surmise a date like that suggested at Khirbet Qumran for the end of Level I, namely the time of the Parthian invasion and the war of the last Hasmoneans against Herod—40–37 B.C.

It is surprising that no remains have been found at Tell el-Jurn from the time of Herod until the third century of our era. Nevertheless, coins gathered from various places in the oasis testify to the existence of a settlement there in the second and third quarters of the first century, until A.D. 68, a settlement alluded to by Josephus (*Wars* IV.7.2). Moreover, the Greek documents found recently by Professor Y. Yadin in the cave of Nahal Hever, which pertain to the period of Roman rule preceding the Bar-Kochbah revolt (A.D. 132–135), explicitly mention Engedi as an estate and village of the emperor, containing a *praesidium* and a market place (*agora*). Letters of Bar-Kochbah found in the same cave are addressed to the heads of his military government in Engedi.

In view of these facts we can only surmise that after the Hasmonean period the settlement's center moved from Tell el-Jurn to another site as yet undiscovered. Moreover, even the remains from the Roman-Byzantine period at Tell el-Jurn tell only of poor and temporary structures and agricultural terraces, not of "the great Judaean village," Engaddi, mentioned by Eusebius, St. Jerome, and Byzantine authors. However, various structures and reservoirs in the oasis, among them an ashlar building halfway between the spring and Tell el-Jurn, as well as a lime kiln near the spring, definitely belong to the third-fifth centuries.

It is therefore probable that the principal settlement of later Engedi stretched east and northeast from Tell el-Jurn, and perhaps reached the seashore. But concrete evidence of this settlement has not remained above ground. Possibly it was destroyed and is still covered with earth, awaiting excavation.

As we mentioned, the expedition to Engedi was not restricted to excavations at Tell el-Jurn but also explored the environs of the spring. A great surprise was the discovery of an enclosure of the Chalcolithic period on the terrace above the spring, about 150 meters to the north. We know, indeed, that the Ghassulian culture (3600–3200 B.C.) reached its greatest expansion in the arid regions of southern Palestine, including the Judaean desert, especially during a late phase of this Chalcolithic culture. But the enclosure at Engedi testifies to a stage of high efficiency and great architectural ability.

This enclosure contains a main building on the north, a smaller building on the east, a gatehouse facing the Engedi spring on the south and an additional gate on the northeast facing the spring of Wadi Sudeir (Nahal David). All are well constructed of stone masonry. A stone fence connects these four structures to make a single unit. At the center of the courtyard stands a small round structure built of small stones, which may have had cult significance.

Especially interesting is the building on the north, which is about 20 meters long. The main door of this quadrangular building (broad-house type) is located in the middle of the long wall which faces the courtyard; the stone socket is intact. Opposite the entrance there is a fenced-off depression in the shape of a hoof, apparently an altar. Here we found remains of animal bones, ashes, and sherds. Among the finds was a clay model of a bull laden with a pair of churns. On both sides of the entrance and on both sides of the hoof-shaped depression are stone benches. Remarkable are regular rows of small depressions in the floor at the two ends of the building; these contained burnt bones, horns, sherds, and much ash. The other building has the same broad-house plan but is much smaller. A smoothed pathway in the courtyard leads to the door in the middle of the long side of this building, where, as in the main building, the socket remained intact. In this building the floor was plastered.

S. J. Schweig

The tower outside the wall at the western end of the tell. Period II (the time of Alexander Jannaeus).

S. J. Schweig

Above: The Chalcolithic enclosure. In the foreground the main building, which may be a sanctuary. In the background the Dead Sea.

Below: General view of the Chalcolithic enclosure. In the foreground is the subsidiary building.

S. J. Schweig

The gatehouse, elaborately constructed, contains a small quadrangular chamber with two doors, one each in the outer and inner walls, with stone benches set along the length of the walls.

The Chalcolithic enclosure raises various interesting problems. It is certainly a sacred place, as shown by its plan and by the pottery seemingly for cult use (mainly bowls and conical cups), as well as by the absence of flint tools and kitchen vessels. The pottery clearly shows relations with the final phase of the Ghassulian culture, well known from the excavations at Teleilat el-Ghassul, northeast of the Dead Sea, and in the Beersheba region (mainly in Tell Abu Matar). It was possibly even the central sanctuary of the inhabitants of the Judaean desert in the Late Ghassulian period. At any rate, nothing like it is known in Palestine or neighboring countries.

This enclosure was certainly not destroyed, but it was apparently abandoned when the Chalcolithic occupation of sites in the Judaean desert came to an end. However, we know nothing about the permanent settlement of this period in Engedi, and this problem also requires investigation.

The Citadel of Ramat Rahel

by YOHANAN AHARONI

The tell of Ramat Rahel is a rather high hill halfway between Bethlehem and Jerusalem. Both of these cities are clearly visible from the site. The mound has become one of the most interesting archaeological sites in the vicinity of Jerusalem, not only because of the connection of its history with that of Jerusalem but because here, for the first time, a royal palace and stronghold of one of the Judaean kings has been discovered. Although its ancient name was unknown, it was obvious even before excavation began that we had a biblical site of much interest. The results of the first season's work (1954) made it clear that the site contained remains of great importance. After five campaigns, the last in 1962, we not only know the history of this place but may even suggest a plausible identification and connect some of its buildings with descriptions in the Bible.

In the course of excavation seven levels of occupation were uncovered. Since the principal building material was stone, as at most of the settlements in the area, the strata are rather shallow, for the stones could be used over and over again. Bedrock is generally only 1.50-2 meters beneath the surface. The older layers suffered from the building activity of later periods, so that in many cases the floors of Byzantine cellars are lower than those of Iron Age structures. However, the principal features of the various strata were eventually disclosed, and even the older levels yielded abundant finds that had survived the ravages of time. Thus it is now possible to ascribe dates to the levels, as shown in the following table:

Level*	Date	Type of Settlement
Vb	Eighth–seventh centuries B.C. (Israelite period)	Early citadel and village
Va	End of seventh–early sixth century B.C. (Israelite period)	Royal palace and citadel
IVb	Fifth–third centuries B.C.	Persian citadel
IVa	First century B.C.–first century A.D.	Herodian settlement
III	Third–fourth centuries	Installations of the Roman Xth Legion
II	Fifth–sixth centuries	Church of the Kathisma
I	Seventh–eighth centuries	Arab village

* The numbering of the levels begins with the latest, at the surface.

77

Helene Bieberkraut

Jar handle with the royal seal impression (four-winged scarab) and the inscription: To the King/Zyph.

Jar handle with two seal impressions. At the right, a royal stamp; at the left, a "private" stamp reading: (belonging) to Nera (son of) Shebna.

EARLY CITADEL AND VILLAGE

No structures or even foundations belonging to the earliest stratum (Vb) were found at first, for the construction of the palace and citadel of Level Va, just above, destroyed all the buildings that had stood on the high area, which was leveled off, here by clearing, there by filling. The existence of the first period came to light with material found beneath the floors of the suceeding level. During the fourth season the wall of a terrace was found underneath a building of Level Va, indicating that there had been no earlier structures here but that the area had been under cultivation. Only in the last season were older structures finally discovered: south of the

inner citadel of Level Va the massive foundations of a fortress were found, and on the northern slope remains of a private house; this had been covered over by the outer wall of Level Va. In this house were found various pottery vessels and two handles of storage jars bearing the seal impression *sbn'/shr*, "(belonging) to Shebna (son of) Shahar." Identical impressions found at other Judaean sites—Lachish and Mizpeh (Tell en-Nasbeh)—provide stratigraphic correlation.

The picture gained of the earliest level is this: a fortress on top of the hill, surrounded by terraced gardens and with dwellings below. Most of the material of this stratum was found beneath the floors of Level Va. From this we can draw certain conclusions.

First, it must be pointed out that the pottery in the fill is mostly rather late in the Iron Age (eighth-seventh centuries B.C.). This indicates that the fortress of Level Va was built, at earliest, in the mid-seventh century B.C., and probably later. Other jar handles with seal impressions were found; three bear the name of one man: *Yhwhyl/ shr*, "(belonging) to Yehohayil (son of) Shahar." This inscription is unknown elsewhere; the person may be of the same family as Shebna, son of Shahar, mentioned above. Of more importance are the royal seal impressions, more than 150 in number, which contribute greatly toward solving one of the oldest riddles in Palestinian archaeology.

Royal seal impressions have been found at various Judaean tells. There are two major types, distinguished by the symbol in the center: in the first group this is a four-winged scarab; in the second it is a two-winged disc, which has been variously interpreted. The inscriptions are identical in the two groups: above the symbol appears the word *lmlk*, "(belonging) to the king"; below appears the name of one of three cities—Hebron, Zyph, or Socoh—or the enigmatic name *Mmst*.

Both purpose and date of this type of seal impression are much disputed, and the material from Ramat Rahel provides new information. For the first time a jar handle bearing a royal seal impression with the two-winged disc and the inscription *lmlk hbrn* was found to bear a "private" sealing as well, the latter reading *lnr'/sbn'*, "(belonging) to Nera (son of) Shebna." It is not known whether the private seals were truly private or not, that is, whether the impressions indicated the property of estate owners or were marks of officials in charge of the royal fiscal system. The latter interpretation would seem the more logical in the case of a private sealing alongside the royal one.

In any event, this double seal impression makes it improbable that these impressions had to do with royal pottery establishments, for if the royal stamp indicates that the jar was the product of a particular royal pottery, what would be the reason for the private one?

A difference of opinion exists as to the earliest appearance of the royal seal impressions, though it has always been agreed that they remained in use until the destruction of the First Temple (587 B.C.). The reason for the disagreement was that at most of the tells where such impressions have been found there was no stratigraphic break during the seventh century B.C., when these cities were prospering in relative peace. The evidence from Ramat Rahel now shows that the royal seal impressions in all their variations belong only to the earliest level (Vb) and were discontinued somewhat before 587 B.C.

These new factors provide material for interpreting the royal seal impressions. It now seems that the four names found on the sealings are those of royal administrative centers, that the seal impressions date from the late eighth and early seventh centuries B.C. (the time of Hezekiah and Manasseh), and the royal seals apparently went out of use before the time of Josiah (640–609 B.C.), who reigned over a much larger area than that of the royal seal impressions (which have not been found beyond the limits of Judah).

These conclusions are of importance for the stratigraphy of other Judaean tells. There are various opinions as to the date of the destruction of Level III at Lachish—whether it was during Sennacherib's campaign (701 B.C.) or during the first campaign of Nebuchadnezzar (597 B.C.). As most of the royal seal impressions from Lachish were found in this level, and only a few in Level II, it may now be asserted

Balustrade of the windows, which decorated the royal palace (restored from fragments).

"The woman at the window"—ivory panel found at Nimrud.

Assyrian "palace ware" beakers and dish found in the storeroom of the royal citadel.

that the later date is untenable. The buildings of Level Va at Ramat Rahel were undoubtedly constructed before 597 B.C., and the royal seal impressions went out of use, as we have said, before their construction.

ROYAL PALACE AND CITADEL

Toward the end of the seventh century B.C. extensive construction was carried out Ramat Rahel (Va), involving destruction of the older buildings. At the summit of the hill rose an upper citadel, approximately 50 x 60 meters, and below this lay the large lower citadel, four to five acres in size.

The upper citadel was surrounded by a casemate wall of extremely fine construction. On the east a gate opened onto a broad courtyard paved with crushed chalk. Of the main building (on the west) little remains today, for this was the highest spot on the hill and bedrock is here close to the surface. Another large building in the northern section served for administrative quarters and storage.

The lower citadel was surrounded by a wall 3–4 meters thick. Although this wall has been excavated at only three points, its outline can be traced on the basis of topography. On the west the wall ran at some distance below the top of the slope. The area immediately within it had been filled in to a depth of several meters; this leveled off and extended the interior, while it also strengthened the wall with its massive bulk. For the excavators it proved important, as it contained uncontaminated pottery of Level Vb, including some fifty royal seal impressions, thus showing that the outer wall was built later, at the same time as the upper citadel. On the northern slope the wall was built over the ruins of an older house which had been filled with stones. In this section of the wall the outer part is well constructed of ashlar masonry. This fact, together with the topography, suggests that the outer gate was nearby. A second gate may have been on the south, but this has not been excavated. Near the northern gate a narrow postern pierces the inner wall; it leads directly outside without passing through the lower citadel. Also nearby is the opening of a tunnel hewn in bedrock to the height of a man; its purpose has not been clarified.

Though only a few places within the lower citadel have been excavated, it is certain that most of its area was open, without buildings. This was, indeed, a fortress—not a town—built for a specific purpose. It did not remain long in use and perhaps was never completed. The lower citadel is so large that it cannot have been built merely to protect the upper citadel. Apparently it was a camp for an army with chariots, a military stronghold on the main highway south of Jerusalem.

The upper citadel, on the other hand, was not of a purely military character, for its architecture and the finds indicate that it was a palace. The outer face of the wall and the buildings which faced the main courtyard were constructed of ashlar masonry finished in a manner very like that of the royal buildings at Samaria, the capital of the northern Kingdom of Israel. Among the debris and between the walls of later buildings, four complete Proto-Aeolic capitals were found, as well as fragments of three or four more—one smaller and carved on both sides. Similar capitals have been found only in cities of the Northern Kingdom (Samaria, Megiddo, Hazor, and on the surface at Medeibi' in Transjordan); this is the first occurrence in Judah. The masonry and the capitals show the royal character of the construction, and it is interesting to note that techniques brought from Phoenicia underwent little change from the time of Solomon to the end of the Kingdom of Judah.

The most interesting and finest architectural members were found at the end of the final season. In the northwest corner of the upper citadel was a heap of debris containing fragments of columns and capitals. After these had been arranged according to shape, it became evident that they comprised a row of small columns, decorated with a drooping petal motif and topped by small capitals of Proto-Aeolic type, joined at the edges of the volutes. Although this seems to be the first occurrence of a row of such columns, a comparison with contemporary Phoenician and Israelite ivories shows that it is the balustrade of a window in the façade of the building. The motif of the "woman in the window," examples of which have been found at sites in Palestine, Syria, and Assyria—such as Samaria, Arslan Tash, Nimrud, and Khorsabad—shows a window with a railing of col-

General plan of Level Va, the royal palace and citadel.

Y. Aharoni, Ramat Rahel *(Rome 1964)*

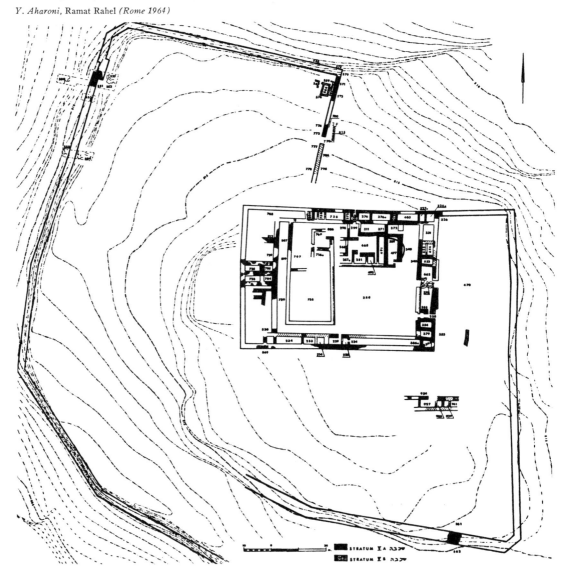

umns like those that are from Ramat Rahel.

The small finds also point to the royal character of the citadel. This material is not abundant because of destruction by later building, though here and there undisturbed corners were found. One such spot, a storage room, contained a heap of crockery which had evidently fallen from a shelf. About 150 pottery vessels, including the finest types of Judaean burnished ware as well as storage jars, cooking pots, and juglets, were found here. Among these were several beakers of Assyrian Palace Ware, the first found in Palestine. Most interesting was a jar fragment painted in black and red, which shows a bearded figure with curled hair, seated on a high, decorated chair. Dressed in an ornamented robe with short sleeves, he stretches out his hands, the right above the left. This drawing recalls the Assyrian style of the same period (ca. eighth-seventh centuries B.C.); comparison with Assyrian reliefs shows that the man depicted is a king. The painting is the work of a skilled hand; the potsherd, however, is of local ware, and the picture, thus far unique in Palestine, appears to have been painted after firing.

Representations of the goddess Astarte as well as figures of animals, common in Judaea in this period, were also found. Also in this level seal impressions appeared on storage jar handles. In place of the royal stamp are rosettes and interesting private stamps, including the inscription: *l'lyqm n'r ywkn*, "(belonging) to Elyaqim, Steward of Jochin." Identical stamps have been found at Beth Shemesh and Tell Beit Mirsim; Professor Albright is undoubtedly correct in assuming that these seal impressions were those of a functionary of King Jehoiachin, the son of King Jehoiakim, who reigned for a very short period during 597 B.C. and was taken into exile by the Babylonians (*Journal of Biblical Literature*, LI, [1932],

Proto-Aeolic capital of the Judaean palace (Level Va).

77-106). This seal provides clear evidence that the citadel was still in use a few years before the destruction of the First Temple; it may confidently be assumed that it too was destroyed by Nebukadnezzar around 587 B.C. The extent of the destruction is shown by the layer of ash and the blackened sherds found at every place not disturbed by later construction. The citadel was never rebuilt.

PERSIAN CITADEL

The site stood in desolation for some time and was reoccupied only in the post-Exilic period. A new citadel was then built on a much smaller scale (IVb) south of the Israelite upper citadel. Several rooms belonging to this later structure have been revealed, but the finds are poor, mainly because of Byzantine buildings immediately above.

The Israelite citadel remained in ruins; yet it was here that the most interesting find of the Persian period was made—a large number of seal impressions on pottery. Persian material may well have been deposited here during leveling operations in Hellenistic or Roman times. This material, found scattered on the surface, consisted of sherds which could not be assembled into complete vessels. Hence, no exact dating can be given. The only possible assumption is that most of the material does not date before the fourth century B.C. or, at earliest, the end of the fifth, and that most of the seal impressions belong to this period.

So far about three hundred impressions have been found. Many are usual types of the Persian province of Jehud (Judah) such as have been found at other sites in the region. Some bear various forms of the name of the province (*yhd*), or the name Jerusalem (*yrslm*) between the points of a pentagram. The seal impressions of these types at Ramat Rahel outnumber those found at all other sites combined. Some, however, are altogether new, such as that with *yhwd* (Jehud). The group called "*phw'* stamps" is of special interest, as it gives the first epigraphical evidence for a governor of Judah under Persian rule. Several have merely *yhwd/phw'*, apparently to be interpreted as "Judah, the Governor." (Professor Frank Cross has suggested reading *phr'* = "the potter" instead of *phw'* = "the governor," but the latter seems preferable.) Two also include the actual name of the governor: *yhwd/yhw'zr/phw'*, "Judah, Jehoezer the Governor"; *l'hzy/phw'*, "(belonging) to Ahzai the Governor." Several duplicate impressions of these stamps provide complete readings and show that the occurrence of these two names is not accidental. The names are typically Jewish, and here seemingly is evidence for two new names of Jewish governors under Persian rule, probably of the fourth century B.C.

The importance of this new information is considerable, especially as we possess extremely little knowledge of Judah during this period. From the Bible we know of three Jewish governors—Sheshbazzer, Zerubbabel, and Nehemiah—who ruled at various times from the end of the sixth century through the fifth century B.C. From the Elephantine papyri we know of a fourth, Bagohi, who ruled in Judah after Nehemiah, near the end of the fifth century. Though this last name is definitely Persian, it is not certain whether its bearer was a Persian or a Jew, for the name (in the form Bigvai) was in use among the Jews who returned from exile in Babylonia (cf. Nehemiah 7:19). It has been generally accepted that after Bagohi only Persian governors ruled in Judah, and that the autonomy of the province was limited to religious matters. Yet here we have epigraphic evidence that Jewish governors continued to rule in the Judaean province and collected taxes in the name of the Persian authorities.

These seal impressions also shed light on

Jar handle of the Persian period (Level IVb) with a seal impression reading: Jehud, Jehoezer the Governor.

the history of settlement at Ramat Rahel. As almost all are connected with tax-collecting, their large number proves that in this period the site was no mere village but an administrative center. From this we can draw conclusions concerning the identification of the site and its function, to be discussed later.

HERODIAN SETTLEMENT

Only quite late in the period of the Second Temple does an ordinary settlement appear for the first time at Ramat Rahel (IVa). The citadel seems to have been destroyed, and smaller structures were built at various places on the tell—workshops, other rooms, and cisterns. These are found above the ruins of the Israelite palace as well, and here and there massive older walls were reused. Thus a number of the rooms of the northern casemate wall were reused in a workshop containing cisterns and basins, and an older postern gate—still intact—was turned into a storeroom. In all these buildings was found pottery of the first century A.D. (Herodian period), and the coins indicate that the settlement lasted until A.D. 69, a year before the destruction of the Second Temple.

In 1931, near the tell, was found a tomb cave of this period. In 1962 several tomb caves were discovered on the rocky slope at the foot of the upper citadel; some had been turned into cisterns in Roman-Byzantine times. One cave was found undisturbed, but

View of part of the excavations: at the left, a casemate wall with postern gate, of Level Va; at the right, a Byzantine magazine built on top of the early storehouse.

part of its ceiling had collapsed in antiquity; glassware and lamps were found within, as well as ossuaries bearing the names of the deceased in Hebrew and Greek.

Beside one cave is a columbarium, with row upon row of small niches hewn in the rock, which remind one of Roman columbaria but are too small for burials. In the center of the cave is a square platform, partly rock-hewn and partly masonry, and on this a complete Proto-Aeolic capital lay with the decorated face upward. One of the volutes had been hollowed out to form a sort of libation bowl. The use of this capital might shed light on the purpose of columbaria, which must have been connected with burial ritual.

INSTALLATIONS OF ROMAN TENTH LEGION

With the destruction by the Romans of the last Jewish settlement, about A.D. 70, Ramat Rahel seems to have been abandoned again, until new buildings were constructed by the Tenth Legion, which was stationed in Jerusalem during the second and third centuries (Level III). Its presence has been proved by tiles bearing the stamp LEG(io) $\overline{X}$ FR(etensis), which were found —some in situ—in one of the basins and in the hypocaust of a bath built over the inner gate of the Israelite citadel. The bath contained several rooms paved in colored mosaics, basins, and a complex plumbing system.

The ruins of a Roman villa built over the main Israelite building were also uncovered. It had a broad, paved peristyle court with rooms on two sides.

CHURCH OF THE KATHISMA

In the fifth century a church and monastery were erected on the site (Level II), incorporating the Roman buildings. The church, relatively large, was built upon the northeast corner of the ancient fortress. The nave and aisles were paved with colored mosaics in geometric designs. A large cruciform stone, evidently the altar, was found in the narthex. Next to the church was a long row of rooms connected by corridors that contained ovens, stoves, and other household equipment. Among the household utensils are storage jars and many small pottery vessels, including lamps with Greek inscriptions. An elongated amphora was discovered lying on its side beneath the stone pavement of one of the rooms. It is unfortunate that the jar was cracked, for its position suggested that it might have contained monastery documents.

In the monastery rooms were various installations such as wine and oil presses. Two large storerooms were built over the storerooms of the Israelite citadel, and as no construction had been carried out here in the intervening period, part of the Byzantine structure lay directly on the massive Israelite walls.

Although no inscriptions were found in the church, it can be plausibly identified. Below the western slope of the tell, beside the old Jerusalem-Bethlehem road, there is an ancient well called by the Arabs "Bir Kadismu." This name is obviously derived from Greek kathisma (seat). The Well of the Seat, Mary's traditional resting place on her way to Bethlehem, is well known from Byzantine sources. The Church of the Kathisma, together with a monastery, was built nearby about A.D. 450, as is known from fifth- and sixth-century sources.

The short distance between the church and Bir Kadismu (about 500 yards), the absence of remains other than the well and the date of the church (which agrees with the sources) all support the assumption that these ruins are those of the Church of the Kathisma.

ARAB VILLAGE

The church and its buildings were destroyed during the seventh century, probably at the time of the Arab conquest. Some of the rooms seem to have been in use even after this, a wall being added here or a new floor laid there. This meager settlement lasted, according to the evidence of the coins, until the eighth century; these few remains are all that exist of Level I, the early Arab period. The site then remained uninhabited until recently, when the modern settlement of Ramat Rahel was founded.

With the character and the history of the site known, it is now possible to suggest its probable identification as ancient Beth-hakkerem. This place is mentioned in ancient sources as being close to Jerusalem. The first mention is in the list of districts of the Kingdom of Judah in Joshua 15:59 (preserved only in the *Septuagint*), where it is located in the district of Bethlehem. The earliest date possible for this list is the ninth century B.C., and it is now clear that the settlement at Ramat Rahel was not founded earlier than this. Jeremiah mentions the name in his description of an enemy drawing close to Jerusalem: "...and blow the trumpet in Tekoa, and set up a signal in Beth-hakkerem" (Jeremiah 6:1). This clearly shows that Beth-hakkerem was a fortified site south of Jerusalem on the road to Tekoa (south of Bethlehem), on a hill from which a beacon would be visible from Jerusalem. No more suitable site for this can be found than the citadel at Ramat Rahel: it is now known that in Jeremiah's time it was of important military and royal character (Level Va). On the other hand, the suggested identification of Beth-hakkerem with Ain Karem, west of Jerusalem, is out of the question, for this village is situated rather low down and is not directly visible from Jerusalem. Additional support for our iden-

tification is the fact that in Nehemiah's time Beth-hakkerem was the residence of a district governor (Nehemiah 3:4); since finds of this period are abundant, it may be assumed that Ramat Rahel was an administrative center at this time.

One of the Judaean kings converted the site into a large fortress, in the center of which he built a magnificent palace. In the light of the archaeological evidence this can only be one of the very last kings, and a reference to the building of a palace by Jehoiakim, the son of Josiah, who reigned 608–597 B.C., is preserved in Jeremiah 22: 13–19. Jeremiah accuses this king of unjustifiably using forced labor in the construction of his palace. The description of the palace resembles in every way that at Ramat Rahel: "... a wide house and large chambers [Hebrew *'lywt* = upper stories] and cutteth

Jar fragment with drawing of a king, from the royal palace.

Helene Bieberkraut

him out windows, cieled with cedar, and painted with vermilion." Since the façade of the main building was decorated with conspicuous ornamented windows, it is not surprising that Jeremiah singled them out.

The remains of the balustrade indicate that the capitals supported wooden beams, and on the stone there are still traces of red paint. Thus it would seem that Jeremiah is describing these very windows. Of course, other palaces in Palestine may have been decorated in the same manner, but the palace at Ramat Rahel is essentially like that described by the prophet, and as it is difficult to believe that the Judaean kings were extensive builders of this sort of structure, the identification seems fairly certain. This raises another question—whether the concluding words of the prophecy in Jeremiah 22:19 (". . . cast forth beyond the gates of Jerusalem") are connected with the location of the palace.

Our excavations may also explain the ancient name, Beth-hakkerem, which means "the house of the vineyard." Since the earliest level (Vb) is composed of a fortress surrounded by terraced gardens and houses, it may be supposed that here was the summer residence of the kings of Judah, within the royal vineyards, about which lay the

houses of the vinegrowers and farmers. A passage in Jeremiah (36:22) states that "the king sat in the winter-house," from which we may conclude that there was also a summerhouse, and this may have been the palace at Ramat Rahel.

Why did Jehoiakim build this palace during his short eleven-year reign? The prophet may also hint at this (22:15): "Shalt thou reign, because thou closest thyself in cedar? Did not thy father eat and drink, and do judgment and justice, and then it was well with him?" It would seem from this that Jehoiakim, who was put on the throne by the Egyptians, encountered popular resentment in Jerusalem, which was openly expressed by Jeremiah (cf. also II Kings 24:4). Instead of following in his father's footsteps and winning the favor of the people by wise and just deeds he ruled with a strong arm, securing himself within his walls. He may have built this fortress overlooking Jerusalem in order to sweep down on the city in case of an uprising. And could these fortifications have been connected with the unsuccessful revolt against Babylon which brought about the end of his kingdom? Whatever the case, the new fortress gave us the unique opportunity of excavating a palace built by one of the kings of Judah.

Arad:

An Early Bronze Age City and a Biblical Citadel

by RUTH AMIRAN AND YOHANAN AHARONI

Arad is known from the Bible as the central town of the eastern Negev during the Canaanite and Israelite periods. At the time of Israel's wandering in the desert "the Canaanite king of Arad, who dwelt in the Negev (South)" (Num. 21:1) controlled a good part of this southern area. He is described as the Israelite tribes' main obstacle in their attempt to penetrate Canaan from the desert, and he is said to have defeated them utterly at the city of Hormah (Num. 14:45, 33:40; Deut. 1:44).

We do not know the exact date of the conquest of Canaanite Arad, but the king of the town is mentioned among the thirty-one rulers who were conquered by Joshua and the children of Israel (Josh. 12:14) and we learn about families of Kenites who came to live in "the Negev of Arad" (Judg. 1:16). Later, Arad appears in the city list of Judah, the second name mentioned in the important Negev district (= Eder of the Masoretic text, Josh. 15:21). As we have no further biblical references to Arad, it is only the excavations which testify to its importance during the period of the Israelite monarchy. The citadels built here by the kings of Israel and Judah protected the boundaries of the kingdom and controlled the main road to Edom and Elath. This road had a primary importance for the kingdom, owing to the copper mines of the Wadi Araba and to trade with South Arabia, where spices and perfumes were purchased. Caravans such as that of the Queen of Sheba, described in the Bible, came to Arad on their way from the south, and here they passed the border of Judah proper. Shishak I of Egypt, who invaded Palestine ca. 920 B.C., five years after King Solomon's death, mentions in his inscription that he conquered the citadel of Arad and a place called Geber, which is probably biblical Ezion-geber, near Elath, at the head of the Gulf of Aqaba. We may assume that one of Shishak's aims in this campaign was to stop Judah's commerce with South Arabia. The latest reference to Arad is in the *Onomasticon* of Eusebius (ca. 264–ca. 340), who mentions a village named Arad twenty Roman miles from Hebron.

Arad is situated in the northeastern section of the Beersheba-Arad basin, on the border of the arid region. It has an average annual rainfall of about 150 mm. The site is located on a hill made of Eocene chalk,

89

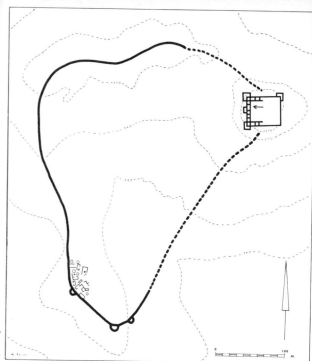

Detail of the Early Bronze Age II wall with a semicircular tower and the passageway from the inside of the city into the tower.

Plan of Tell Arad, showing both sites: the Israelite Citadel mound and the area of the Early Canaanite city with its defensive wall. Arrow points to Israelite sanctuary.

overlooking the loess-covered basin that extends to its west, south, and east. In the north, beyond a small shallow basin, is the southeasternmost spur of the Judaean mountains.

Arad is a dual site: a large walled city (25 acres) dating to Early Bronze Age II (29th–27th centuries B.C.) and a small compact mound (one acre) with remains of fortresses dating to the periods from the Judaean kingdom down to early Ommayad times. A gap of some seventeen to twenty centuries separates the two parts of the site, and during this long time the area was part of the desert around it. The two sites are fundamentally different in regard to the specific reason for their existence in this arid place. Another long gap—some twelve centuries—elapsed between the abandonment of the fortress-mound and the establishment of the new town of Arad in 1961. During that time the desert was again in full control of the area.

THE CANAANITE CITY OF THE EARLY BRONZE II

The city spreads out on the gentle slopes of a horseshoe-shaped formation, eroded into the sides of the hill. It is fortified by a stone wall (2.30 m. broad and about 1170 m. long) built all around the crest of this configuration, which was the most suitable line for defense. The choice of this topography is unique and seems to permit only one explanation: it allows the drainage of the maximum amount of runoff water into the city area, at the bottom of which is an artificial depression that most probably was the reservoir for storage of this rain water.

Much information has accumulated during five seasons of excavation concerning the history of the city, its stratigraphy, the ingenuity involved in planning, its architecture, its mobile furniture such as pottery, metalwork, and objects of other materials. The knowledge of planning has been noted

The Early Canaanite city. Living quarters, showing streets and parts of the insulae of the houses.

The Arad house: entrance in the long wall, benches around the walls, post-base to carry the roof, and a small outdoor kitchen-storeroom at the left of the entrance to the main room. There is a courtyard or an open square in front.

in the water-supply system. Further evidence of town planning and architectural style may be seen in a number of features. First, the semicircular towers attached to the city wall seem to be at a regular distance of 20–25 m. from each other, to judge from a stretch of about 160 meters, where seven of them came to light. Second, there seems to have been a clear distinction of the functional division of the city into living quarters and areas for public buildings. The living quarters extend along the upper parts of the slopes, while the public buildings seem to have been concentrated in the lower central area adjacent to the water reservoir. The public buildings excavated thus far face the center of the city and have a thick wall at the base that joins them. One of the buildings may very well be identified as a temple, from a comparison of its plan with excavated temples of Early Bronze Age II at Ai and Megiddo. Third, in the living quarters there are streets and squares sepa-

rating the blocks of houses. Finally, the most intriguing feature of Arad architecture—from the cultural level a most pronounced architectural style—is that of the dwellings.

The Arad house-type consists of one large room, often with a small one annexed to it, and a courtyard. The large room is always quite broad, with the entrance approximately in the middle of the long wall. The door socket is on the left of the entrance on the inside, benches are all along the walls, and often a post-base is found in the center of the room or near the center, to carry the roofing. The size of the room ranges from 7.30 m. x 5.10 m. to 4.30 m. x 3.30 m.; the larger size is more common. In most of the houses both the main room and the annexed kitchen-storeroom have been found full of household furnishings, mainly pottery but also stone implements such as mor-

Pottery of the Early Bronze II period from the Canaanite city. Both types have been found in Egypt in First Dynasty context, hence are important for dating.

tars and grinding stones, clay receptacles for grain, copper tools, and various small objects like jewelry. Large quantities of charred grain have been found, sometimes *in situ* at the bottom of large hole-mouthed jars (pithoi) or within broken receptacles of clay or even in a stone mortar.

The city existed through four strata that did not occupy more than 150 to 200 years, to judge from the pottery, which is of both local and Egyptian origin. Each of the four strata produced evidence for relations with Egypt, in the pottery vessels as well as in other objects. Considering the Egyptian evidence (or rather, hints) of importing various oils from Canaan into First Dynasty Egypt, we may safely conclude that the Arad-Egypt relations as shown in the pottery vessels (which must, of course, be considered as containers for the stuff shipped in them) was of a commercial character. The goods that could have been sent to Egypt are easier to imagine than those that might have been imported to Arad from Egypt. In the Egyptian vessels found at Arad and in Canaanite vessels found in tombs of the First Dynasty in Egypt we have more than just evidence that commerce was one of the factors of Arad's economy: we have here proof of the contemporaneity of the early periods of Canaan and Egypt. It seems that the whole duration of the life of the city corresponds more or less to that of the First Dynasty of Egypt.

The earliest of the four cities (Stratum IV) was an unwalled settlement, making use of various sorts of natural caves and rock cavities for its habitations. One such dwelling was found beneath the foundations of the city wall, thus giving us stratigraphic-chronological evidence for the date of the incipient settlement immediately preceding the walled city. The pottery found in Stratum IV consists of local wares of Early Bronze Age I and some Egyptian pottery typical of the very beginning of the First Dynasty. One synchronism is thus established, though much more detailed work will be required.

With Stratum III begins the real city, large and walled, coinciding with the beginning of Early Bronze Age II, which is generally recognized as the period of large-scale urbanization of the country, both north and south. There are many large cities, from Qadesh in Upper Galilee to Arad in the south. The planning and architecture described above pertain to Strata III and II, mainly to II, of which up to now we know more. In both strata there came to light pottery types which have been found previously in royal tombs of the middle of the First Egyptian Dynasty. The painted style, which displays red-painted bands of dotted triangles and lozenges covering the shoulder of the vase, has turned up at Arad on various types of jars, both large and small. In quantity it exceeds all that was found previously. However, we cannot yet state that the center of production of this painted ware was Arad, and we do not know whether the painted jars and jugs found in Egypt originated at Arad itself. There is still too little evidence to draw final conclusions.

The jar with the pillar handle, which turns up in quantities at Arad, has its coun-

Clay casket—imitating perhaps the house of the period—from the Canaanite city.

terpart in one of the royal tombs at Saqqara (middle of the First Dynasty). The pillar handle sometimes has a hole through it, or incisions on its cuplike top—devices apparently meant to save every drop of the costly liquid in the jar, while the top of the pillar handle served as a place for the dipper juglet. Such a jar seems easy to identify as an oil jar, and one specimen found in the burial chamber of an Egyptian royal tomb strengthens this conjecture.

Arad is furnishing us with new material and new problems about this early period in the history of the ancient Near Eastern civilizations.

RUTH AMIRAN

THE CITADEL MOUND OF THE
ISRAELITE PERIOD

As there are no remains at Tell Arad from the later Canaanite period, there arises the question of the location of the Canaanite city mentioned in the Bible. There is hardly any doubt that Tell Arad is the site of Israelite Arad; this not only is borne out by the preservation of the name at the tell and the precise indication of Eusebius, but has been further strengthened by the discovery of the name Arad (*'rd*) inscribed on a bowl seven times in ancient Hebrew letters. This is one of the few instances in Palestine when an inscription with the name of the place being excavated has been found during the excavation, and it would be difficult to believe that the occurrence of the name is accidental. But the question still is: where must we look for the king of Arad and his city at the time of the Israelite conquest?

On the basis of the archaeological survey, the only major tell in this area which was inhabited during the later phases of the Canaanite period is Tell Malhata (Tell el-Milh), some 12 km. southwest of Tell Arad. This is the only place which can be taken into consideration as the main stronghold in the area during the Late Bronze Age, but if it was Canaanite Arad, how can we explain the shift of the name in the Israelite period to another tell, 12 km. distant, while Tell Malhata was still occupied? Fortunately the list of cities in the inscription of Shishak comes to our aid in solving this vexing problem. In it two citadels named Arad are mentioned, "Arad Rabat" (Arad the Great) and "Arad of the house (family) of Yeroham." The Shishak list proves, therefore, that in the period of Solomon there existed in this region two citadels called Arad, one the major fortress and the other inhabited by the Yeroham family, the

name of which is perhaps connected with biblical Jerahmeel and the "Negev of the Jerahmeelites" (I Sam. 27:10). It seems now that archaeology provides the explanation for this: apparently Solomon built two citadels in this area, one on the site of Canaanite Arad, then inhabited by the Yeroham family, and the other on the site of the Early Canaanite town to the north of it. He chose the latter for its strategic situation on the main road to the Wadi Araba and probably also because of its traditional rôle as a high place during the Early Israelite period. We shall return again to the last point.

Fortresses of various periods were discovered on the citadel mound. These were destroyed and rebuilt about ten times between the time of Solomon and the Roman period.

To begin with the last mentioned, the Roman citadel was part of the early *limes* (border) fortification of the Roman empire on the edge of the desert before the overthrow of the Nabataean kingdom (A.D. 106). At the beginning of the Arab period this fortress was converted into a larger building, which was perhaps partly used as a *khan* (inn) for travelers. In one of its rooms a treasure of glassware and other objects was discovered, which was hidden there when the place was abandoned.

During the Hellenistic period a solid tower was built, whose foundations have been preserved up to a height of 5–6 meters, and around it smaller rooms were built. At its foot a deep plaster-covered water pool was found.

The strongest and most imposing fortresses built at this site belong to the Israelite period. Some of them are built of ashlar masonry, an example of which has not hitherto been found in the Negev. From this it may be deduced that Arad was the main royal citadel in the area; it defended

the borders of Judah and dominated the
important road to the Araba, Edom, and
Elath. Remains of six Israelite citadels have
been revealed, dating from Solomon to the
end of the First Temple: one from the
tenth century, two each from the ninth and
eighth centuries, and one from the end of
the seventh century. The last two were surrounded by casemate walls with projecting
towers. An imposing fortress of the eighth
century, from approximately the time of
Uzziah, was built partly of ashlar masonry,
and the rich finds give evidence of its wealth.
In the ninth century, perhaps during the
reign of Jehoshaphat, the fortress was surrounded by a massive wall four meters thick,
which may be classed among the strongest
walls of this period known in Palestine. The
excavation of the fortress of the level, which
probably dates to the days of Solomon, is

*Air view of the citadel mound at the end of
the first season: (1) Roman wall; (2) Israelite
wall; (3) the area of the sanctuary, which was
discovered at the end of the second season.*

Ashlar masonry of the Israelite citadels.

Iron Age jars and juglets after their restoration.
The white part of the scale at lower left is 10 cm.

still in an early stage, and its plan is not yet defined. However, it is already evident that this was the earliest citadel, built on top of an artificial filling. Below this, traces of a settlement were found, with some silos and remnants of houses. This settlement, which belongs to the beginning of the tenth century B.C., was apparently an unfortified village and was erected immediately on top of remains of the Early Bronze Age.

The abundance of pottery found indicates that those who lived in the citadel were not only soldiers but also merchants and artisans. Hundreds of vessels were found on the successive floors of the citadel's rooms and its court. It is obvious that the place was subjected to a number of sudden conquests and that its inhabitants were unable to save many of their possessions. In the courtyard were several industrial installations, some of them probably connected with metalworking and perfume distilling. Some weights found, a *pim* and several inscribed 1, 2, 4, or 8 shekels, point to commercial activities.

Worthy of mention are cult and art objects such as Ashtoreth figurines, a Hebrew seal, and a decorated shell that probably served as a cosmetic palette. The precise stratification provided by Arad and the wealth of pottery from the different strata will be the basis for a more definite chronology of Judah in the Iron Age.

Fragments of a bowl inscribed seven times
with the name 'rd (Arad), in reversed lettering.

S. J. Schweig

A fact of great importance is the abundance of written material preserved because of the aridity of the climate. The inscriptions, written in ink on potsherds (ostraca), are partly in ancient Hebrew-Phoenician letters, from the Israelite strata, and partly in Aramaic script, from the Persian period. Most of them are fragments of dockets and business documents; some are letters. In one letter parts of fifteen lines have been preserved. Found in a level of about the time of Hezekiah, it is the most ancient Hebrew letter hitherto discovered. Unfortunately it is incomplete, although several names and many words are readable. Some of the best preserved ostraca belong to the fourth century B.C.; these contain lists of names and goods. The script is identical with that on the ostraca discovered at Ezion-geber, and this points again to the connections between the two places.

This rich epigraphic material needs thorough study before any conclusions are possible. However, since here for the first time a series of ostraca extending from the ninth to the fourth century has been discovered at one site, the material makes an important contribution to establishing the chronology of Hebrew palaeography.

The highlight of the discoveries in the Israelite citadels was a sanctuary, which was uncovered on the last days of the second season. Thus far only part of the Holy of Holies has been excavated. Three steps led to its entrance, which was flanked by two stone altars, the larger of which is 51 cm. high. The altars are beautifully dressed and smoothed, and in concave depressions in their upper surfaces were found the remains of some organic material, apparently burnt offerings. In the entrance, between the altars, was a gutter sloping from right to left. In the room itself was a raised platform (*bama*) of stone and around it stood three stelae (*masebot*). The largest of these is well cut and smoothed and on its face are traces of red color.

Although the excavation of the sanctuary is just beginning, some vital facts emerge quite clearly. This is not a small shrine or high place, but a well-constructed building of large dimensions. Judging from the walls uncovered to date, it seems that the sanctuary included three adjoining rooms, the entrance facing east and the Holy of Holies to the west. This is exactly the principle of the plan of the Solomonic Temple in Jerusalem, according to its description in the

Hebrew seal inscribed ldrsyhw bn' . . .
(belonging to Derashyahu son of . . .).

One of the Aramaic ostraca.

S. J. Schweig

Bible. Since the sanctuary is within the area of the royal citadel at Arad, there is hardly any doubt that this is a royal Israelite sanctuary, the first one discovered through scientific excavation.

The sanctuary existed during the ninth and the first half of the eighth century and was repaired several times. We have not yet penetrated to the earlier levels in this area. However, its final stage is already clear: a casemate wall which cuts through the rooms of the sanctuary dates its destruction to sometime in the second half of the eighth century. It is probable that the destruction is to be associated with the joint Aramaean-Israelite-Edomite attack on Judah in the days of Ahaz, in 734 B.C. (cf. II Kings 16:6; II Chron. 28:17), and that the fortress above, surrounded by the casemate wall, was built by Hezekiah. It is interesting that Hezekiah is the first king of Judah about whom we are told that "he removed the high places and brake the images (*masebot*)" (II Kings 18:4, 22), while even a virtuous king like Jehoshaphat did not interfere with the worship in the high places (I Kings 22:43).

The discovery of the Israelite sanctuary raises many problems which must wait for the more complete excavation of this unique building. However, a royal sanctuary could hardly have been built here without an earlier tradition. We have in the Bible an interesting passage stating that the Kenite Hobab family, related to Moses, settled down in the vicinity of Arad (Septuagint version of Judges 1:16). We owe to Professor Mazar the ingenious suggestion that the biblical emphasis on this special family and its relation to Moses hints at its important rôle in connection with Yahwistic worship at various places. This idea may become most fruitful for the solution of some problems of early Israelite history and religion, and it makes the role of Arad in the Israelite period more understandable. The prominent hill of Tell Arad was probably chosen by the Hobab family as their central place of worship in the region of Arad. This is probably a further reason why Solomon chose this place for his main fortress in the area, giving it the name of Arad Rabat. The traditional high place was converted into a sanctuary within the royal citadel, using the honored Kenite priests who traced their genealogy to Moses. The sanctuary is, of course, an important part of the royal citadel, which was the administrative and military center in this border region. Exactly the same motives apparently guided Jeroboam in the construction of his two main royal sanctuaries at Beth-el and Dan, both on the border of the kingdom and both venerated through ancient traditions.

Some of our conclusions are of course hypothetical. It is already clear, however, that Tell Arad is one of the most interesting and promising sites in southern Israel.

YOHANAN AHARONI

Holy of Holies of Israelite sanctuary, with altar at each side of entrance.

Front view of Temple, with "Molten Sea" at left, Altar of Burnt Offering at right. The restoration of the altar follows Albright's interpretation of Ezekiel 43:13-17. Archaeological evidence for details of decoration is lacking; note, however, the stepped-pyramid and ramp features that are customary in many Babylonian ziggurats.

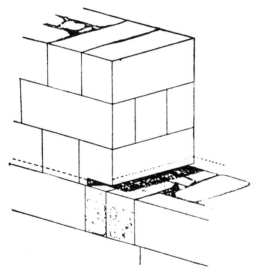

Reisner et al., Harvard Excavations at Samaria, 1908–1910

Phoenician masonry. The great limestone blocks used in the Temple walls and raised basement (another Babylonian architectural stylism), many 12 and 15 feet long, were of uniform tier height (approximately 1½ feet). They were laid without mortar in the style of masonry current in that time, as is clear from excavations at Megiddo and Samaria. The drawing shows a part-ashlar wall uncovered at Samaria.

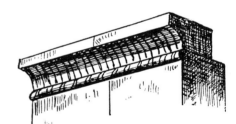

Perrot and Chipiez, Egypt I, *fig. 67*

Cornice at Karnak, Egypt. Phoenicians of Solomon's time traveled widely. Everywhere they went they were both teachers and learners in the arts. They did not imitate; they incorporated what they learned into their own modes and styles. Phoenician architecture of the tenth century B.C. showed individuality. These people had, however, borrowed from Egypt, notably Egypt of the earlier Amarna period. The Egyptian "streamlined cornice" used on the Howland-Garber model was employed on the Karnak temple some three centuries before the time of Solomon and is illustrated by the Phoenician temple of Amrith (Lebanon) which was dated by A. Reifenberg (Ancient Hebrew Arts, New York, 1950) on epigraphical evidence to "the time of the Kings."

A Reconstruction
of Solomon's Temple

by PAUL LESLIE GARBER

The Temple which the Phoenician king Hiram of Tyre in the tenth century B.C. designed and constructed for King Solomon is the Bible's most famous building. References to it, its predecessor the Tabernacle, and its successors the temples of Zerubbabel and Herod, appear in more than half of the Old Testament books and in nearly half of the New Testament books. Extended descriptions of the first Temple and its furnishings are given in I Kings 6–8, II Chronicles 3–4, Jeremiah 52, and Ezekiel 40–42. The structure, according to the Book of Kings, took seven and a half years to complete. It stood from about 950 to 587 B.C. as the jewel of Jerusalem. Its fabled splendor was due to the excellence of its materials and to the skillful workmanship that went into its construction, as well as to its unique theological presuppositions as a God-house.

The appearance of this place of worship has attracted the imagination and creative efforts of many artists, draftsmen, engineers, architects, historians, and model makers as well as students of the Bible. The earliest known European efforts were by Bh. Lamy (Paris, 1720) and A. Altschul (Amsterdam, 1724). More than thirty different works on the Solomonic Temple were published during the nineteenth century.

Lacking factual information, early reconstructions were conceived almost exclusively by artistic taste and imagination. Archaeology relating to the Bible is an achievement of the twentieth century. Slight as is this new-found body of data, reconstructions of Solomon's Temple can now be made more accurately and objectively than in any previous time in history.

During the years since 1952 when this article was first published, proposed restorations of Solomon's Temple have continued to appear. Some, such as the drawings (1964) of W. H. E. Drummond Roberts, a British architectural engineer, do not take into account findings of either biblical scholarship or archaeology and thus need not be taken seriously. Less commendable are such drawings as those of Eva Avi-Yonah in *Views of the Biblical World* (Jerusalem, 1959, Vol. 2, 213), and the drawings of Charles F. Stevens, which appeared first in *The Biblical Archaeologist* (Vol. 18 [1955], 43–44) and since widely reprinted. These reconstructions are published in such a manner that they appear to have a scholarly character but

Temple model from "northwest" corner. It is generally assumed that Solomon's Temple, like many of the ancient world, was positioned with reference to the sun's rising and setting. If the Temple was built on an east-west axis with the Holy of Holies at the west, the slanting rays of the rising sun would shine first through the open tall doors of the Temple, shedding its light far back through the dark interior. Here was housed the structure's most meaningful religious symbol, the Ark made in the wilderness under Moses' direction to hold the stones upon which were engraved the Ten Commandments.

Wooden "pallet" construction of the Temple. The parts of the Temple that were made of wood suggest the use of "pallet" construction, which we might describe as an early, if not the earliest, form of prefabrication. A pallet in this sense is a large, self-supporting piece so constructed that it may be covered with boards and used as a floor, ceiling, or wall panel. These could have been manufactured outside the Temple area, carried into the structure, and put in place silently. It is not improbable that, as I Kings 6:7 states, Solomon's Temple was erected without the sound of an iron tool.

Nails might have been used in making the pallets. Copper spikes were discovered at Ezion by Dr. Nelson Glueck. Measurements taken from these spikes, now in The Smithsonian Institution, were used by Mr. Howland to make the model's spikes to scale.

Above left: Pillars before the Temple façade. The two free-standing columns that stood before the porch of the Temple and bore the enigmatic names Jachin and Boaz are seen in the front view of the model and in the cutaway side view.

Above right: Incense burner from Megiddo. The Kings description of the chapiters for Jachin and Boaz is remarkably illustrated, as Professor H. G. May first suggested, by this "incense burner," which modern investigators found in a colored wall painting at Megiddo. This made available for the Howland-Garber reconstruction not only an authentic design for the chapiters but also an accurate way of duplicating the colors. Strands of pomegranates, carefully described in Kings, have been arranged around the chapiters. Each has two hundred pomegranates in two strands of one hundred each. Each pomegranate, made to scale (1/16 of an inch in diameter), was individually cast following the pattern of a metal pomegranate, so designated by the Oriental Institute excavators of Megiddo.

there is no discussion of study methods or evidence, as is expected in any serious work of scholarship. A critique of the Stevens drawings has been made in the *Journal of Biblical Literature* (Vol. 77 [1958], 123–132), followed by an exchange between the present author and William Foxwell Albright and G. Ernest Wright. The hope was expressed that future archaeological evidence may point the way to more reliable reconstructions of the Temple. A brief summary of some of the most recent investigations appears in Martin Noth's *The Old Testament World* (English translation: Philadelphia: Fortress Press, 1966, 173–179). Noth omits reference to Y. Aharoni's discovery at Tell Arad (see article) of an Iron Age Israelite temple, which has been interpreted as possessing an *un*-roofed "porch," with Jachin and Boaz inside rather than outside the Holy Place and functioning as support for the roof. Should future evidence even partially support Aharoni's initial conclusions, a newer "look" for Solomon's Temple may be in the making.

The Howland-Garber model began with a teacher's search for a print of an authentic reconstruction of the Temple of Solomon to hang in his classroom. He was directed to the article "Solomon's Temple Resurrected," in *The Biblical Archaeologist* (Vol. 4 [1941], 40 f.), by the editor, G. Ernest Wright. This preliminary assemblage of archaeological data was substantially enlarged by four and a half years of the teacher's studies, including one summer on a Carnegie Foundation grant. The finished model represents 3,600 man-hours of the model maker's time and skill. The scale is ⅜ of an inch to the cubit; the model measures about 15 inches from the court pavement to the top of the cornice. The model remains on exhibit at Agnes Scott College, Decatur, Georgia, where in the fall of 1950 it was first shown to the public.

Some of the methods of reconstruction used in the Howland-Garber model and part of the archaeological sources drawn upon are best seen by illustration. A set of color slides and filmstrip, together with a more detailed black-and-white filmstrip, are available from Southeastern Films, 79 Spring St., N.W., Atlanta, Ga. 30305.

The Temple of Solomon was not a place for "congregational" meetings. Those permitted inside were few in number. It may have been, however, that worshipers standing in the courtyard, priests and laymen alike, could have seen through the outer and the inner doors the Ark and its attendant giant cherubim. This possibility was suggested first by the completed Howland-Garber reconstruction in the frontal view shown here. Confidence may thus have been strengthened that His "eyes were open toward this place whereof Thou hast said, 'My name shall be there; to hearken to . . . prayer.'" (I Kings 8:29)

Column base from Tell Tainat. The Bible does not mention bases for these columns, but from similar structures stone bases may be assumed. This carved stone column base is from the eighth century B.C. palace excavated at Tell Tainat (ancient Hattina) in northern Syria, and now in the Oriental Institute, University of Chicago.

The Oriental Institute

Interior of the Temple. The Temple was in ground plan a house of two rooms oriented on the long axis. The entrance was on the short side through an open PORCH which sheltered the doors. The larger room, the HOLY PLACE, was 60 feet long, 30 feet wide, and 45 feet high. The inner room, the HOLY OF HOLIES, was a cube of 30 feet. A lowered ceiling and a raised floor in the inner room explain the difference in the height of the rooms. □ Fabricated cedar of Lebanon I-beams span the HOLY PLACE and support the ceiling pallet. The late Dr. J. A. Montgomery wrote in his volume on Kings, "The crossing of the rafters at right angles formed hollow squares, in technical phraseology, coffers; these may have been further set forth by decoration as in modern architecture." □ The SIDE CHAMBERS in the model are entered from the interior rather than, as usually understood, from the outside. This interpretation follows a study of the Hebrew text by Professor Leroy Waterman. As apparently the SIDE CHAMBERS were used by priests for storage and by the king as national "treasure vaults," an interior entrance to the vaults and the elimination of outside windows for the chambers seem to provide a likely arrangement. □ The STAR OF DAVID design of interlaced triangles, known from a graffito found at Megiddo in the Solomonic stratum, has been incorporated in the flooring of the model's HOLY PLACE. The pattern of bracing is quite a useful one for such a large flooring pallet (60 x 30 ft.). □ "He who thrones [or, is enthroned upon] the cherubim" is a known designation for the God of the Hebrews in the Old Testament. His presence may have been thought invisibly enthroned over the Ark, which stood between cherubim. These were sometimes regarded as guardians at the gates to the Garden of Eden. They have also been considered God's aids in moving through the heavens, functional parts of His "throne." In any case, the colossal (15 feet high; wingspread 15 feet) carved and gilded statues gave cosmic dignity to Him to Whom, according to Isaiah 6:3, seraphim (*i.e.,* cherubim) continually cry:

"Holy, Holy, Holy is the Lord of Hosts;
"The whole earth is full of His glory."

Within the HOLY PLACE was furniture from the Tabernacle, the TABLE OF SHEWBREAD, on which the priests daily arranged twelve loaves of unleavened bread, and the INCENSE ALTAR, here made by following the dimensions and shape of an altar found in Iron Age Megiddo.

Bronze door plaque. The shafts of the free-standing columns were 27 feet high and about 4 feet in diameter. Kings describes them as single castings of "brass," that is, copper alloy. We do not know that the ancients were able to make single castings in such large sizes; in fact, the history of metal technology would argue against such a possibility. We do have repeated instances where castings of metal plates—such as the bronze door plate shown here—were made to be fastened by stud-headed spikes to some wooden wall or post. This suggests that Solomon's pillars may have been made of cylindrical cast copper bands slipped over a built-up wooden post as a core support. Such a column would have given the appearance of a single sleeve or pipe of metal but would be made in a way we know was possible in the time of Solomon.

Limestone pivot stone. Archaeology's best suggestion to date for a "cornerstone" in Solomon's Temple is a door socket. The Temple doors swung on metal-tipped pivots set in stone sockets. From earliest times this device was used for large doors in Egypt and Mesopotamia. Valuables and records were deposited beneath such stones at the time of the structure's dedication. The exposed surfaces of the sockets bore, as in this example from the Gimilsin temple at Ur (20th century B.C.), words of dedication or, in other instances, of exorcism. Thresholds were thought to need special attention that the house might be guarded from enemies, both human and spirit. I Kings 16:34 refers to the city gates of newly rebuilt Jericho as having been "set up . . . upon Segub, his Hiel's youngest son" to offset Joshua's curse (Joshua 6:26).

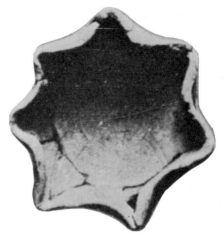

W. F. Albright, Tell Beit Mirsim, I, plate 23B

"Seven-branched" lamp. If the menorah form of the lampstand was used as early as the period of the Israelite monarchy, a surviving example is yet to be known. Clay lamps made as bowls to hold oil and with seven wicks to each lamp are commonly found in Iron Age I sites. It may confidently be assumed that they were in use in Solomon's time.

Metal stand from Megiddo. There is no textual evidence regarding the appearance of the lampholders, as the word "candlestick" more specifically means. This Megiddo stand with a tripod base—an inverted Proto-Ionic capital at each foot—served as a pattern for the Howland-Garber model reconstruction. Others like it are known, some dating as early as the twelfth century B.C.

The Oriental Institute

E. G. Howland

Wainscoting of the Holy Place. Carved wainscoting went completely around the interior walls of the HOLY PLACE. Decoration by exact repetition of motif seems to have been conventional with Phoenician artists. The designs reached 7½ feet from the floor. The border of open lilies and buds follows the I Kings 6:8 description, "knops and open flowers." Oversize unearthly figures, facing "trees of life" and carved on towering pilasters, effectively created an "other world" atmosphere. "In-lay," according to Dr. Wright, is a more adequate rendering of the verb in Kings, which is usually translated "over-lay." So the floor was not "over-laid" with gold; rather, carvings such as these were highlighted by skillful use of gold inlay.

Pilaster capital. This stone capital from Ramat Rahel (about the time of Solomon) suggests the Greek Ionic capital. A number of datable examples from the Near East, including the Jerusalem area and Megiddo, assure us that the design was employed in the Orient centuries before the earliest Greek usage. The artist of the Megiddo expedition suggested these capitals for use on pilasters. The ceiling height of the HOLY PLACE was 45 feet. The effect of tall pilasters (see the interior picture) made of East India sandalwood (close-grained and yellowish in color)—five equally spaced along the 60-foot HOLY PLACE walls—was to add to the sense of height in the room. See also the illustration of the doorway leading into the HOLY OF HOLIES.

Doorway leading to the Holy of Holies. It was suggested by Professor Kurt Galling of Halle, Germany, that Solomon's inner sanctuary, like those of known Canaanite temples, had a floor elevated above that of the rest of the Temple. This feature is seen also in the palace chapel at Tell Tainat in northern Syria. The partition between the HOLY PLACE and the HOLY OF HOLIES has not been made the thickness of boards, as I Kings 6:16 might seem to imply. This impression may have come from observation of the cedar paneling. The phrase "a fifth part," applied to the doorposts of this doorway in Kings 6:31, is here interpreted as referring to the cross-section of the door jambs and lintel, that is, being shaped so as to have five exposed faces. This was done by beveling the corners of the squared doorposts. The beveled faces shown here are colored azure blue and decorated with rosettes of gold. Functionally such a door jamb permitted the doors to swing in a wider arc and to reveal to viewers from the HOLY PLACE a more inclusive sight of the HOLY OF HOLIES—its sacred Ark flanked by the giant cherubim. Note that wall panels may have been fastened to the masonry walls by beams attached to their reverse sides being wedged into slots prepared in the stones. With expansion of beams, due to absorption of moisture, the wood is fitted snugly and the paneling is secure.

E. G. Howland

G. Loud, The Megiddo Ivories, *plate 4*

Ivory from Megiddo. We may no longer think of biblical cherubim and seraphim as plump winged infants. They were considered in Solomon's time as hybrid creatures—part lion, part bird, and part man. An ivory carving found at Megiddo shows a personage of some prominence seated "between" the cherubim, presumably one carved on each side of the supports of his "throne."

The "Molten Sea." On the pavement in front of the Temple stood this great bowl, the "Molten Sea." As described in I Kings, chapter 7, it was 15 feet in diameter and 7½ feet high. It was made of cast copper alloy, about three inches thick, and its brim was "wrought like the brim of a cup, like the flower of a lily." The large reservoir appeared to rest on the backs of twelve yearling calves; these animals were thought to be symbols of fecundity and power. As such they were highly suitable as sacrificial victims (Micah 6). The calves were grouped in four sets of three, headed toward the major points of the compass. The arrangement perhaps signified, as Dr. Albright has suggested, "the round of the seasons through the year."

The Altar of Burnt Offering. The presentation through burning of selected portions of valuable animals was a high moment in worship for the ancient world in Israel and elsewhere. The practice suggested human sacrifice and it demanded burning places called altars. There are as yet no sufficient data to make more than a "mock-up" of the Solomonic altar. Certain details from II Chronicles 4 and Ezekiel 43 are clear; others are far from being self-evident. Why were dressed stones not permitted? Why were there no steps? From what source came the notion that altar "horns" sometimes provided sanctuary for fugitives? Why is no mention of the altar made in the Kings account of Solomon's Temple?

A Graffito Star of David. Until stratigraphic excavation gave us knowledge of this double triangle crudely scratched on the unfinished back of a masonry block from Solomonic Megiddo, it was widely believed that this symbol was no older than the European Middle Ages. Now the Star of David is known to have been utilized in Palestine far nearer David's time than had previously been thought.

The Holy Place floor-pallet design. The discovery of the graffito Star of David permitted an experiment in a suitable design for the pallet that serves in the model as the floor of the HOLY PLACE. Placing this large (30 feet) self-supporting piece in position could have been one of the final acts in the finishing of the Temple construction. Its pattern provides an added element to the Israelite character of the house. Functionally it serves to lock in place at the bottom the wooden carved wainscoting that covers the inner face of the stone Temple walls.

The Oriental Institute

E. G. Howland

Jaffa's History Revealed by the Spade

by J. KAPLAN

Among the ports of Israel, Jaffa was of primary importance in ancient times. Situated at the center of the country's coastal strip, on the top of a high hill with a distant prospect, the city has been since antiquity a way station for conquerors faring from Egypt northward or from the northern countries southward. It was also the first stop for pilgrims to the Holy Land on their way to Jerusalem. It is not surprising, therefore, that Jaffa is frequently mentioned in the Bible and in numerous ancient records.

The earliest mention of Jaffa in Egyptian sources is in connection with its capture by Pharaoh Thothmes III in the fifteenth century B.C. The name occurs in the list of cities he captured in the Land of Canaan, whose names are engraved on the walls of the temple at Karnak. It is mentioned again in the Harris Papyrus, which is a folk tale describing the capture of Jaffa by stratagem, in a manner reminiscent of the story of Ali Baba and the forty thieves and the legend of the Trojan horse. Jaffa is mentioned subsequently in two of the Tell el-Amarna letters, which inform us that in the fourteenth century Jaffa was an Egyptian stronghold containing royal granaries. In Papyrus "Anastasi I," a satirical letter apparently of the thirteenth century, an Egyptian royal official gives an account of his experiences in Jaffa. The Bible refers to the town in the Book of Joshua in connection with the frontier of the tribe of Dan, which crossed "over against Jaffa," and twice in regard to the bringing of cedars from Lebanon to build the Temple at Jerusalem: these were transported "on rafts to the Sea of Jaffa." A fourth allusion is in the story of the prophet Jonah, who sought to flee from God through this port. Some believe that the legend of Perseus and Andromeda (the story relates that she was chained to the rocks off the shore of Jaffa to be devoured by the sea monster but was saved by the legendary hero Perseus who sped to her rescue) goes back to the twelfth century B.C., when the "Peoples of the Sea" invaded the coast of Israel and settled there. Besides, the name of Jaffa is engraved on the "prism stele" of King Sennacherib of Assyria, found in his palace at Nineveh; it relates that on his way to fight King Hezekiah of Judah he took Jaffa and a number of towns in its vicinity, an event which occurred about 700 B.C. The inscription of Eshmunezer, king of Sidon, probably be-

View of the excavations of the Jaffa citadel (Area A), looking toward the south.

113

Photohouse Prior

longs to the beginning of the fourth century
B.C.; it relates that he received in gift as an
expression of gratitude from the "Lord of
Kings" (king of Persia) two harbor towns
on the Palestinian coast, Jaffa and Dor.
Other sources confirm the settlement of
Sidonians at Jaffa at this time: these are
the inscription found at Jaffa which refers
to the establishment of a Sidonian temple,
and the account of the coastal towns attributed to the Greek voyager Scylax. From this
period onward Jaffa is frequently mentioned
by the Greek and Roman historians and,
above all, in Jewish and Christian literature.

Such was the information available until
excavation commenced at Jaffa. The city's
secrets were long sealed in the depths of the
earth because from the eighteenth century
on the area was densely covered by Arab
buildings, and only at the beginning of the

1950s, after a considerable part of these had
collapsed and been demolished, was it possible to proceed to archaeological investigation. The first scientific excavation was carried out in 1950 by the late P. L. O. Guy
on behalf of the Department of Antiquities,
and afterward digging in Guy's test pit was
continued by Drs. Bowman and Isserlin for
the University of Leeds. From this excavation it became clear that the ancient settlement did not extend over the entire area of
the hill. In 1955 systematic excavations were
begun by the writer for the Museum of
Antiquities of Tel Aviv-Jaffa. By 1963 six
seasons of digging had been carried out, three
in the eastern part of the Jaffa citadel (Area
A), two in the area of the *Hammam*, or
Turkish bath (Area B), and one near the
Church of Saint Peter (Area C). The results of these excavations, together with the

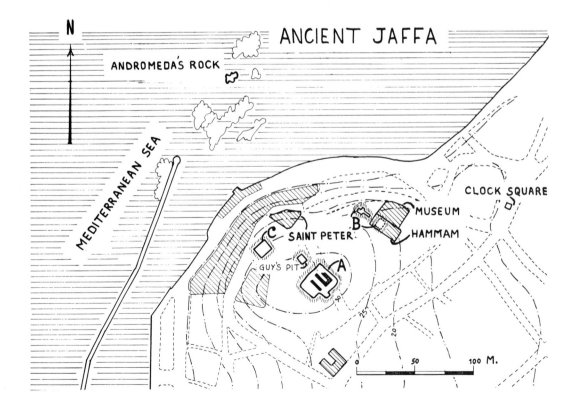

Nat Supprin

The gate of Ramses II, with the sill and two side walls (Area A). At the right is a stone of the jamb in situ; *at the left the foundation of the jamb, preserving the hole for the door pivot.*

information furnished by ancient documents, have added new chapters to the history of Jaffa.

In the eighteenth century B.C. (the Hyksos period) a great square enclosure was established within a rampart of beaten earth. Remains of this rampart were disclosed in the southern part of Area A and in the area excavated west of the *Hammam* in Area B. Investigation in Area A showed that the city's citadel stood here in all periods down to our own times. Most of the structures belonging to the first century B.C. and later had been demolished during the Crusades and in the modern Arab period (in certain spots modern remains were found lying directly on the Hyksos rampart).

There are some remains of buildings dating from the seventeenth–fourteenth centuries B.C. as well as deposits of pottery found *in situ*. Among these are imported vessels—red-on-black wares, from Cyprus, bichrome wares and wares of the Tell el-

Amarna period. An important discovery was made during the clearing of the thirteenth-century gate of the citadel located in the eastern part of Area A; the lower part of the gate was preserved, with a number of dressed stones belonging to both jambs lying near it. On these were found the titles and part of the name of Ramses II of Egypt, engraved in hieroglyphs. The discovery furnishes a reliable date for occupation Level V in the stratigraphic series of Area A and supplies a key for determining the dates of the other occupation levels found here.

A road four meters wide extended from this gate and ran between two entrance walls, eighteen meters long, into the citadel. These walls were of sun-dried bricks on foundations of small undressed masonry blocks. The entire gate area and the entrance walls were found to have been burned down in a violent conflagration; it may be supposed that this destruction occurred at the end of the reign of Ramses II, in the third quarter

*Four blocks of the jamb of the gate of
Ramses II, with part of his name and his five
titles inscribed in hieroglyphics.*

of the thirteenth century, when Egyptian power had weakened. This is the period when, in the opinion of many scholars, the country was conquered by Joshua. We have no literary evidence which might help to confirm the conjecture that the destruction at Jaffa was caused by the Israelites, who at this time destroyed neighboring Gezer; the latter, 17½ miles from Jaffa, is mentioned in the list of the Canaanite kings whose towns Joshua captured; the matter is still under consideration.

Some two meters above the burnt layer was found the threshold of another citadel gate, belonging to Level IV. Here, too, there were two parallel entrance walls lead-ing into the city; these were erected exactly on the building lines of the burnt structures of Level V, which remained buried beneath them. From this it is evident that no great length of time passed between the destruction of the Ramesside gate and the building of the new gate above it. Among the finds in this level may be mentioned the bronze pivot for the door, which was found *in situ*. Both the gate and the entrance walls of Level IV were burned, and it may be supposed that this event took place at the beginning of the twelfth century, when the "Peoples of the Sea" invaded the coastal area. It is thought that these peoples, as they streamed southward toward Egypt, burned all the maritime cities on their way, and Jaffa seems to have been unable to escape the fate of the rest.

Philistine remains were discovered in Area A, in the form of an ash pit and a courtyard floor containing potsherds. These were found in the debris of the burnt and shattered entrance walls of Level IV. East of the threshold of the Level IV gate were found traces of a stone glacis which overlay and concealed the burnt gate. Another glacis, of the ninth century B.C., was discovered in Area B, under the interior floor of the *Hammam*. It sloped up from east to west and its external revetment was made of small stone slabs. Beneath the latter were found alternate layers of sand and beaten earth, and underneath these was a layer of sun-dried bricks. Under these bricks were still other layers of sand and beaten earth. The function of the brick layers appears to have been to compress the sand and beaten earth layers beneath. The series of sand, beaten earth, and brick layers rested, as it subsequently appeared, on the eastern side of the Hyksos rampart which was found deep in the soil west of the Turkish bath.

Remains of the Persian period survived chiefly in Area A. Here a section of a wall of dressed masonry of the fourth century B.C. was uncovered, sunk into the burnt entrance walls of Level IV. It should be noted that the pottery of this period included numerous sherds of Attic ware. A fragment of a fortress found in Area A belongs to the Hellenistic period; built of dressed blocks, it dates to the third century B.C. Belonging to the same period was a ruined catacomb disclosed in Area C at a deep level. Its walls were made of dressed blocks laid as headers and stretchers. The debris in the court of the catacomb yielded half of a Greek dedicatory inscription incised on a marble slab. This much-defaced inscription preserves the names of Ptolemy Philopator (221–204 B.C.)

and his wife Berenice. A fragment of wall exposed in Area A was of the Hasmonean period (late second century B.C.); upon it abutted parts of a building whose floor was paved with seashells. Additional remains of this period were found in Area C, including repairs to the ceiling of the third-century B.C. catacomb, which had been refurbished at this time and supported on stone arches set 30 cm. apart. It appears that at this time

View from the top of the Hammam *dome (Area B) over the brick facing of the ninth-century* B.C. *glacis. In the trial trench cut at the upper left can be seen, in cross-section, a layer of whitish sand between two layers of brown beaten earth.*

Photohouse Prior

the restored catacomb was used as the cellar of a dwelling built over it.

Remains dating from the end of the first century B.C. onward were preserved chiefly in Area C. Among those of the first century of our era are the courtyard of a dwelling and part of an adjoining room whose front wall was preserved to a height of two meters. Near the door leading into the room, as was normal at this period, was a plastered cistern. The finds in the court and in the cistern showed that the house had probably been abandoned in the year 66, at the outbreak of the war with Rome. These included bronze coins, *terra sigillata*, and a stamp for bread or cheese on which the name "Ariston" was incised in Greek. Above these building remains was exposed another occupation level containing numerous signs of destruction by fire. The date of this level was fixed by a hoard of coins found on the cellar floor of one of the dwellings, as well as by three identical Greek inscriptions on limestone mentioning the name of the inspector of weights and measures *(agorano-*

mos) of the Jaffa market, Judah, who held his post in the reign of Trajan (98–117). Four additional occupation levels were cleared in Area C, datable between the third and the sixth century. Among these may be mentioned the court of a fourth-century building with a floor made of large slabs of stone taken from the seashore. In another corner of the excavated area was a mosaic pavement belonging to the end of the sixth century.

Our account of the history of Jaffa has taken us on a long journey. The work continues in investigation of the later periods —Moslem, Crusader, Mameluke, and Turkish. Although remains of these periods have been disclosed in Jaffa, so far they have been discovered haphazardly and in relatively small areas on account of the destruction caused by nineteenth-century building. It is to be hoped that remains of this sort may yet be found in an undamaged state and that finds will be forthcoming which can adequately represent these periods in the Museum of Antiquities of Tel Aviv–Jaffa.

Six Campaigns at Biblical Shechem

by JAMES F. ROSS AND LAWRENCE E. TOOMBS

The low mound covering the remains of ancient Shechem rises from a fertile plain at the eastern entrance to the narrow valley between Mt. Ebal and Mt. Gerizim. A city located here was in a position to control important trade routes from Egypt through Jerusalem (forty miles to the south) to the centers of culture in Syria and Phoenicia. The difficulty of defending a site overshadowed by two mountains was more than offset by the presence of an abundant water supply, provided by the fine spring at the southeast corner of the tell, or mound.

Egyptian texts of the XIIth Dynasty indicate that Shechem was a strategic city of international importance as early as 1800 B.C. Abraham's first contact with the inhabitants of Palestine took place at Shechem (Genesis 12:1–7), and the stories of the Hebrew patriarchs show that during the eighteenth and seventeenth centuries B.C. Shechem was a center of Canaanite religious and political life. The Tell el-Amarna letters (1400–1350 B.C.) speak of Shechem, under its prince Lab'ayu, as playing an important role in the intrigues against Egyptian control of the Palestine area. The city is not listed among those conquered by the invad-

ing Israelite armies under the command of Joshua, but immediately after the conquest (ca. 1250–1200 B.C.) it appears as the rallying point for the twelve-tribe Israelite confederacy and as the site of a covenant renewal ceremony (Joshua 24). During the tribal period Shechem was the scene of an attempt to make one of the sons of Gideon king (Judges 9). In the struggle associated with this premature experiment in monarchy the city was destroyed.

During the early Israelite monarchy Shechem retained its position as the most important city in the kingdom after Jerusalem. Rehoboam went there to be crowned king in the northern part of his territory, and the city was for a short time the capital of the independent northern kingdom after the disruption of the monarchy following the death of Solomon. When the capital was moved to Samaria, Shechem remained the center of an administrative district until its destruction by the Assyrian armies of Shalmaneser V (724 B.C.).

The ruins of such an important city could not escape the attention of the archaeologists. On the basis of its location and the remains of walls visible on the surface the

The palace area as it appears from the north. At the left is the area occupied by the streets, and at the upper left the Samaritan house (II on the plan). The temple forecourt is in the middle background, while the temple itself is at the upper right.

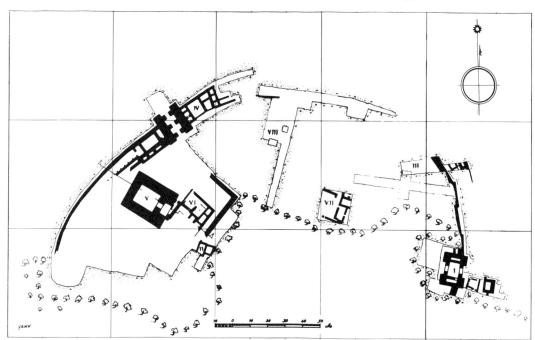

General plan of the areas excavated by the end of the 1960 season.

tell was identified in 1903 as the site of Shechem. A series of German expeditions (1913–14, 1926–27, 1928, 1932, and 1934) cleared the face of a massive defense wall and the foundations of an impressive temple; in addition, extensive trenches were cut into the north and east sides of the mound. The results of these expeditions were never adequately published, and the dates of the fortifications and temple structure remained uncertain.

The Drew-McCormick Archaeological Expedition began its work with a short season in 1956, followed by longer and more intensive campaigns in 1957, 1960, 1962, 1964, and 1966. The work was governed by three aims: to clarify the problems remaining from the earlier excavations, to develop a complete picture of the history of the city, and to provide a training ground in the field for students of Palestinian archaeology.

The earliest inhabitants undoubtedly clustered around the spring that now supplies the village of Balatah, outside the area excavated by both the German and American expeditions. But there is ample evidence for early occupation elsewhere on the tell. In areas used later for the fortress temple (V on plan) seminomadic people of the early fourth millennium B.C. dug shallow, clay-lined pits, which they probably covered with tents of animal skins. After these had been abandoned, floors of packed earth were laid; these were renewed from time to time. These people were really only "campers"; they constructed no buildings and were apparently much less advanced than their contemporaries at Jericho and elsewhere. Nor have any buildings of the Early Bronze (3000–2100) or Middle Bronze I period (2100–1900) been discovered, although there is evidence from scattered pottery that the site was occupied during these centuries.

The real birth of Shechem (the name is found in Egyptian texts from the nineteenth

century B.C.) began with the Hyksos, a people of mixed racial origin including Semitic elements. They occupied Palestine and moved on to rule Egypt for more than a century and a half (1720–1550). The beginnings were modest; so far only a few walls and a packed earth floor with a sunken, stone-lined pit have been found, dating from the first half of the eighteenth century. But the Hyksos were not slow to fortify this advantageous site. They surrounded the city with an immense earthen bank, approximately eighty feet wide and twenty feet high, and consolidated its slope with a plastered surface. The bank was probably surmounted by a defensive wall, which was destroyed when later builders sheared off the top of the bank to use its earth for fill. In the acropolis area the Hyksos constructed a massive stone wall separating what was to be the sacred area from the rest of the city (the L-shaped wall to the right of VI on the plan) and erected the first system of defense walls. Inside this fortified area the new settlers erected an extensive structure with a central courtyard, which is probably to be interpreted as a temple. Between its eastern wall and the L-shaped wall there was left a space for a street and drain. This "courtyard temple" was rebuilt at least twice during the Hyksos period; nine superimposed cobblestone streets have been discovered. Only a few walls of the first of these structures have been excavated, but its successor is relatively well preserved. Built in the last half of the eighteenth century B.C., it consisted of at least nine rooms of which three, bordering on the streets, were workrooms. One room was provided with two clay ovens, a kneading block and a stone-lined pit, probably for grain. Other rooms were carefully paved with large flagstones; several burials in storage jars were found under the floors. All contained the bodies of children, interred in jars, often in a simple stone structure for protecting the burial. They were not, as at first suspected, foundation sacrifices, since, in those cases where the evidence was preserved, they were seen to be cut through the floor after the building had been completed.

After about fifty years the temple was again rebuilt, and several rooms were enlarged. There is some evidence of burning between the second temple and the third as well as between the first and second, but the ground plan remained basically the same; indeed, several walls of the older temple were simply reused or widened. The central courtyard remained in the same position as in the first two structures. Few distinctive features of the third building remain; almost all the rooms were excavated by the Germans to a point below floor level. An impressive northern court is worthy of mention, however; it had six heavy pillars at its north end and one in the center. Otherwise only bare stone walls remain; these probably had a mud-brick superstructure like the walls of the earlier palaces.

Finally, the Hyksos commenced still a fourth building. But of this only two high walls remain, and it is unknown whether or not it was another temple. We can say that these walls mark the end of a building tradition, for about 1650 B.C. the city was destroyed and Hyksos building in this particular area ceased (VI on plan).

After the destruction of 1650, Shechem was rebuilt on a larger scale. In order to provide more living space within the walls an enormous engineering project was undertaken to extend the city limits about forty feet to the north. On this side the tell merged gradually into the slopes of Mt. Ebal and offered no suitable elevation on which to found a wall. The engineers therefore constructed an artificial mound against the south slope of the mountain by bringing in up to twenty feet of earth fill. This mass of earth was held in place by a huge retaining wall with a free-standing mud-brick superstructure that served as the outer line of defense. Within its circuit a slighter wall was erected, and the two were connected at intervals by a system of cross walls to form a casemate. This double circumvallation was investigated on the north (IV on plan) and on the east of the city (I and III on plan). In one place the outer wall survives to a height of at least twenty feet and has stones as large as 3 x 4 feet in its outer face. The wall merits the term "cyclopean," which has long been applied to the section exposed by the Germans on the north side of the city. Opposite the slopes of Mt. Ebal in the northwest sector of the cyclopean wall the builders inserted a monumental gateway (58 x 65 feet), divided into two sections by three sets of massive stone orthostats. So effective was this heavily defended entrance that it was rebuilt several times, and continued in use into the Late Bronze Age.

Formidable as these defenses were, within fifty years they required additional strengthening. The main line of defense was moved twenty to forty feet farther up the slope of the tell. It consisted of a massive outer wall, ten feet thick, connected to a slighter inner wall, as in the earlier plan. The disused cyclopean walls now functioned mainly as retaining walls for a sloping packed earth rampart.

The most striking feature of the new defense system was the east gate. In front of the gate a wide approach road, paved at first with cobblestones and later with brick, led up to the gateway. This road completely covered the casemate defenses of the earlier period. The gate itself consisted of two huge rectangular towers (each 23 x 42 feet), the masonry of which compares in size with that of the cyclopean wall. Space was provided in them for guardrooms flanking the entry way.

In its brief existence of fifty years the gate was destroyed three times, and the accumulated debris raised the level of the road between the towers above that of the city, so that a set of steps had to be built up to the gate level from the city side. The last years of Hyksos Shechem must have been stormy. Two major assaults on the city came in quick succession. In the first of these the gateway was breached and destroyed, and it had barely been rebuilt when the final attack came. The last surfacing of the stairway shows almost no sign of wear. And in this final period the width of the gateway was decreased by the addition of four pairs of basalt orthostats, set on deep foundations.

Throughout the gate area, over the stairs, and in the guard towers, evidence of the final destruction of Middle Bronze Shechem was startlingly clear. Decayed mud brick, burned beams, fallen plaster, and a jumble of building stone were piled in the guardrooms to a depth of twelve feet, and four human skeletons, literally buried in ash and debris, lay on the steps. This spectacular destruction is attributed to the Egyptian armies, which followed up their expulsion of the Hyksos by an invasion of Palestine about 1550 B.C. It effectively put an end to Shechem as a Hyksos city.

During the period just described the city was dominated by the largest temple yet found in Palestine (V on plan). Its foundations were laid in the fill brought in to extend the city limits northward, and the building was clearly designed to serve as a fortress as well as a place of worship, thus giving the name "fortress temple." In plan the temple is a rectangle with outer dimensions of 68 x 84 feet and with foundation walls seventeen feet thick. It was approached from the east by a forecourt occupying the same area as the courtyards of the earlier structures. The wide doorway gave access to a small room, beyond which lay the rectan-gular cella. The orientation of the temple is twenty-eight degrees south of east (approximately the direction of the rising sun at the winter solstice), similar to that of the Israelite temple in Jerusalem. None of the temple furnishings have survived.

The mass of debris left by the Egyptian destruction complicated the task of rebuilding Shechem. The Late Bronze inhabitants took the line of least resistance and made no effort to clear the Hyksos walls for reuse. Instead they moved back to the line of the innermost wall of the preceding period and used it as the foundation for their own much weaker defenses. At the east gate they built two new towers. Only the southern one survives; it consists of two small adjoining rooms under the lowest floor of which was found the intentionally buried skeleton of a small animal, probably an ass. A wide avenue, paved with flagstones, led up a slight incline from the gateway into the city. On its south side a large open space, beautifully surfaced with cobblestones covered with hard plaster, probably served as a military parade ground or public meeting place. Toward the end of the Late Bronze Age the guardrooms were modified, and the open square disappeared. Now only a narrow alley separated the enlarged guardrooms from the houses. In this form the structures continued in use into the period of Israelite occupation. No destruction level such as that found at Hazor marks the transition from Canaanite to Israelite times. Two small excavations on the north side of the tell (VI.2 and VIII on plan) tended to confirm this fact, since each produced evidence of new building at the beginning of the Israelite period, but not of violence. Three major fields (VII, IX, XIII) which reached Late Bronze levels in 1964 and 1966, revealed a more complex situation than the small soundings. The evidence of these fields indicates that there may have been localized acts of destruction which did not, however, affect the defenses of the city as a whole.

The peaceful passage of Shechem from Canaanite to Israelite control is an important historical datum. The absence of the city from lists of Joshua's conquests and its importance as a center for early Israelite tribal life have been interpreted as indicating that Shechem was in friendly hands when the Israelites entered Palestine. The archaeological data lend considerable support to this theory.

The heyday of Late Bronze Shechem was the first half of the fourteenth century B.C., the period of Lab'ayu of the Tell el-Amarna letters. This time of prosperity was ended by a general destruction of the city. In the debris a splendid bronze figurine of the Canaanite Baal was found.

The two succeeding Late Bronze phases were marked by a lower level of material culture, although the continuity of the religious tradition is indicated by a series of female fertility figurines and by a house shrine with a crude brick altar and the flaring base of a libation stand.

During the 1960 campaign an important fact came to light in the area of the fortress temple (V on plan). It had been thought that the Hyksos fortress temple was directly overlaid by the foundations of an Israelite granary, but careful excavation within the cella revealed that an intermediate phase existed between the temple and the granary. This building, which is dated by the associated pottery, was evidently the Late Bronze temple of Shechem, none other than the structure mentioned in Judges 9 as "the Temple of El (or Baal) Berith," the God, or Lord, of the Covenant. The fragmentary state of the walls and the numerous pits found everywhere in the cella are eloquent testimony to the destruction of the sacred place when Abimelech, son of Gideon, took revenge on the city for its revolt against him.

A bronze statuette of the Canaanite god Baal.

These pits contained pottery of the early Israelite period (Iron IA, about 1200–1100 B.C.). If this pottery can be more precisely dated it will help to establish one fixed point in the otherwise obscure period of the Israelite judges.

The forecourt, its level raised about two feet, was reused in connection with this Late Bronze temple. On the surface were found two stone sockets, one on each side of the entrance, in which sacred stones had been set up in ancient times. Farther east is an altar platform where sacrifices were offered. Near the front edge of the platform had once stood a huge flat limestone slab, six feet high, set in a stone socket. We found both the socket and the slab broken and thrown down from the forecourt. Ingenuity and brawn, assisted by a steel tripod and much shouting, raised the stone and its socket to their original position. The slab is one of the largest of the few surviving examples of the *masseboth*, the sacred stones of the Canaanites.

A new period in the history of Shechem began after the death of Solomon, with the division of Israel into Samaria (or Ephraim) and Judah. Jeroboam I, the first monarch of the northern kingdom, fortified the city as his capital (I Kings 12:25) but then moved to Penuel and eventually to Tirzah. Only fragmentary evidence of Jeroboam's work has been discovered. But later Israelite houses have been found, one of the ninth century and one of the eighth. The latter (VII on the plan) measured approximately 30 x 40 feet, with narrow corridors along three sides surrounding a large central room and some smaller chambers. Just outside this house a beautiful cylinder seal was found, and an amethyst seal found in a disturbed Hellenistic level is probably also from this period, to judge from the script.

In the same general period the Israelites also began to use the site of the pagan fortress temple once again; for seven centuries it had been abandoned, although the early Israelites had dug pits and silos through the temple floors. Now a granary with walls of unhewn stones was erected. It measured approximately 50 x 60 feet, and had a corridor along one side with three narrow rooms occupying the remaining width of the building. The whole structure was set into a thick layer of plaster laid over the walls of the temple. Quite possibly this was a government warehouse; there is evidence that Shechem was now the head of an administrative district.

Israelite houses occupied Fields VII and IX continuously from about 900 B.C. to 724

Cypro-Phoenician jar, finely painted and burnished, found in association with the Israelite house of the eighth century B.C.

Amethyst seal and impression dating from the eighth century B.C. *The inscription reads* LMBN, *which probably means: "Belonging to [the Lord] is [my] Maker."*

B.C. (Strata IX B-VIII). Those of Field VII were built on a terrace along the southeast slope of the hill which led down from the temple area to the east gate. These buildings apparently owe their large size to the fact that they were centers of industrial activity. The Stratum VII A house had a large open hearth, and a number of cisterns and storage bins. That of Stratum VII B possessed a wine pressing installation (see illustration).

This period of the city's history came to a violent end when the Assyrians under Shalmaneser destroyed it (724 B.C.). The floors of the latest Israelite house are covered with broken, burned brick and collapsed ceilings, along with fragments of storage jars that had once stood on the roof. Israelite Shechem was a thing of the past;

the pious now made pilgrimages to the temple in Jerusalem (Jeremiah 41:4–5).

Shalmaneser did his work well. The city was virtually abandoned from the time of his invasion until the fourth century. Fragments of Greek pottery and an early coin show that there was some occupation, but Shechem was not to enjoy its former glories until after the death of Alexander the Great. The latter defiled the city of Samaria by turning it into a rest camp for his veterans; the Samaritans thereupon moved to the site of ancient Shechem because of its proximity to their holy mountain, Gerizim (see John 4, where in place of Sychar we should probably read, with the Syriac, Sychem).

There are four definite phases of Samaritan occupation at Shechem. They probably

represent a series of building operations carried on by the same people and their descendants, with intermediate destruction at the hands of the rival claimants to Palestine: the Ptolemies, the Seleucids, and the native Maccabees. In the first period (ca. 325–250 B.C.) the defenses were strengthened by building an earthen rampart down the slope from the east gate and new brick walls on the seventeenth-century guardroom of the gate. A small building containing an oil or wine press was erected over the remains of the Israelite guardroom. And on top of the tell new houses were laid out over the brick-filled ruins left by Shalmaneser. Because of later pits dug into their rooms it is difficult to discern their plan. We have found, however, a carefully plastered shallow basin

which was used either as a wine press or for moistening clay in the making of pottery; near it was a storage jar sunk into the cobblestoned pavement.

The next period (250–200 B.C.) saw a new series of houses in this central area; three well-preserved rooms have been found, as well as a street on their west side. And now the Samaritans began to occupy more of the tell. They constructed a beautiful house near the site of the now forgotten temple and palaces (II on the plan). It had carefully prepared thresholds and door jambs; in its remains were found the key to one of the rooms and a clay-seal impression from a papyrus document. These houses were destroyed by the Seleucids; in one was found a cache of Ptolemaic silver coins (tetra-

Seal impression found outside the Samaritan house (II on plan). Impressions on the reverse show that it was once affixed to a papyrus document.

At left: A wine press, vat, and storage jar in an Israelite house from about 750 B.C.

Hoard of silver Ptolemaic coins left by a refugee fleeing Shechem when it was captured by the Seleucids. The latest coin is of Ptolemy V, dated to 193 B.C.

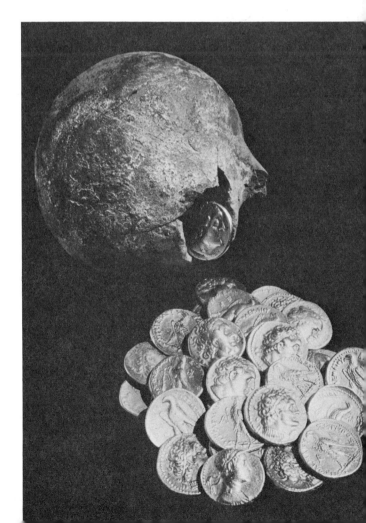

drachms) left behind by a refugee fleeing from the city.

When they returned, the Samaritans once again looked to their defenses. The first half of the second century saw the erection of a rough stone tower down the slope from the east gate, perhaps intended to screen the ancient gateway itself. New houses were built in the center of the tell, but of these only a few disconnected walls remain.

The last period of Shechem's history (ca. 150–100 B.C.) was again filled with violence. John Hyrcanus, one of the most powerful of the Maccabean kings, is reported to have utterly destroyed the city in 128. But according to the evidence from the coins, Shechem survived for a few more years; she probably held out until toward the end of the century, when John delivered the *coup de grâce.*

One of the mysteries of the Shechem area was the location of the Temple of Jupiter, built by Hadrian on Mt. Gerizim and pictured on coins minted at Neapolis. Tell er-Ras, the northernmost peak of Mt. Gerizim, has an artificially created crest on which large architectural fragments could be seen. Field XII, opened on Tell er-Ras in 1964, uncov-

ered the ruins of a rectangular building (73 x 46 feet) the style of which, together with the pottery recovered from the foundation trenches, indicates that the structure is undoubtedly the Hadrianic temple. Deep excavation against the foundations showed that the Roman building stood on the remains of a structure of Hellenistic date. It is likely, though not absolutely certain, that the Hellenistic building is the temple of the Samaritans. The Roman building was approached by a monumental stairway, which ran from near Neapolis all the way up the mountain to the peak. Its lower part consists of rock-cut steps, but as the temple is approached these widen to broad terraces where the pilgrims could rest and refresh themselves after the long ascent. Traces of mosaic flooring, marble paving, and pleasure gardens testify to the former magnificence of the ascent to Hadrian's temple.

During the Roman period the mound itself lay uninhabited; the people settled either in a village by the spring or in the Roman "New City" (Neapolis, now Nablus, where a small colony of Samaritans still lives). Today there remain only the small Arab village of Balatah and the ancient walls revealed by the archaeologists' trenches.

Ashdod: A City of the Philistine Pentapolis

by MOSHE DOTHAN

Tel Ashdod, situated near the remains of the village of Isdud, has always been identified with ancient Ashdod. It lies two and a half miles inland from the coast, on the edge of sand dunes bordering the sea, and comprises an acropolis of about seventeen acres and a lower city covering a much larger area. The summit of the mound is fifty-two meters above sea level and rises about twenty-two meters above the surrounding area.

The first settlement was built on a natural isolated hill, mainly on a sandstone base covered by a thin coating of earth. It is not yet possible to determine the exact extent of the city because of the accumulation of sand dunes on the west and the cultivation of fields both in ancient times and at present. But our surveys lead us to believe that at the time of its greatest extent the city covered at least ninety acres. During the last few centuries the villagers of Isdud had been digging into the rich organic soil of the mound to fertilize their fields and to make mud brick for their dwellings. While this destruction of part of the site proved a great loss for us, it also revealed some important phases of stratification even before our excavations began.

The main aim in our first three seasons was to establish the duration of the settlement and its stratification. Altogether about three quarters of an acre were excavated, in nine different areas, the most significant results being achieved in the Areas A, B, D, G, H, and K. Area D is in the lower city and all the rest are on the southern, northern, and western edges of the acropolis. It has been possible to make a provisional correlation of the stratigraphy of the various areas. This included twenty strata of settlement, from Early Bronze Age II (2900–2600 B.C.) to the end of the Byzantine period (seventh century A.D.).

Micha P.

Steatite scarab of Ramses II, probably the pharaoh of the Exodus, found in the last Late Bronze Age at Ashdod.

Section through part of the mound, showing levels from Philistine at the bottom to Roman at the top. Below: Plan of Ashdod.

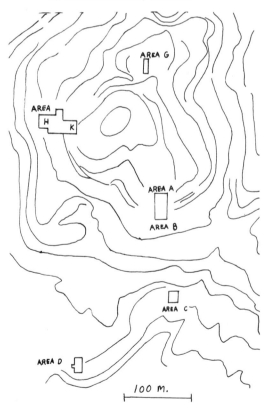

Until recently the earliest non-biblical source for the history of ancient Ashdod dated no farther back than the eleventh century B.C. (*Onomasticon* of Amenope), but documents discovered at Ugarit now indicate the important rôle played by Ashdod in the fourteenth and thirteenth centuries B.C. (C.F.A. Schaeffer, *Ugaritica* IV [Paris 1963], 140 ff.). They show Ashdod was one of the three Canaanite cities that had commercial relations with Ugarit, the other two being Akko and Ashkelon.

The Bible, of course, furnishes considerable information about Ashdod. As we know from Joshua 15:45–47, it was apportioned to the tribe of Judah. But the conquest of Ashdod is not mentioned at all, either in the Book of Joshua or in the Book of Judges. Ashdod always appears as one of the five chief cities of the Philistines. According to the Book of Samuel, the Ark of the Covenant was brought to the temple of Dagon in Ashdod, and remained there until the inhabitants were stricken by a great plague (I Samuel 5:1 ff.). Ashdod is not mentioned in

Micha P.

the Bible again until the time of Uzziah (783–742 B.C.), who "brake down . . . the wall of Ashdod: and built cities about Ashdod and among the Philistines" (II Chronicles 26:6). In 712 B.C. Sargon II of Assyria sent a military expedition against Ashdod because the city refused to pay tribute (Isaiah 20:1). When the rebellion was crushed, the kingdom of Ashdod was annexed by Sargon and became an Assyrian province. Its inhabitants were exiled and others were settled in their stead. The fullest account of the conquest appears in the annals of the Assyrian kings. The vicissitudes of the people of Ashdod up to the Babylonian conquest are mentioned by several of the prophets (Jeremiah 25:20, Zephaniah 2:4, Zechariah 9:6). Eventually the region became a Babylonian province and later a Persian one. After the return of the Jews from the Babylonian exile, the city is reported to have been the enemy of Judah (Nehemiah 4:7). At the same time there appears to have been considerable intermarriage between Jews and Ashdod women, and their descendants are said to have spoken the Ashdod dialect (Nehemiah 13:23, 24). This is the last biblical reference to Ashdod. The history of the Hellenistic city is chronicled mainly in the books of the Maccabees and by Josephus, who also mentions its history in later times.

On the last day of our last season we decided to cut a small section below what seemed to be natural rock. The results of such a small trial dig must necessarily be treated as provisional until a larger area is excavated, but so important for the early history of Ashdod are the discoveries we made that they should be mentioned. The cut was made below the earliest Late Bronze Age II city defenses, on the northern edge of the tell. Here two settlement strata were found. The lower one revealed some stone-wall foundations, the remains of one or possibly two rooms, with a deposit of ashes, bones, and potsherds on the floors. Most of the sherds are characteristic of Early Bronze Age II. Without knowing the extent of this earliest settlement of Ashdod, we can only conjecture that it was one of many that sprang up in this period of rapid urbanization.

This section of the Early Bronze II settlement was completely destroyed and subsequently covered by thick debris. It shows no traces of habitation for nearly a thousand years. The next settlement appeared in our vertical section as a black layer containing sherds of Middle Bronze Age II. The section does not show distinct traces of structures; at this time Ashdod may well have been only a Hyksos outpost on the Via Maris.

The establishment of Ashdod as a large walled city can be traced back to the beginning of the Late Bronze Age, about 1550 B.C., when the city apparently covered the entire acropolis. The earliest pottery belongs to a local bichrome type. An important small find is a cylinder seal of the late Mid-

Micha P.

Typical Philistine bowl found on floor of the Philistine fortress, eleventh century B.C.

dle Babylonian period, inscribed with a cuneiform text. Although it was found in a late stratum (Area G), it belongs to this time. Traces of foundations of what seem to be the earliest city walls surrounding Ashdod were found in Area B, small sections of two superimposed city walls in G. However, only in the next stratum (early Late Bronze Age II) was the excavated area large enough for us to reach more definite conclusions. Here we uncovered stone foundations of large brick buildings within the city. Besides the local pottery we find bichrome ware and Cypriot imports, especially monochrome ware. This was a period when Egyptian rule was firmly established in Canaan under the Pharaohs of the XVIIIth Dynasty—Thutmose IV and Amenophis III—and before the time of unrest and strife in Canaan, which is reflected in the famous Amarna letters.

In the next two strata in Area B a large public building was uncovered, consisting of rooms built around a central courtyard, with mud-brick walls 60–70 cm. thick. Sufficient evidence was found to show that in both strata the buildings had the same plan. It

resembles the buildings common to this period in Canaan, such as those at Megiddo. The pottery shows that there was considerable trade and commerce between Ashdod and the Mycenaean cultural area, as well as Cyprus. It includes local wares, both cooking pots and painted vessels, Mycenaean III B ware, the well-known Cypriot "knife-pared" juglets, white-slip and base-ring ware. Other artifacts include stone tools and vessels, scarabs, weapons, and clay female figurines, which may represent goddesses.

The last Bronze Age stratum in Area B could not be thoroughly evaluated because of destruction wrought by modern villagers. Some grain silos and floors of dwellings are still preserved; associated pottery enables us to date this stratum to the thirteenth century B.C.

On the western side of the acropolis (Area H) we reached Late Bronze strata only in a small section, revealing the two upper layers of this period. In contrast to Area B, the structures of the uppermost stratum are well preserved, with the brick walls still standing up to one meter in height. An Egyptian scarab with the name of Ramses II belongs to this level, although it was found in later debris. We know from the evidence of the vertical section cut between Areas A and B, and also from Area H, that a thick burnt layer indicates the destruction of the last Late Bronze Age city in the second half of the thirteenth century. The same total destruction was observed in the corresponding stratum at nearby Tel Mor, a town which probably served as an inland harbor for Ashdod. This destruction could be attributed to the campaigns of one of the conquerors of the southern coast of Palestine, such as Merneptah, or to local warfare between the Canaanite cities. The destruction of both Ashdod and Tel Mor could, however, also be attributed to a wave of Israelite conquests (especially of the tribe of Judah), even though the Bible does not expressly mention such events.

Since the excavations have as yet barely touched the lowest strata in Area A, representing Iron Age I, we cannot be sure what happened here after the destruction of the Late Bronze Age city. The two upper strata in Area A were excavated on a somewhat larger scale. A corner of a fortress belonging to the Philistine period was uncovered. The walls (1.25 m. wide) of this rectangular mud-brick building have been preserved to a height of up to two meters. A section of the entrance gate was uncovered in the eastern wall. Most of the pottery found in the fortress dates from the eleventh century B.C. Unfortunately much of the building was destroyed in modern times, long after its first destruction in the early tenth century B.C. The evidence gathered from excavation in Area H (1965) corroborates the stratigraphy of Area A. There are three Philistine strata with different types of structures and traces of the brick city wall, almost completely eroded. In the uppermost level is a circular, or apsidal, structure within rectangular walls.

We can now tentatively reconstruct the historical background of the Philistine period on the acropolis. In the twelfth century the Philistines constructed their buildings on a ruined site of Iron Age I. However, it was only in the beginning of the eleventh century that a fortress was built. The archaeological evidence is thus in accord with biblical sources: the Philistines reached the peak of their power in the first half of the eleventh century, that is, before Saul's ascent. The destruction of the fortress may have been the result of one of David's raids on the Philistines.

A large, roughly circular pit filled with discarded Philistine pottery was cleared in Area C (outside the acropolis). Hundreds of sherds painted in black and red, mostly over a white wash, were found here. The designs include spirals, Maltese crosses, checkerboards, lattice patterns, wavy lines and stylized swans painted on bowls, beer jugs, and stirrup jugs.

The three campaigns have increased our knowledge of the Philistines, but this is merely a beginning. So far, we have investigated only the edges of the acropolis, which was probably the main seat of Philistine power in the city. Area G (on the northern edge of the tell) opened up a further line of inquiry. Here remains of the Philistine settlement were found, and a section of its city wall. Over six meters wide and built of sun-dried bricks, this served as the defense wall for the later Philistine settlement.

The most important details concerning Iron Age II were supplied by Area D in the lower city, where four superimposed settlements were discovered. Our knowledge of the earliest settlement is slight; typical of its pottery are a highly burnished krater decorated with black bands, and two-handled cooking pots.

A section of a brick wall at least three meters wide and belonging to the last three of these settlements indicates that the city was well defended. We are best acquainted with the cities of Strata VIII and VII, belonging mainly to the eighth and seventh centuries B.C. The most important building in Stratum VIII is a small brick temple with several rooms, the main one rectangular. In the long side of this room an altar juts out from the wall. About one meter square, it is built of bricks and whitewashed. The pottery types include red burnished bowls with bar handles, a large storage jar, and juglets, some burnished. Of special interest is a large quantity of cult vessels and figurines found near the altar, in the debris that covered the floor, and in refuse pits nearby. Among them were bowls, some standing on seven small knobs (perhaps used as incense burners)

Micha P.

Main shrine of the small temple in Area D, Stratum 8. In the middle is an altar built of brick and plastered.

Below: Highly burnished krater (bowl) decorated with black bands (Iron Age II). Right: An elegant burnished juglet.

Micha P.

Micha P.

Figurines from the shrine in Area D.
Above: A female figurine of the plaque-like
Astarte type—with one hand held to the
breast. Below: A harpist.

Illustrated London News

and miniature clay offering tables, to which figures of deities or humans were probably once attached. These continue the early Philistine tradition. Most of the cult figurines were hollow pottery heads of bulls, cows, rams, and other domestic animals. Most were broken, but from some examples still attached to fragmentary hollow pottery rings and from comparison with specimens from Gezer, Megiddo, and Cyprus, we know that they belonged to *kernoi*, ring-shaped vessels with small vessels or figures attached at intervals.

The male and female figurines are of several types. A striking characteristic of the former is the prominent nose. Of special interest is the figure of a harpist. The female figures are mainly of the Astarte plaque type. A pottery mold for a figurine found in Area D indicates that the figurines were made near the temple.

The lower city was destroyed in the eighth century B.C., probably in the reign of Uzziah. In the following stratum (VII) we found in the temple area mainly refuse pits full of ashes, sherds, animal bones, and some pottery wasters. To the north of it were uncovered ten pottery kilns; the pits probably served as refuse dumps for them. One of the kilns, which may have been used for pottery storage after it had fallen into disuse, contained four hole-mouth jars of the later part of Iron Age II. The pottery—mostly carinated flat-based bowls and juglets—belongs on the whole to the same period.

This settlement probably represents a quarter inhabited by artisans, mainly potters.

An inscription on a jar fragment in Hebrew characters of the eighth century B.C. belongs to this settlement, although it was found in another area. Written in what seems to be a local Phoenician or "Philistine" dialect, it should probably be translated as ". . . [the] potter." This is the first

Fragment of pottery jar with inscription in Hebrew characters.

evidence of the "Philistine" Ashdodite language and script.

This city quarter was sacked: mass graves with heaps of skeletons bear witness to terrific destruction. This may have been one of the two recorded conquests of Ashdod; the first was by Sargon II of Assyria, in 712 B.C. Three fragments of basalt stele bearing cuneiform characters, found scattered in Areas A and G, form part of a monumental inscription of a type found in Sargon's capital, Dur Sharrukîn (Khorsabad). The stele appears to have been erected to commemorate his victory over Ashdod. Another possibility is that the settlement of Stratum VII was laid low by Psamtik I of Egypt (663–609 B.C.), who, according to Herodotus (ii 157), besieged Azotus (Ashdod) for twenty-nine years.

The topmost stratum in Area D (VI), which follows this destruction, dates from the seventh century B.C. As yet little is known about it, except that it was also destroyed. There are few indications for the date ending this occupation, but the latest pottery is of the late seventh or early sixth century B.C. It is possible, therefore, to associate the final destruction of the lower city with one of the campaigns of Nebuchadnezzar, earlier than or contemporary with that against Jerusalem. After the conquest Ashdod came under Babylonian rule and its prince went into captivity in Babylonia. During our last season, late Iron Age II buildings were found on the acropolis—on the northern side a section of casemate city wall and on the western edge part of a very large building on a stone foundation that could have served as an administrative center of the Assyrian or Babylonian city.

The next stratum (V), of the period when Ashdod was the capital of a Persian province, was uncovered mostly in 1965. A large building of Area K, only partly excavated, may be a public building of this period. In other areas a deep layer of ashes covers the remains of the Iron Age II settlement, and few traces of buildings are discernible. These must have been almost completely demolished by extensive building operations in the Hellenistic period. Local pottery of the fifth century B.C., such as large deep bowls with ridged sides and ring bases, was found everywhere; of special importance are many fragments of Attic red-figured vases. The Achaemenid art of Persia is represented by a gold earring in the shape of an ibex.

The Hellenistic city of Stratum 4 was excavated on a large scale mainly in Area A and on a smaller scale in Areas G and K. The layout of several buildings and streets uncovered here indicates some town planning. The main building seems to have been part of the agora, or market place. On the floor of one room were found many large pottery jars and some lead weights; in a corner of the room we came upon what seems to have been a cult place. There were two upright plastered stones and a flat stone which had probably been laid across the uprights. Nearby were two miniature stone altars. The place was full of charred wood, among which were found some coins, metal weapons, and a lead plaque representing a deity, perhaps Atargatis.

At a later stage of Stratum IV, on the floors of a new occupation level, were *terra sigillata* bowls, glazed bowls, and lamps. Analysis of the finds on the various floor levels will enable us to reconstruct a detailed stratigraphy and chronology of the city during Ptolemaic and Seleucid rule (third–second centuries B.C.). Most valuable in this respect are the Rhodian amphora handles.

During the Maccabean revolt Ashdod was attacked several times by the Jews, and Jonathan, Simeon's brother, is said to have destroyed the famous temple of Dagon. It seems that the city was finally conquered by John Hyrcanus (135–104 B.C.). The burned buildings of Stratum IV can probably be related to this conquest.

Stratum III was also excavated mainly in Area A. It appears to begin with the reign of Alexander Jannaeus, some of whose coins were found. This city was mainly a continuation of its Hellenistic predecessor. Some of the streets were blocked off and houses were divided by new partition walls, but the general layout was retained. The finds include many pottery vessels such as deep bowls, cooking pots, large storage jars, jugs and juglets, spindle-shaped bottles, stands, and especially *terra sigillata* bowls. On some of the bowls are incised inscriptions in Greek (such

as ZH, "Live!".). Among other imported vessels, so-called Megarian bowls should be mentioned.

The city seems to have been destroyed sometime in the first century of this era. There appears to be a certain gap after the First Jewish War against the Romans, when Ashdod recovered its autonomous status within the *Provincia Judaea*. Archaeologically, this period is probably represented by Stratum II; this, however, comprises mostly Late Roman and Byzantine material. It was to a great extent destroyed by the inhabitants of Stratum I. Stratum II (Areas A, G, K) includes small houses on stone foundations and an enormous pit, probably a refuse dump for workshops in the vicinity.

By this time a settlement already existed beside the sea, where the Iron Age port of Ashdod had been founded This new town, called Azotus Paralius, had begun to replace the metropolis. The meager remains of houses, grain pits, and other agricultural installations show that the mother city had declined into a large village (Stratum I, sixth–seventh centuries). From surface surveys and previous finds we know that it spread onto a neighboring hill. Here many marble architectural fragments were found, and this is probably also where the well-known inscribed slab belonging to a synagogue was discovered long ago.

With this last phase of occupation, ancient Ashdod ends its long history.

The main course of the stepped tunnel cut through the solid rock of the hill
leading from an opening inside the city wall to the spring at the base of the mound.
In the left wall there is a lamp niche. There is a total of 93 rock-cut steps in
this stairway.

Gibeon:
Where the Sun Stood Still

by JAMES B. PRITCHARD

Eight miles north of Jerusalem there stands the Arab village of el-Jib, which since 1838, when Edward Robinson made his topographic explorations of Palestine, has been considered a likely candidate for the location of the biblical city of Gibeon. The city is listed by the Egyptian King Shishak as one of his conquests toward the end of the tenth century B.C., and the historian Josephus tells that Cestius, the Roman governor of Syria, camped there in his attempt to take Jerusalem A.D. 66. Yet most of what we know of Gibeon's history is to be found in some forty-five references to it or its people, which appear in eight books of the Old Testament.

Prominent among the biblical traditions about the Gibeonites are those involving Joshua. In the ninth chapter of the book that bears his name there is the account of how he was deceived by the Gibeonites who, by disguising themselves as the inhabitants of a distant country, obtained a covenant of peace from him. Faithful to his word, even after he had discovered the fraud, Joshua responded to the Gibeonites' plea for military aid against the five Amorite kings who had besieged the city by going

immediately to their rescue. It was on this campaign that Joshua gave the order, "Sun, stand thou still at Gibeon," that he might have added time to take vengeance upon his enemies.

Another memorable incident is the gruesome contest at the "pool of Gibeon" between the young men of Joab and the young men of Abner, which is described as ending without a decision: "And each caught his opponent by the head, and thrust his sword into his opponent's side; so they fell down together" (I Samuel 2:16). Joab murdered Amasa there; and the seven descendants of Saul were sacrificed by the Gibeonites in order to put an end to a three-year famine. Solomon is said to have offered a thousand burnt offerings at the high place at Gibeon before the famous Jerusalem temple was built. Gibeon had but one prophet, Hananiah by name; but alas, he was found to be a false prophet.

The location of the ancient city, remembered for such dramatic incidents, at the modern el-Jib, as proposed by Robinson, did not go unchallenged. In 1926 Professor Albrecht Alt reassessed the evidence used by Robinson and staunchly rejected the Gibeon-

139

Wine-jar handle inscribed with the name "Gibeon" followed by gdr, *found in the great pool during the first season of excavation. This and 55 other inscribed handles provide evidence for the identification of the site of el-Jib with the biblical Gibeon.*

el-Jib identification. During the thirty years that followed, Gibeon's location on the present-day map was a subject of debate. We began excavations at el-Jib in the summer of 1956 with the hope that we might find some new evidence for the solution of this topographical problem. For five summers, between 1956 and 1962, excavations were made under the auspices of the University Museum of the University of Pennsylvania. We shall describe the results of these five campaigns in terms of four major discoveries.

The first evidence for the identification of the site appeared as a complete surprise toward the end of our first season. It consisted of a jar handle found in a refuse dump. On the handle was scratched the word gb'n, "Gibeon," in archaic script of the seventh century B.C. During the remaining days of the 1956 season and throughout

most of the 1957 campaign handles inscribed with Hebrew letters continued to be found, until we had amassed a total of fifty-six examples. The usual formula of these inscriptions consists of the name Gibeon followed by an enigmatic word gdr, possibly to be translated as "vineyard of," and then one of the following personal names: Hananiah (Nera), Azariah, and Amariah. Each of these names is common in the Bible. In a slightly different arrangement appear the less common names of Shebuel and Domla.

In the debris that had produced these jar handles there was some additional evidence of importance. More than forty clay stoppers that obviously had been intended to fit into the mouths of the jars to which our handles belonged—several handles still had the mouth of the jar attached—and a funnel for filling the jars suggested the possibility that the refuse was from an industry for making a product for which the jars with inscribed handles had been the containers.

What the jars had held is a question we shall leave for later discussion. But at the end of the 1957 season two conclusions seemed inescapable. First, the jars had been inscribed for export from Gibeon, which, to judge from the presence of a funnel in the associated context, must have been located at the site of el-Jib. Secondly, the maker had taken pains to put his name and address on the label of his product, either to assure the consumer of its quality or to facilitate the return of the empty jar when the contents had been consumed. Although there were some unsolved problems, the finding of the name Gibeon at the site of el-Jib seemed to be sufficient evidence to settle the debate over the location of the biblical city.

When Joshua discovered the deception of the men of Gibeon he condemned them to become "hewers of wood and drawers of water" (Joshua 9:27). From evidence recovered during the first two seasons for two ancient water systems used by the Gibeonites to carry water up into their heavily fortified city it would seem that at least the second of these two professions was properly associated with the people of Gibeon.

One water system was partly discernible when we began to work at the site. Today there is a copious spring flowing from the base of the east side of the hill, the major source of water for the village. Cut into the rock from which the water flows is a large cistern room as well as a horizontal passageway, or feeder tunnel, that leads some 112 feet into the rock of the hill; obviously the latter was cut in order to provide a better channel for the flow of water from its source to the cistern room. By an opening from the south side of the cistern room one enters a stepped tunnel cut from the solid rock leading upward until it opens into the city behind the thick city wall. There are, in all, ninety-three steps by

which the inhabitants of the city had easy access to the spring at the base of the hill on which the city stood. The device was a costly but extremely effective defensive measure. When the city was under siege and the gates securely locked the Gibeonites could block the outside door to the cistern room and have a protected access to the city's principal water supply. Indications are that the construction of this tunnel dates from about the tenth century B.C. To judge from the wear on the steps and the smooth sides of the tunnel, polished by the hands of the carriers who braced themselves in their descent, it had a long use. Similar constructions are known at Gezer, Megiddo, and Ibleam in Palestine, and at such distant places as Mycenae, Athens, and Susa.

The second water system at Gibeon was thought to be a pool when we first encountered it. Cut from the solid limestone of the hill, it is cylindrical in shape and measures thirty-seven feet in diameter and thirty-five feet in depth. There is also a spiral stairway, five feet wide, which begins at

Section of the stepped tunnel, the feeder tunnel, and the cistern room, which could be shut by a stone barricade.

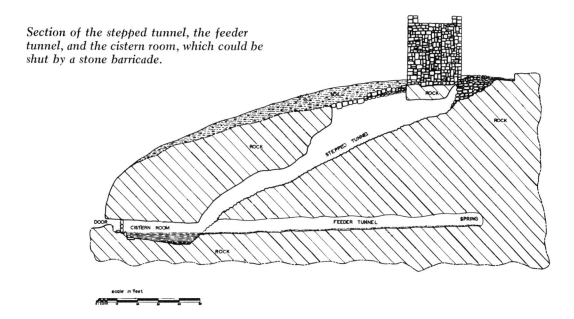

The pool stairwell, with its spiral stairway of 79 steps that lead to the water chamber, 80 feet below the surface of the rock. The 56 inscribed jar handles were found in the debris that filled this pool.

Plan of the two water systems and the city wall which protected the entrance to the tunnel and the pool stairwell inside the defensive system.

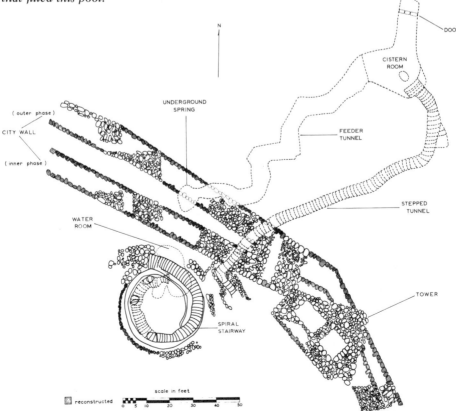

DOOR

CISTERN ROOM

N

UNDERGROUND SPRING

(outer phase)

CITY WALL

(inner phase)

FEEDER TUNNEL

STEPPED TUNNEL

WATER ROOM

TOWER

SPIRAL STAIRWAY

reconstructed

scale in feet

0 5 10   20   30   40   50

the northeast and winds clockwise along the edge of the cutting. But the stairs do not come to an end at the bottom of the pool; the steps continue downward into a tunnel that winds corkscrew-like, following the curve of the rim of the pool, to a depth of forty-five feet below the floor of the pool. At the very bottom of the seventy-nine steps there is a reservoir of water, eighty feet below the rock surface of the hill. There had been no access to the water that flows into it since the tunnel had been filled in some 2,600 years earlier. Two jars, dated to about the first part of the sixth century B.C., lay in the water—evidence for the last use that had been made of this water system.

It was only with the final clearance of the tunnel and the water chamber at the bottom that the purpose of this construction became clear. The Gibeonites had excavated about 3,000 tons of stone to make a stairwell within the city walls to insure access to the water source under the hill. One can only guess why the planners of this stairwell were so ambitious in the beginning as to remove the core of their circular stairway to make a gigantic pool. Did the water table drop from the level of the bottom of the pool, so that later users were forced to cut a tunnel downward to reach it? Or does the monumental cutting of the pool from the first thirty-five feet represent the work of a strong ruler, and the modest tunneling below constitute that of his successor who could not command the resources of his predecessor? As yet there is no evidence for the sudden change in plan during the construction of the pool stairwell.

Although one cannot be sure, it is entirely possible that this impressive landmark at Gibeon may have been the "pool of Gibeon" mentioned in II Samuel 2:13 as the scene of the contest between the men of Joab and the men of Abner. A by-product of the removal of debris that had clogged this water

system was the discovery of the inscribed jar handles. Apparently the pool of the stairwell became the city's dump into which had been thrown these and other objects, which witness to the culture of the Iron II Age.

The discovery of what appears to have been one of the principal sources for the prosperity of Gibeon during its most flourishing period was not made suddenly. But gradually there appeared from a number of clues the picture of Gibeon as a center for wine making, a kind of "Bordeaux" of ancient Palestine. The first intimation had been the jars with inscribed handles found during the first two seasons. In the 1959 season we were surprised to find a puzzling cylindrical cutting in the rock. The circular opening is about three feet in diameter; below the rim the cutting has been enlarged to a diameter of over six feet and then carried down to form a jug-shaped tank that is six feet deep. Eventually no fewer than sixty-three of these cuttings were found in two large areas of bare rock. Some of them had stone covers in place; others had been left open and had been filled with debris during the centuries of abandonment.

What was the function of these underground tanks? They could not have held water or any liquid in bulk, since the porous limestone walls of all but a few of them had never been plastered. The moisture in the live rock from which they had been cut makes it unlikely that they could have been used to store grain: it would have become quickly subject to mildew.

The first suggestion that they might have been used for storing wine at a constant temperature of sixty-five degrees Fahrenheit —we measured the temperature during the hottest summer months—came when we discovered shallow cuttings in the rock nearby which seemed suitable for wine presses. Shortly afterward a large storage

A part of the winery area, with openings to the cellars and other cuttings
in the live rock of the hill. The modern village of el-Jib is at the upper left.

jar, with a capacity of 9¾ gallons, was
found within one of the tanks which had
been closed by a stone; then fragments of
the same type of jar turned up in great numbers. Gradually it dawned upon us that these
cuttings were in all probability cellars for
the storage of wine placed in large jars. There
it had been kept under natural refrigeration
until it was removed jar by jar as it was
needed for consumption or export. There
were facilities for storing in excess of 25,000
gallons of wine in the jars which could be
fitted into the sixty-three cellars. And finally,
the presence of the word *gdr*, which is actually used in the Bible (Numbers 22:24) for

A storage jar from the Middle Bronze II
period is hoisted from the tomb of the
cemetery at the west of the hill.

the wall that encloses a vineyard, on the inscribed jar handles suggested that wine was indeed the product of the industrial areas at Gibeon and that it was exported to a wider market.

From the very first season we searched for the cemetery of the ancient city, but it was not until 1960 that a native woman of el-Jib told us that there were tombs on her farm land to the west of the tell. It was indeed the burying ground during the Middle and Late Bronze ages. By the close of the excavation we had discovered and cleared fifty-five tombs, of which forty-six contained datable tomb goods. All of them had been cut from the solid rock of the west side of the hill, outside the limits of the city wall. Each had a cylindrical shaft, averaging a little less than four feet in diameter, cut to a depth of from three to twelve feet. At the bottom of the shaft there is a doorway leading to the tomb chamber, in which was found the burial deposit.

The burials were made in three major periods. The earliest was that of the simple burials of the Middle Bronze I period; there were twenty-six of these. Within the tomb chamber there was generally a single skeleton, accompanied by a limited repertory of tomb goods: lamps with four nozzles, funerary jars, daggers, spear points, and beads.

In the Middle Bronze II, or Hyksos period, twenty-nine of the tombs had been used for burials, most of them multiple interments. Tomb goods were much more lavish: delicately fashioned pots, bronze daggers, beads, and carved bone that had been used as inlay on wooden boxes.

The last major use of the cemetery was in the Late Bronze Age, during the fourteenth century B.C. and slightly later. Seven of the tombs had the distinctive pottery of this period, some of it imported from Cy-

The bezel of an 18-carat gold ring with two animals that suggest a Persian origin; found over the foundation of a destroyed city wall.

An adz head and a dagger of bronze from Middle Bronze Age tombs in the cemetery.

prus. Although there were these Late Bronze Age burials in the cemetery, no structures on the tell have yet been found belonging to this period.

The history of the biblical city of Gibeon, although better known than it was when we first began excavation, is far from complete. Much of the evidence has been irretrievably denuded from the top of the wind-swept hill on which the city stood, and much of it remains to be uncovered in land that, for the present at least, is under cultivation in the olive orchards and vineyards of the peasants who eke out a livelihood in the village of el-Jib. Enough has been excavated to make it certain that Gibeon was a great city in Israelite times, as it had been in the Early Bronze and Middle Bronze periods before, that the epithet of "drawers of water" was well deserved, and that the city was a center for the production of wine in the period when the prophet Jeremiah was in conflict with the false prophet Hananiah, "who was from Gibeon."

POST-BIBLICAL PALESTINE

Nabataean pottery. Above: A bowl of the
early period. Right: A bowl of the middle
period; note the increasing heaviness of
hand in applying the paint. Below, right:
Two-handled juglet, showing the use of very
dark paint and extremely conventionalized
design. Below, left and center: Two pottery
vessels whose shapes seem to be uniquely
Nabataean.

The Nabataeans in Petra

by CRYSTAL M. BENNETT

If one looks today at a map of the region around Petra, in eastern Jordan, one gains little idea of the great importance this city possessed in ancient times. Petra was the capital of the kingdom of the Nabataeans, who, in the three centuries before Christ and the two which followed, built up one of the greatest trading kingdoms in the Middle East. They became masters of all the North Arabian routes; along these were brought the spices, gums, scents, silks, and other luxuries so much in demand by the Greeks and the Romans. Petra lay almost in the center of this vast network of routes, which ran from South Arabia to Damascus and the Mediterranean; it became the greatest emporium of its time.

At the height of its territorial expansion in the first century B.C. the Nabataean kingdom stretched from Damascus to Medâ'in Saleh; it also included a large part of the Negev of Palestine and had harbors on the Mediterranean. This vast territory was ruled during the first half of the first century B.C. by Aretas III, a king who was sufficiently influenced by Greek culture to be called the "Philhellene." It was probably at this time that Petra began to take on the aspect of a Hellenistic city.

It was inevitable that the kingdom controlled from Petra should arouse the cupidity of the Roman Empire. Apart from its importance as a buffer state between the nomadic tribes of the Arabian hinterland and the settled coastal regions, its great wealth was a magnet. Throughout the centuries just before and after Christ it combated all attempts to bring it under the Roman aegis, and the Nabataeans waxed prosperous under able, shrewd leaders. It was only when the royal power weakened under their last ruler, Rabbel II, and when the Roman Empire was controlled by one of its greatest empire-builders, the emperor Trajan, that this proud kingdom lost its independence. Petra was finally incorporated into the empire A.D. 106 as the province of Arabia. Thereafter, Petra began to acquire all the attributes of a Roman town—a colonnaded street, a theater, temples, and baths—and it differed from other Romanized eastern towns only in its unique setting.

In the late third century the economic and political difficulties which beset the empire as a whole were reflected in Petra; gradually it sank into obscurity. A Greek inscription in the Urn Tomb, dated to A.D. 447, refers to the consecration of a chapel by a bishop of Petra, but by the time of the Moslem invasions, in the seventh century, the city was only a shadow of its former greatness. Two twelfth-century Crusader

149

castles in the vicinity attest to a transitory interest in the area. Thereafter, for six centuries, Petra lay forgotten. In 1812 the young Swiss explorer John Burckhardt penetrated its fastnesses and slowly Petra became known to the outside world as a weird, fascinating place, with extraordinary monuments carved out of the living rock—testaments to a long departed, sophisticated civilization.

Petra lies in a basin about twenty miles northwest of Ma'an and about sixty miles, as the crow flies, north of the Gulf of Aqaba. East and west of it rise sandstone mountains and craggy cliffs, dominated on the west by Umm el-Biyara, "Mother of Cisterns," some thousand feet above the floor of the basin. From the western edge of this great peak extends the whole panorama of the Wadi

Part of the famous gorge called the Siq, looking west. Observe how the rock faces close in.

Araba. A natural, almost impregnable fortress, this mountain has been identified with biblical Sela, stronghold of the Edomites. North and south of the basin rise gaunt hills cut by deep wadis, accessible to men and pack animals but difficult terrain for staging a surprise attack. The cliff faces are honeycombed with caves and rock shelters which were useful for storing the Nabataeans' precious cargoes.

The multicolored striations of blue, white, yellow, and black give the sandy rocks a scenic brilliance and magnificence. The colors change with the play of light so that Petra never presents the same aspect for more than a few minutes. This ever-changing color presents a challenge to the photographic skill of visitors, whose number daily increases. With the setting sun they depart; the echoes of the clatter of horses' hoofs and the shrill cries of the Arab guides gradually die away. Night falls swiftly; the mountains become dark-purple to black, with a glow here and there from fires within the Bedouins' caves and tents. Petra retires once again into its secret world.

The usual approach to Petra today is from the east. The path follows the winding, downward course of the wadi through a pleasant valley, where the first of the Nabataean rock-cut tombs are to be seen on either side of the path. Gradually the rocks close in and the path narrows. This is the Siq, where close observation reveals traces of the large stones which once paved the entire route. In Roman times a dam was thrown across this narrow gorge and the flood waters of the wadi were diverted away from the road. Rock-cut channels, which brought drinking water into the city, are still visible on both sides of the path.

As the rock walls soar to a height of nearly one hundred meters and curve inward, the light diminishes until only an infinitesimal slit gives an indication of daylight. At the western limit of the seemingly endless Siq, which centuries of gushing waters have carved out, one of Petra's most beautiful monuments comes into view. The Khasneh, or Treasury (dating probably from the second century A.D.), protected from the elements by its girdle of rocks, is one of the finest preserved examples of Romano-Nabataean architecture, carved from the living rock. The impression it makes on the traveler when he emerges from the Stygian darkness of the Siq, or when the sun's first rays suffuse its façade with a warm rose-red color, is unforgettable.

From here the path widens and many more examples of rock-cut tombs may be seen, ranging from the austerely simple to the magnificent but sometimes overpoweringly ornate façades such as that of the palace tomb. Glimpses may also be had of Nabataean cult monuments. Carved in the sides of the tombs and on the plain rock faces are small niches, often containing a rectangular block of stone or an obelisk, symbol of the chief Nabataean god, Dushara. Elsewhere, steps or paths lead up clefts to the summits of the nearby mountains, on several of which are open-air sanctuaries, the "high places" of the Nabataean religion.

It was Petra's funerary architecture which, in the late nineteenth century, aroused the interest of such scholars as Brünnow and Domaszewski, whose work, *Die Provincia Arabia*, remains a classic. Subsequent research, notably that of Wiegand in 1916, also tended to concentrate on the architectural remains, though in this case more attention was paid to the free-standing buildings, which we now know to be associated with Petra's incorporation into the Roman Empire. While adding much to our knowledge of its art and architecture, these works did not make a significant contribution to understanding the history of Petra as a city.

Archaeological excavation began in the

El Khasneh, also called the Treasury, showing almost baroque features. Since this photograph was taken the fallen columns have been restored by the Jordan Department of Antiquities.

early 1930s, but the main interest at that time was not primarily the city area. From 1954 to 1956 the Department of Antiquities of Jordan sponsored a program of clearance and preservation in the heart of the city, but analysis of the stratigraphy was outside the scope of the work. A detailed knowledge of Petra's history and of the development of Nabataean material culture was still lacking.

The chief aim of the recent excavations has been to fill this gap. In particular, stratified evidence has been sought of the city's history while it was still the capital of the independent Nabataean kingdom.

The main street of Petra follows the course of the Wadi Musa, which runs westward through the heart of the city. Little now remains standing of the many buildings which once rose up on terraces on either side of the paved, colonnaded street. The only surviving free-standing monument of any size is a temple of the second century A.D. known as the Qasr el-Bint, which is approached from the street through a triple-arched gateway.

Trenches excavated alongside the street disclosed the earliest remains, a series of walls resting on sterile gravel. Made of wadi boulders and *terre pisée* (rammed earth), these belonged to small rectangular rooms. The floors are of beaten clay; a conical clay oven was found in this level. Accurate dating of these structures must await detailed study of the pottery. The evidence, however, of imported black-glazed lamps and of the coins of Aradus in Phoenicia—locally minted Nabataean coins are not known until the first century B.C.—suggests a date in the third century B.C. Preliminary study of the pottery and coins associated with successive building phases implies that this primitive type of building did not go out of use until the early first century B.C. No other examples of this type of construction have been found anywhere else in Petra.

These early levels also revealed objects which are highly important for the light they throw on Nabataean religious practices and on the association of these people with far-flung areas. Several small incense burners of stone or clay were discovered, similar to others from Mesopotamia, southern Arabia, and southern Palestine but differing in the decoration, which is much less elaborate on the Petra examples. Where it exists it is a simple design impressed or incised on the sides. Cubes or obelisks carved to represent deities are common at Petra and are known at other Nabataean sites. Unique, however, are crude portable stone idols. Comparison with "face idols" from the Hadramaut and the Yemen suggests connections with those areas.

At some time in the first century B.C. the inhabitants of Petra became conscious of town planning and of the superiority of solid stone structures over their primitive buildings. Increasing contact with the Hellenistic world may have inspired in them a desire for a more sophisticated way of life. The first requisite was to extend the area available for building, and an artificial terrace of loose gravel, some fifteen meters broad, was built against the northern side of the earlier buildings, along the bank of the wadi. Part of this increased width was used for a road running parallel to the wadi. This was resurfaced with gravel many times before a colonnaded street was superimposed in Roman times on exactly the same line; the deposit from these resurfacings is 1.50 m. thick.

Between the gravel roads and the edge of the wadi have been found the remains of a row of buildings of well-dressed ashlar masonry, the exact sequence of which has yet to be elucidated. Two facts are certain, however: they belong to the same general phase as the gravel road resurfacings, and they were roofed in the "arch and slab" tech-

View looking west toward the temple called Qasr el-Bint. The wadi is to the right of the colonnaded street.

Crude anthropomorphic idols found in early levels at Petra.

nique, hitherto known mainly in Byzantine contexts in the southern Hauran and in the Negev at Sbeita and Abda. That the beginning of this technique dates back at least to Nabataean times is now proved.

Complementary to the work on the street was the excavation of another area, in the southern part of the city. From the street—the city's main artery—the ground rises sharply until it overlooks the Wadi Farasa, which is the southern boundary of Petra. This high ground, known locally as Katuteh, levels out to a plateau formed in part by use as a rubbish dump.

Excavation revealed a house which had been completely covered by Roman rubbish tipping, a circumstance which helped preserve the walls to a height of over three meters. The house plan comprises a narrow central court some thirty meters long, with smaller rooms opening off the two long sides on the east and west. The imposing main entrance (2.75 m. wide) is in the north wall, that is, on the city side. A smaller entrance lies to the west of the main door. On the south side there are no signs of doors or windows. This suggests that the back wall of the house might have been incorporated into the city's defenses, for this wall lies on the crest of the steep slope leading down to the wadi; unless an artificial platform had been built over the slope this was the only possible defensive line.

The eastern and western walls of the building, of fine ashlar masonry, present an imposing appearance externally. Far less attention was paid to the interior faces. The cross walls also show the same lack of attention, but this was certainly deliberate. Many fragments of painted wall plaster, both molded and plain, prove that these interior walls were faced with an ornamental stucco veneer. This is a technique well known in Hellenistic and Roman architecture; the house at Katuteh illustrates the fusion of Nabataean and foreign building methods.

In the western rooms small pilasters project from the centers of the cross walls, possibly to support a roof in the "arch and slab" technique. However, since no voussoirs or slabs were found, the possibility of a wooden roof cannot be excluded. There are two drains: one leads from one of the west rooms to a covered outlet beyond the main west exterior wall; the other drained water from the courtyard through an outlet beneath the main entrance.

The house was built on top of a deep fill of stratified rubbish which contained sherds of imported *terra sigillata*. These, together with other pottery and coins, suggest a date of about A.D. 25 for its construction. The house continued in use, with various repairs, alterations, and modifications, throughout the first century. It is certain that it was abandoned about A.D. 106. One visualizes the proud, wealthy Nabataean owner of this fine residence resenting the loss of his capital's independence and removing himself to an area where the Roman presence was not so acutely felt. The abandonment of the house suggests that the southern limits of the town contracted after the Roman annexation, and a study of the town walls on the northern perimeter of the site shows that the city area was reduced in this direction as well.

During succeeding centuries the abandoned building at Katuteh was occasionally used by squatters, who erected crude cross walls at various places, especially in the western rooms. They were makeshift affairs which could well have provided temporary mangers for animals. Perhaps also to this period should be ascribed infant burials in pots, found against some of the cross walls. Later the building was used by the Byzantines as a burial ground, after the walls had been completely covered by rubbish.

The hundreds of objects found in and under the building are important for tracing the development of Nabataean culture and for assessing the extent to which it was influenced by contact with the Oriental, Hellenistic, and Roman worlds. The lamps, many of them locally made, clearly show western influence. Over one hundred were found in the house, including some fine examples of imported Roman ware of the first century A.D. The clay figurines, many representing camels and horses, also illustrate the steady absorption of classical influences by the Nabataeans.

The pottery, however, is of the greatest importance. The chronology of its development has never before been established. Of eggshell thinness and at the peak of its development akin to the finest porcelain, it is one of the Nabataeans' greatest achievements. So much pottery has now been found in stratified levels that it is at last possible to trace accurately the full development of this unique ware. The earliest painted examples come from trenches beneath the Roman street and under the Katuteh building, but a considerable quantity was also found in a homogeneous and extensive tomb group. It first appears during the first century B.C., and the shapes of the vessels—shallow curving bowls for the most part—recall contemporary Hellenistic pottery. The decoration, however, is something new. In its earliest period the floral and leaf patterns are applied in a light red-brown paint to the pink surface of the rather creamy clay, with an almost feathery brush work of the greatest delicacy. During the middle period, covering most of the first century A.D. and part of the second, the designs become less naturalistic and more stylized; the paint tends to be darker and the pottery itself is thinner and somewhat metallic. The decoration on the latest examples is even more conventionalized, and the now almost black paint is applied to the vessels in a heavy-handed fashion; this style probably belongs to the third century. Throughout all this time shallow bowls and plates continue to be the commonest painted shapes, though cups and juglets are also found. Although the link with Hellenistic ware is clear, close parallels are hard to find.

So common are painted sherds that they tend to distract attention from the plain Nabataean pottery, which is almost as fine. On the whole, the vessels are similar to contemporary Palestinian pottery, but several shapes seem to be uniquely Nabataean, notably a narrow cup with a wide, flat rim, a small basket-shaped vessel, and a so-called "inkwell," whose exact function is not known.

While the trenches on the Roman street and on Katuteh have provided the most important evidence, several smaller areas have also yielded interesting information. One trench was dug in the road at the foot of the triple-arched gateway, which before work began was buried in debris to a depth of several meters. The function of this gate has been variously interpreted as the main entrance to the city from the west, as a triumphal arch dedicated to a Roman emperor, or as the monumental entrance to the precincts of Petra's most important temple (Qasr el-Bint). The present excavations have proved that the third interpretation is correct. The evidence lies in the agreement of the gateway's orientation with that of the temple and its close similarity in architectural decoration, as well as in the fact that emplacements for doors were found, showing that it was a true gate, not just a triumphal arch. The period of the gateway, which had also been in dispute, has now been established. Its plan, with four free-standing columns on pedestals, shows that it can hardly date before the reign of Hadrian and is more likely to be Antonine or Severan. This agrees well with the stratigraphic evidence, which proves it to be later than the colonnaded street. The fact that no coins later than A.D. 106 were found beneath the street suggests that it is of Roman construction. This is borne out by the street's affinities with others and by an important inscription found in 1956. This seems to belong to a building bordering the colonnade; it dates to A.D. 114. Such a date is probable for the laying out of the street as part of a building program inaugurated within the Roman provincial town that Petra had become.

An architectural study of the Qasr el-Bint by G. H. R. Wright (*Palestine Exploration Quarterly*, 93 [1961], 124–135) provided an opportunity to sink a trench at the northeast

Part of the triple-arched gateway, looking east. Much of the debris has been removed by the Department of Antiquities.

corner of that building in order to establish its true floor levels. Contrary to previous belief, the temple stood on a podium about two meters high. The front part of this had evidently been faced with white marble veneer, of which one large slab still remained *in situ*. The surrounding area was paved with limestone blocks all the way east to the triple gate. Much of the podium, including the steps leading up to the temple, had been pillaged later for building purposes.

The suggestion made earlier that domestic buildings might have been incorporated into the defenses of the Nabataean city is reinforced by a discovery made in a small trench laid down in the northern part of the city overlooking the Wadi Abu Olleqa. Remains of a stone building were found, with its western wall lying on the presumed line of the city wall, just as in the case of the Katuteh building. Another interesting feature of this building was a small circular cobbled area, with six pilasters placed at regular intervals around its wall. The presence of drains suggests that this formed part of a small bathhouse in a residential building, which appears to have been in use in the first century A.D.

As we have said, knowledge of Nabataean architecture has hitherto been restricted largely to the funerary monuments of Petra. Excavations have helped to redress the balance. The Nabataeans begin to emerge as architects for the living as well as the dead. When the study of all that has been found is completed, a fuller picture can be painted of these people who came mysteriously from the desert to build up one of the great merchant kingdoms of history and to offer their own special contribution to the culture of mankind.

The Scrolls from
the Judaean Desert

by FRANK M. CROSS, JR.

In April 1948 came the first electrifying announcements of the discovery of ancient manuscripts in Palestine. The first statement, from the American School of Oriental Research in Jerusalem, described pre-Christian manuscripts: a great scroll of Isaiah, a commentary on Habakkuk, and a sectarian "Manual of Discipline," all in the possession of the Syrian monastery of St. Mark in old Jerusalem. A second announcement, that scrolls of similar date from the wilderness near the Dead Sea had been bought by the Hebrew University in Jerusalem, followed almost immediately. In the latter group were a sectarian hymn book, a fragmentary exemplar of Isaiah, and a document called the "War Between the Children of Light and Darkness."

Earlier, Professor W. F. Albright, who is *facile princeps* in matters of early Jewish palaeography, had been sent photographs from the great Isaiah scroll. In a letter to Dr. John Trever, a fellow of the American School, he wrote: "My heartiest congratulations on the greatest manuscript discovery of modern times. . . . I should prefer a date around 100 B.C. . . . and there can happily not be the slightest doubt in the world about

the genuineness of the manuscript." Professor E. Sukenik, the principal in the purchase and study of the Israelis' part of the find, reached like conclusions as to the date and significance of the scrolls in his possession.

The story of the initial finds is now clear in essential details. In the spring of 1947 two Bedouins were tending their flocks on the crumbling cliffs that border the northwest shore of the Dead Sea in the region of Wadi Qumran. One of their animals strayed. In the search for it, a shepherd, Muhammad edh-Dhib by name, tossed a stone into an opening in the rock. Instead of the expected smack of rock against rock he heard a crash and a sound of shattering. Later, when the fear of jinn or hyenas finally gave way to the lure of buried gold, the shepherds crept into the cave and found decayed rolls of leather in strange elongated jars. These were the fabulous Dead Sea manuscripts of what is now labeled Qumran Cave One.

In the year between the Bedouins' discovery and the first press releases there was confusion, blundering, and intrigue such as is often associated with spectacular chance finds. After having been passed about in the tents of tribesmen, the tattered rolls came into the hands of a Syrian shoemaker of Bethlehem. Through his mediation these scrolls as well as later finds were offered for sale and ultimately came to the attention of western scholars.

It was not until early in 1949 that Mr. Lankester Harding, Director of Antiquities in Jordan, and Père R. de Vaux of the École Biblique et Archéologique Française in Jerusalem were able to make scientific excavations in the cave. In the meanwhile Syrians had made at least one clandestine dig and perhaps more. Nevertheless, pottery finds were sufficient to date the deposit roughly, to confirm palaeographic data, and to tie the various purchased lots to the Qumran cave.

The discovery and excavation of Qumran Cave One was merely the first and most exciting of a series of cave finds and related discoveries. In the region of Qumran alone some ten caves have produced inscribed material, while twenty-five give evidence of late Hellenistic and Roman occupation. Touched off by the Qumran finds, Bedouin, police, and archaeologists have ranged over forgotten precincts of the desert of Judah, leading to several series of discoveries of ancient documents unrelated to those of Wadi Qumran. The most important finds were made in the vicinity of Wadi Murabba'at, southwest of Qumran. Here a large corpus of secular and biblical documents has been recovered, belonging mostly to the era between the two Jewish revolts against Rome, between A.D. 70 and A.D. 135.

There is room for only the briefest account of discoveries and research in the area of Wadi Qumran. Of the ten "producing" caves, One, Two, Four, and Six were discovered by Bedouins between 1947 and 1952; Three, Five, and Seven–Ten were found by archaeologists in the years 1952–1955. Cave Three is famous for its copper scrolls. These scrolls, originally a single document, are together some two and one-half meters long, engraved with a monumental script of the first century A.D. They were found to contain a list of buried treasure (see *The Treasure of the Copper Scroll* by J. M. Allegro, 2nd ed. 1964).

After the close of the expedition systematically searching the area around Khirbet Qumran, Bedouins again took the field in the summer of 1952 and discovered Cave Four, the largest of the caches of manuscripts. Archaeologists rushed back to the desert in time to halt clandestine digging before the cave had been completely exhausted. In September 1952 they completed controlled excavations with good results: enough undisturbed fragments were found in the lowest deposits of the cave to insure the provenience of material bought from the Bedouins. Save for the discoveries of Cave One and Cave Four, the remaining caves produced quite minor finds. The produce of Cave Four represents the remains of some three hundred manuscripts. Unlike the carefully wrapped scrolls of Cave One found sealed in jars, the hoard of Cave Four had to be excavated out of the accumulated deposits in the cave; virtually all the manuscripts, therefore, are very fragmentary and in an advanced state of decay.

It is not yet possible to give a complete catalogue of the manuscripts of Cave Four. Tens of thousands of fragments have been recovered and are slowly being pieced together. The process is exceedingly tedious. Some manuscripts are preserved in no more than one or two fragments of encrusted, time-blackened leather. Others contain parts of more than forty columns of text. Their poor state of preservation handicaps attempts to clean and flatten the twisted and shrunken pieces; many can be read only on long-exposed infrared plates. About one third, approximately ninety manuscripts,

Cave One at Qumran.

are biblical, all of course from the Old Testament. Only Esther is missing, no doubt by chance, from this ancient Jewish library. All other books (reckoning by the Hebrew canon) have been identified in one or more copies. Especially popular are Isaiah, Deuteronomy, and Psalms, each represented by ten or more exemplars; it is noteworthy that these books are among those most frequently quoted by New Testament writers.

Another large portion of the documents belongs to the category of apocryphal and pseudepigraphical works: Tobit in Aramaic and Hebrew, Enoch in archaic recensional forms, an early Testament of Levi (not directly related to the Testaments of the Twelve Patriarchs), Jubilees, and Ecclesiasticus (from Cave Two). There is another group of sectarian works: the Discipline of the Community, the sectarian hymns, the War Scroll, all known from Cave One, reappear. In addition there are copies of the so-called Zadokite or Damascus Covenant document already partly known from two incomplete medieval manuscripts. There are also commentaries on a large number of Old Testament books. One of the most exciting is on Nahum, a well-preserved manuscript acquired only last year. Finally there are miscellaneous documents, all wholly unknown previously, together with fragments of the Septuagint, lists of Messianic "proof-texts," and even some Aramaic contracts and name lists. Most of the non-biblical documents, even if known, appear now for the first time in their original Semitic garb.

In the midst of the cave sites, some two miles south of the northern tip of the Dead Sea, on a marly plateau that huddles under the brow of the great cliffs where Wadi Qumran breaks through to the sea, lies an ancient ruin called Khirbet Qumran. The site has been known since its description by De Saulcy in the mid-nineteenth century. Recent explorers had supposed it to be a small Roman fort; it was remarkable for its cemeteries of more than twelve hundred tombs. With the first discoveries of manuscripts in the area, attention was focused on the ruin, and four excavation campaigns (1951–1955) have been carried on by Père R. de Vaux and Mr. Lankester Harding.

Thanks to a combination of literary evidence, not least that of the adjacent caves, and spectacular archaeological data, the identity of the site as the Essene community center or "city in the wilderness" has been established beyond reasonable doubt. The Essenes were the historian Josephus' "third party" in Judaism in the time of Jesus Christ, an apocalyptic community competing with the more conservative Sadducees and Pharisees for the allegiance of pious Jews.

The first two seasons opened the central building complex of the site. It included a fortified tower; common rooms for study, storage, and work, including a scriptorium with a plaster writing table some five meters long; inkpots, benches, and basins for ritual washing. It is probable that at least some of the manuscripts in the caves came from this center; the fact that manuscripts from caves both north and south of the site are on occasion written by a single scribe supports this supposition. Early excavations established the general chronology of the Khirbet. The community was founded in the time of John Hyrcanus I (135–104 B.C.) or at latest Alexander Jannaeus (103–76 B.C.), in the early Hasmonean era. Three

main periods of occupation followed: the first continued until the time of Herod the Great (37–4 B.C.) when an earthquake, probably that of 31 B.C. recorded by Josephus, destroyed the Qumran structures. After a gap in occupation during much of Herod's reign, the community re-established itself, perhaps in the time of Herod Archelaus (4 B.C. to A.D. 6), and prospered until the dark days of the First Jewish Revolt against Rome (A.D. 66–70). The Essene center seems to have been destroyed by the Tenth Legion in the year 68. The site was then transformed into a military fort and occupied by a Roman garrison, no doubt protecting Jericho against Jewish guerrilla action, which centered in the wilderness to the south and southwest. This was the final period of construction of Khirbet Qumran. After abandonment as a Roman post, there was a brief occupation by squatters in the days of the Second Jewish Revolt (A.D. 132–135), followed by permanent abandonment.

In 1954 the quarter south of the central complex was opened. A massive and complicated water system was disclosed, with more than ten large cisterns and settling basins connected with an aqueduct from high in the wadi. The cisterns are structurally identical with contemporary Roman cisterns. Although there has been some speculation that these were baptisteries, there is little reason to connect these cisterns with the well-known practice of the sect; more probably "living" water was utilized for baptisms. In any case the aridity of the region requires extensive water-conserving installations if a community of any size is to survive. A large communal eating hall was excavated, and a pantry containing over a thousand pieces of pottery used for the communion meals of the sect.

In 1955 the western quarter was opened; it proved to be a domestic complex. In one room more than five hundred silver coins were found in jars hidden under the floor. The coins are of Tyrian stamp, spanning in date the first century B.C.

We have remarked that the people of the scrolls were Essenes, an apocalyptic sect within Judaism. They are known to us from Pliny, who tells us of their community center between Jericho and Engedi ('Ain Gedi), from Philo of Alexandria, and especially from Josephus, who seems to have had a flirtation with the sect in his idealistic youth.

Of the three major parties within Judaism —the Pharisees, Sadducees, and Essenes— we hear in the New Testament only of the first two. This is extraordinary, since the literature of the Essenes is quoted in the New Testament. It is clear that reworked Essene documents were current in the early Christian community. There is also evidence that the Essene sectaries were a fruitful field of evangelization, that they in turn had influence on the formation of institutions of the Apostolic and sub-Apostolic Church. In any case, we must suppose that the non-mention of the Essenes in the New Testament arises not from ignorance, but from lack of antipathy; we hear of the other Jewish parties largely in polemical passages.

The Essenes had their origins in the party of the Pious, the Hasidim of the national revival in the Maccabean era (ca. 175–135 B.C.). As a separatist party, the Essenes appear under the early Hasmoneans. It now appears from new documents, as already maintained by a number of scholars on the basis of older evidence, that the chief creative personality in the sect, one who held the title or office of "Teacher of Righteousness," flourished in the reigns of John Hyrcanus and Alexander Jannaeus. In this time the sect was persecuted, formed cells in many villages of Judah, and developed its chief center in the desert south of Jericho.

The scriptorium of the Essenes at Khirbet Qumran.

It may well be that in this period part of the sect retreated from persecution into Syria. Their communal life flourished until the Jewish War against Rome in A.D. 66–70. After this they disappear, leaving only the ruins of their ancient desert retreat and the litterings of manuscripts on the floors of caves.

Two aspects of scroll study are especially interesting for students of the Bible. One has to do with the bearing of the new materials on the textual study of the Old Testament. Most of the biblical manuscripts antedate by more than a millennium the traditional Hebrew text which has been the basis of our English Bible. The second is concerned with the significance of the new Essene documents for New Testament studies. No doubt this is the most exciting as well as the most controversial side of scroll researches. We shall deal with each in turn.

The discovery of a virtually complete manuscript of Isaiah from about 100 B.C. in Cave One caused extraordinary excitement among students of the Old Testament. It was not merely the fact that specific readings in the Book of Isaiah could be improved. More important, the great barrier to our knowledge of the archaic Hebrew text was breached—the Rabbinic recension of about A.D. 100, which in effect eliminated all variant texts. The Isaiah scroll was received with some consternation by those who had presumed that the pre-Christian Hebrew text was fluid, and that the traditional (Proto-Masoretic) text was formed in the medieval period, whereas those who had held that the received text rested on an archaic and stable textual tradition were delighted to find their views confirmed. For the text of Isaiah at Qumran (now represented in ten or twelve scrolls) shows few important variations from the medieval text; it contains thousands of variants but few making significant changes in meaning, and even fewer that can be shown to be superior to the Masoretic readings.

From this evidence scholars have generalized that not only in Isaiah, but in the entire Old Testament, the text was stabilized early, and that late recensional activities were of only slight effect. This conclusion, of course, powerfully supported textual scholars of conservative persuasion.

There was one difficulty. Evidence already existed that the text of Isaiah, unlike that of other books, was stabilized early or at least the tradition of the later text was in existence before the authoritative traditional text was promulgated, about A.D. 100. This evidence was to be found in the Old Greek translation of the third-second centuries B.C., the so-called Septuagint. The Septuagint translation differs widely in content in many books from the traditional Hebrew text. Some scholars maintained that the Septuagint was translated from Hebrew manuscripts which belonged to a radically different and often superior textual tradition. More recently, scholars had been dealing more conservatively with the Masoretic text, more radically with that of the Septuagint. The variant renderings of the Greek translators were explained away as due the ignorance, errors, or theological prejudices of the translators. Obviously this is in part true; many such changes do exist. It had become increasingly popular, however, to suppose that the great bulk of the differences was to be so explained. Now it seemed that the Qumran Isaiah bore out this position.

But to return to our difficulty. As it happens, Isaiah in the Old Greek is *not* one of those books where the traditional renderings and those of the Septuagint clash. Isaiah in Greek appeared to have been translated from a manuscript quite close to the Proto-Masoretic tradition. However, it was difficult to be certain, since the translation of Isaiah is among the poorest in the Greek Bible. This meant that the Book of Isaiah was a particularly poor ground upon which to test textual theories to be applied to other books, or even to the entire Bible. What was needed, rather, was manuscripts in Hebrew from other books where the Septuagint translation was good, where it was extremely literal when it followed Masoretic readings, but where it frequently branched radically from this later standard text. This was the case, for example, in the historical books, especially Joshua, Samuel, and Kings. Ideally, of course, the scholar needed samplings from the whole of the Old Testament in order to reconstruct a valid history of its transmission. For detailed readings in a single manuscript are less important than samples of text types in reconstructing a more nearly original text of the Old Testament, the goal of textual study.

The recovery of remnants of nearly a hundred biblical manuscripts in Cave Four came, therefore, as incredibly good fortune. Here at last was the basis for sampling the textual types extant in virtually every book of the Old Testament. Here was a substantial basis for establishment of the archaic, pre-Masoretic history of the Hebrew text.

The first manuscripts studied were those of Samuel. Two fragmentary columns of so-called 4Q Samᵃ (Samuel MS No. 1 from Qumran Cave Four) were immediately published. Later, in lots purchased from clandestine Bedouin operations, fragments from nearly every column of this manuscript were identified.

The results were shocking. The text of Samuel contained in the three scrolls from Qumran is widely at variance with that of the traditional Masoretic Bible; it follows most frequently the rendering of the Old Greek of Samuel. There are also many unique readings, some more nearly original than any previously known.

Other historical books follow suit in presenting the tradition of the Septuagint. It now becomes clear, at least in these books, that the Septuagint's divergent text was due far less to "translation idiosyncrasies" than to the archaic form of the text it translated. For example, in six fragments of the most archaic Samuel manuscript (late third century B.C.), the Septuagint is followed thirteen times when the Greek disagrees with the Masoretic tradition, against four cases when the Qumran text agrees with the Masoretic tradition against the Septuagint: three to one in favor of the Greek tradition.

Palestine Archaeological Museum

Fragments of Samuel from the earliest of the Qumran manuscripts, dating from the later third century B.C. *(4Q Samᵇ).*

The question of which text is original is another problem, to be decided in individual readings. The point, however, is that while we had previously only one clear line leading back toward the original text, we now have three converging lines: the Masoretic tradition, the Qumran tradition, and the Hebrew tradition underlying the Old Greek translation. The latter has always been known, of course, but had become increasingly suspect as a useful witness to the old text; now it is vindicated as faithful in the historical books, and it must be taken seriously in all textual study.

The state of the text in other books is more complicated. In the Pentateuch at least three different textual types are now known to have existed at Qumran. One is nearly identical with the Proto-Masoretic tradition; another is closely parallel to the Samaritan Pentateuch; still a third follows the Septuagint version. Many manuscripts are mixed in type.

For the study of the Old Testament text, therefore, the grand Isaiah-manuscript did not reflect the real complexity of the textual tradition in the pre-Masoretic, pre-Christian era. New finds should chart new courses by which scholars will progress toward a more accurate, more intelligible Old Testament.

It is difficult to exaggerate the importance of the Essene documents for the study of Christian origins. In the early stages of investigation some distortions and premature syntheses were made, which now have broken down under the weight of new material, most of it as yet unpublished. Of these the most flamboyant and provocative theories have centered about the rather obscure figure of the "Teacher of Righteousness." For example, the distinguished Semitist of the Sorbonne, A. Dupont-Sommer, has gone so far as to portray him as the prototype of the Christian Messiah, martyred, risen from the dead, incarnate divinity, returning Messiah, redeemer of the world. Part of his construction is based on or bolstered by the use of Christian editions of Essene documents, especially the Testaments of the Patriarchs. Such procedure is unsound since these editions swarm with Christian interpolations and revisions. Further sifting of new and old data now suggests that the Teacher, while persecuted, was not martyred, and in any case is given no divine prerogatives; as for his being the expected Messiah of the "end time," this problem is enormously complicated by new, conclusive evidence that the Essenes expected two Messiahs, a priestly Messiah of Levi, and a royal Messiah of David, as well as an eschatological Prophet (cf.

John 1:2–24). There is no explicit identification of the Teacher with either Messiah; as the evidence now stands, he is probably not to be identified with any of these figures. The most that can be said is that the Teacher is thought to be predicted in scripture as appearing in the "last times"; since the Essenes considered themselves to be living in last times, and assigned the fall of Jerusalem in 63 B.C. to last times, this is at best a highly ambiguous datum.

If there are but superficial parallels between the Essene teacher and Jesus of Nazareth, there are intimate parallels between the Essene and primitive Christian communities. These are to be found in their theological language, in their theology of history, in their liturgical institutions, and in their ecclesiastical organization. In these areas the Essene documents are radically important for our understanding of Christian origins and for the exegesis and definition of New Testament expressions and concepts.

The Essenes and the Christians apply similar terms to themselves; they are the people of the "New Testament," who have chosen the Way (cf. Acts 9:2, etc.). Love of God and neighbor is the sum of the law. They are the poor in the world, the children of light, the elect of God who shall judge Israel and the nations at the end of days.

The central "sacraments" of the Essene church were its baptism and its communion meal. The baptism of the Essenes, like that of John, was, upon repentance of sins, into an eschatological community. Contrary to the early Christian institution, the Essenes seem to have practiced continual lustrations as well as baptism on initiation into the covenanted community.

In the liturgy of the communion meal of the Essenes, we discover material of the first importance for understanding the eucharistic practice of the early Church. There follow excerpts:

"When [God] begets the (priestly) Messiah, he shall enter with them, [for he is] the head of the whole congregation of Israel; and all the fa[thers of the Aa]ronids, the priests who [are invited to] the feast . . . shall sit be[fore him], each according to his rank.

"Then [shall enter the Mess]iah of Israel, and the chiefs of the thou[sands of Israel] shall sit before him, [ea]ch according to his rank . . .

"Wh[en] they solemnly meet at the [tab]le of communion, [or to drink the wi]ne, and the communion table is arranged and the wine [is mixed] for drinking, one [shall not stretch out] his hand on the first portion of bread or [of the wine] before the (Messiah-) Priest; for [he shall b]less the first portion of the bread and of the win[e, and he shall stretch out] his hand on the bread first of all. Afterwar[ds the Messiah of Israel shall [stre]tch forth his hands on the bread; [and after giving a bles]sing, all the congregation of the Community (shall partake), ea[ch according to] his rank.

"And they shall follow this prescription whenever [the meal is ar]ranged, when as many as ten meet together."

The agape (love feast) of the Essenes is here clearly set out as the liturgical anticipation of the Messianic banquet. This element in the New Testament accounts of the Lord's Supper and in the later eucharistic practice of the Palestinian church was very strong. In the Markan account we read, "Truly I say to you, I shall not drink again of the fruit of the vine until that day when I drink it new in the kingdom of God" (14:25); in the Lukan version it is even stronger, especially if one follows the shorter "western" text (22:14–19a); and it appears as well in the Pauline and later formulae, "For as often as you eat this bread and drink the cup, you proclaim the Lord's death *until he*

comes (I Cor. 11:26); *marana-tha*, "Come (our) Lord," and "the holy vine of David thy servant which was made known to us through Jesus. . . ." (Didache 9:2; 10:6. Cf. Rev. 19:9.)

The Christian community (Acts 2:46, etc.) ate common meals regularly, partaking of the food in joy. Indeed these banquets of joyous anticipation led to the excesses referred to in Jude 12 and I Cor. 11 and to the later reforms which in turn led to the separation of the Eucharist proper from the regular common meals of the faithful.

What is the background of the institution of common meals of the entire community, eaten in anticipation of the Messianic banquet? The Passover, the other element in the background of the Lord's Supper, can give no suitable historical context. It is a yearly feast of memorial, eaten in private in families, and is not, properly, an eschatological festival. The Essene meal gives the first suitable answer.

This is not to suggest that the Church merely took over an Essene meal. Within the Lord's Supper are notable original elements: the formulae, which transform the old Passover into the feast of the New Covenant, memorialize the sacrifice of the body and blood of the victim, the pledge of the covenant. And there is no reason, I think, to suppose that the combination of the two elements, the memorial of the sacrifice and the anticipation of the Messianic banquet, does not go back to Jesus himself.

Detailed parallels in language and liturgical practice by no means tell the whole story. Still more important is the common theological world view of Essenism and Christianity. Both live in the end of days. Both live in a world in which the powers of righteousness and the power of evil are engaged in warfare: God against Satan, spirit against flesh, the "world" against the Kingdom, the sons of light against the sons of darkness.

These two common elements, the eschatological structure of their community life and the "ethical dualism" of their thought, have origins in the Old Testament apocalyptic literature but cannot be explained simply in terms of such origins; they have parallels in Rabbinic Judaism but are not of a piece with it.

The Essene community recognized in the events of their own days the signs of the coming consummation of history. The Old Testament prophecies of the last days are realized in the history of the sect and in the outer events of Israel. They are living in the last generation. Those with "knowledge" should now recognize that the final war has begun. They must decide, understanding by faith the fulfillment of prophecy, expectant of the full consummation.

"When these things come to pass in Israel to the Community (the Essenes) . . . they will separate themselves from the midst of the abode of evil men to go into the desert to prepare there the way of the Lord, according as it is written, 'In the desert prepare ye the Way (of Yahweh), make straight in the wilderness a highway for our God.' "

Thus the Essenes understand themselves to be in the situation of John the Baptist. Jesus' early teachings are in much the same eschatological framework. The man in the early Church is in a somewhat new "historical" moment. He lives in a "later" time. He knows that with the advent of the Christ "the world has come to an end" and the powers of Sin and Death are broken. Yet in some sense these too are ambiguous, "historical" events, to be understood in faith. He is to take part in the Kingdom proleptically, anticipating the coming day when ambiguity will end, the world be transformed, and end brought to wicked flesh, and the kingdom of God fulfilled.

The Essenes therefore search the scripture and interpret their prophecies "historically."

As several scholars have pointed out, Essene exegesis has no precise parallels either in Hellenistic or Pharisaic Judaism, in allegorical philosophizing or in legalistic interpretation. But it falls precisely into the pattern of the New Testament exegesis of the Law and the Prophets.

The life of the sect is understood as life in anticipation of the kingdom of God. The spirit of Truth abides in its camps. This is the spirit of Unity. The Essenes call themselves the Community, literally the Unity. The Johannine phrase, "that they may be one," "become perfectly one" (John 17:11, 21, 23), uses typical Essene diction.

This eschatological unity or community of the anticipated kingdom is made concrete not only in the common meal but in sharing of goods. Entry into the Essene community meant giving up all private property. In the New Testament church, especially in Palestine, a similar practice appears: "Now the congregation of the believers were of one heart and soul, and no one said that any of the things he possessed was his own, but they had everything in common" (Acts 4:32; cf. 4:32–5:11). "And all who believed were together and had all things in common. . . . And day by day, attending the temple together and breaking bread together (in common meals) in their homes, they partook of food with glad and generous hearts" (Acts 2:44–46).

Approaching from a slightly different angle, we learn that the Essenes were soldiers in the Holy War of the end time. They divided themselves into armies, divisions, companies, and squads. Being engaged in the War of God, they followed the ancient ritual prescriptions of the Old Testament for Holy War, keeping the purity of their camps. They refrained from sexual intercourse and marriage, kept the stringent sanitary regulations of Holy War, and all the rest. Theirs was not a genuine asceticism but an eschatological asceticism. They did not eschew marriage as such, but marriage in the present circumstances. Compare in Paul's letter to the Corinthians the following passage: "I mean, brethren, the appointed time has grown very short; from now on, let those who have wives live as though they had none . . . and those who buy as though they had no goods, and those who deal with the world as though they had no dealings with it. For the form of this world is passing away" (I Cor. 7:29–31).

The mention of the state of war brings us to a final point. According to Essene doctrine the world is in the grip of two warring spirits, created by God from the beginning: the Spirit of Truth and the Spirit of Lying (or Perversity; cf. I John 4:1–5). The Spirit of Lying is none other than Belial, the Prince of Darkness, Satan. The Spirit of Truth is otherwise called the holy spirit (not precisely identical with the Holy Spirit), the prince of light, the angel of truth. All men have their "lot" in one of these spirits and thus are children of light or children of darkness (cf. John 8:42–47). The "Prince of Light" or Spirit of Truth is appointed to the help of the children of light. He is identical with the Paraclete (Advocate) of John (John 14:17; 15:26; 16:13; I John 5:6–8). His func-

tion, "to witness," "to intercede," to speak, yet "not on his own authority," now becomes intelligible. The origins of the idea are found in the Heavenly Court of God in the Old Testament where, in scenes of judgment, Satan as prosecutor stands over against the angel of the Lord as advocate or witness. In the elaborate angelology and dualism of the Essenes, partly under Iranian influence, Old Testament origins are blurred and the two angels become the two opposing principles of light and darkness, truth and error. In the New Testament the dualism is partially resolved, but reflections of an Essene structure of thought still survive. This is especially clear in the Johannine Advocate, but also to a lesser degree in the special function of the Spirit in Acts and in Paul.

In these new texts we are in the conceptual world of the New Testament. The New Testament and the Essene writers draw on common resources of language, theological themes and concepts, and share common religious institutions. They breathe the same atmosphere, confront the same problems. We can now enter into this rich, variegated world of sectarian Judaism in the first century A.D. with new boldness and understanding; the strange world of the New Testament becomes less baffling, less exotic.

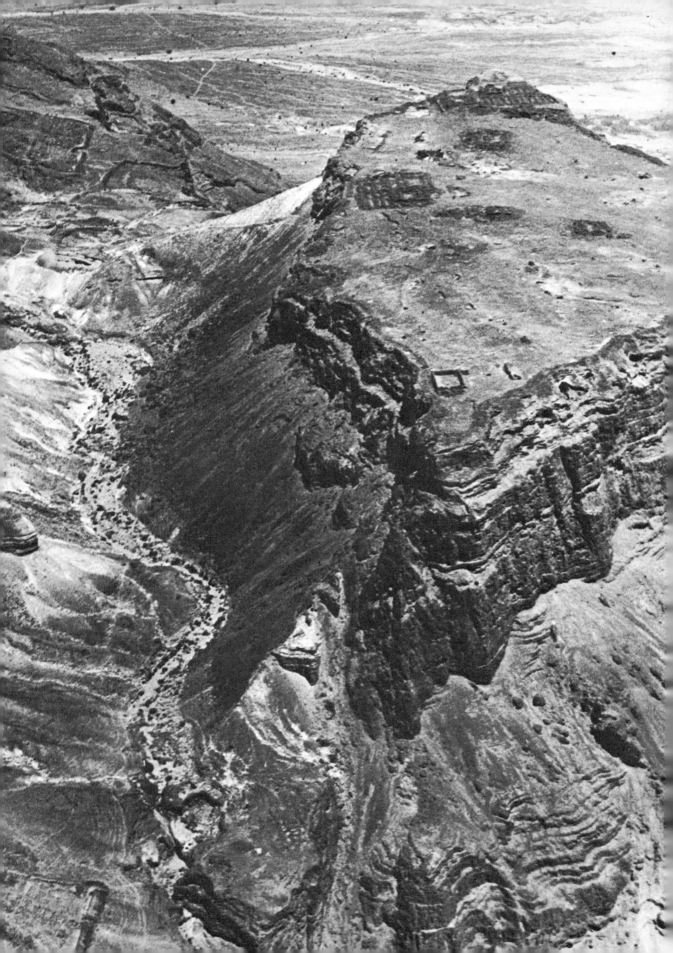

Masada:
A Zealot Fortress

by YIGAEL YADIN

The rock of Masada, rising some thirteen hundred feet above the western shore of the Dead Sea, is a place of majestic beauty. Here, beginning about 37 B.C., Herod the Great erected a palace and a fortress, with the purpose of obtaining a potential place of refuge against possible attack by Cleopatra of Egypt. And here, not many years later, one of history's most dramatic episodes took place, when 960 men, women, and children of the Zealot sect preferred to kill themselves rather than surrender to the besieging Romans.

The only source of information about Masada in ancient literature is the history written by Josephus, who was himself one of the Jewish commanders at the beginning of the great revolt against Rome but later went over to the enemy.

The Masada excavations are perhaps the largest archaeological enterprise ever attempted in the Holy Land. In two campaigns, one of seven months and one of four, almost all the buildings were excavated. Only a small section was left undug in order to give visitors a "before and after" impression.

Herod's "Hanging Palace," once thought to be on the west edge of the rock, was cor-rectly identified in the 1950s by Israeli youths who climbed up the north side of the hill. The excavation of this three-tiered palace was very difficult. The remains of a rectangular building were revealed on the upper terrace, with a semicircular porch extending out to the very edge of the cliff. The rooms had wall paintings and mosaic floors. The middle terrace, sixty feet below, comprised a circular pavilion and a colonnade. The lowest terrace was even more elaborate, with a double colonnade surrounding a square area, and wall frescoes imitating marble and precious stones.

On the top of the rock a number of other buildings of Herod's time were excavated. Just south of the Hanging Palace are the ruins of long narrow halls, which were storerooms. As a result of earthquakes, the walls had been overthrown, and these had to be cleared before excavation could begin. In view of the major significance of Masada, we decided to essay a new technique, that is, to reconstruct the walls first, and then to excavate the rooms. This experiment proved a great success.

In the rooms were hundreds of broken jars containing remnants of food; each kind of food was kept in a separate room. The stor-

Masada from the air, a view that shows how difficult it would be to storm the fortress.

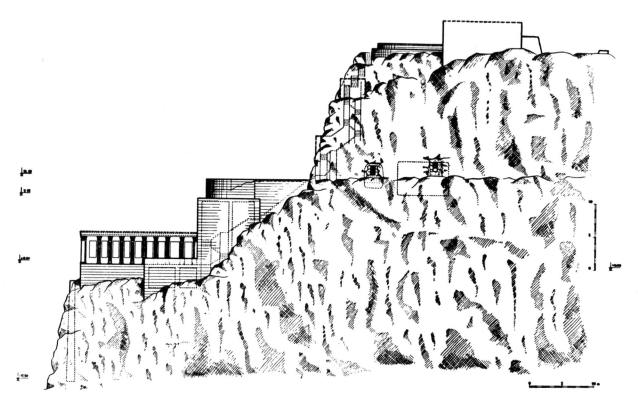

Reconstruction of the Northern Palace of Herod, seen from the west, showing the extraordinary engineering feat involved.

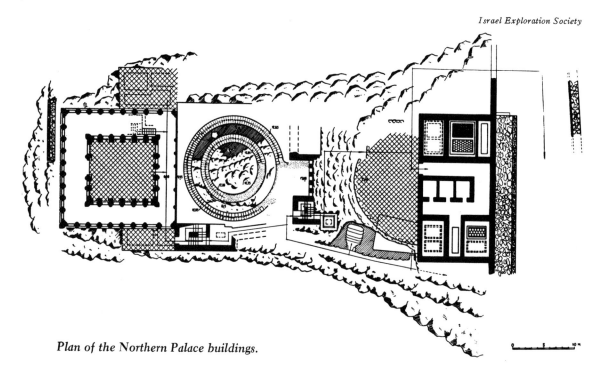

Plan of the Northern Palace buildings.

View from Masada toward the Dead Sea, showing the rectangular camp of the Roman Tenth Legion.

age jars often bore labels describing their contents in Aramaic or Hebrew.

Near the storerooms we found a public bath of Roman type—the largest of its kind known in that part of the world, with much of its installations and adornments still intact.

The largest building on Masada is the Western Palace, Herod's principal residence, complete with throne room, reception halls, service quarters, workshops, and huge storerooms. Here were found two mosaic floors with representations of fruit and geometric designs, perhaps the finest uncovered in Israel. Other small palaces and a swimming

pool were nearby. To make life possible on this rocky height, great cisterns with tremendous capacity were carved into its sides.

After Herod's death in 4 B.C., a Roman garrison was stationed at Masada, and this occupation continued until A.D. 66, when a large-scale Jewish revolt broke out all over the land. At this time the Zealots made a lightning raid on Masada and wiped out the Roman garrison. As fighting continued throughout the country, many more Zealots came to Masada, thus strengthening the Jewish garrison there. Four years later Jerusalem fell to the Romans, the Temple was

Lowest terrace of Herod's Hanging Palace showing painting on walls.

Multicolored mosaic from floor in Herod's western palace.

View of a storehouse during reconstruction of the walls.

pillaged, and eventually Masada was left as the one bit of territory that could not be taken by the conquerors.

For seven long years, from 66 to 73, the Zealots living on Masada, led by Eleazar ben Yair, defied the Romans. They made their dwellings in the chambers of the casemate wall and installed partition walls, stoves, and cupboards. They also built additional dwellings, most of them close to the wall. Parts of the palaces were also used as living quarters, possibly for the leaders. The most important finds relating to the Zealots were made in the chambers of the casemate wall. Here were found large quantities of domestic utensils and remains of mats, shoes, and clothing. Some of the rooms contained stones that the besieged had collected to roll down on the Romans, as well as hundreds of stone balls that had been fired into the fortress by the enemy's catapults. Numerous bronze and silver coins were found there, including great hoards of silver shekels inscribed "Jerusalem the Holy—Shekel of Israel."

During these seven years the Zealots constructed a synagogue, two ritual baths, and a religious schoolroom. Beneath the floor of the synagogue we found two biblical scrolls —parts of Ezekiel and Deuteronomy. This is not only the earliest synagogue known, but the only one to survive from the period when the Temple was still standing.

This period ended in the spring of A.D. 73 when the Roman governor Flavius Silva decided to lead the Tenth Legion against the rock in a final assault. Provisions were hauled from miles away by Jewish prisoners of war who had been taken captive years before. Silva organized his camps and set up a wall all around Masada, making it impossible for the Zealots to flee. Then he erected a huge ramp and at the head of it siege towers and catapults. The last stage of the drama was approaching. The Romans now began to use a battering ram but the defenders hurriedly built a second wall and filled the space between the two walls with earth. The pounding of the Romans only made the earth more compact. Silva then ordered the soldiers to attack with flaming torches, and the defenders realized that the end was near. That night, urged by Eleazar, they died by their own hand—all except two women and a few children who had hidden themselves and remained to tell the story.

After the defeat of the Zealots, the Romans left a garrison there for at least forty years, as we know from the coins found on the site. Later, Byzantine monks established themselves on the rock for a short period. Following them the hill remained unoccu-

pied, except for brief periods of exploration, until our large-scale excavations began in 1963.

Besides the finds already mentioned, we found hundreds of coins dating from the time of the revolt, bearing the inscription "For the Freedom of Zion." Some of these were in the remains of Herod's Hanging Palace, where we also discovered arrows and bronze scales from suits of armor. Among the debris in this building were the skeletons of a man, a woman, and a youth. These undoubtedly had been some of the heroic defenders of Masada.

Our most exciting prize was, of course, the fragments of fourteen parchment scrolls.

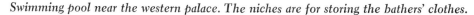

Swimming pool near the western palace. The niches are for storing the bathers' clothes.

*Sandal of Zealot woman, removed
from the site.*

They include parts of the books of Genesis, Leviticus, Deuteronomy, Psalms, and Ezekiel; in text and spelling they are identical with the traditional Hebrew Bible. One fragment was a part of the long-lost Hebrew original of the Book of Jubilees, which had been preserved only in Ethiopic, Greek, and Latin manuscripts. Similar fragments were found at Qumran. Another major find was a copy of the lost Hebrew original of Ecclesiasticus ("The Wisdom of Ben-Sira"), one of the most important books of the Apoc-

rypha. Definitely the most important find, however, was a portion of a scroll identical with one of the Dead Sea scroll fragments from Qumran. This single find is of the greatest significance for the study of the Essenes as well as the Zealots; it seems to show that the Essenes took part in the revolt along with the Zealots.

Besides the scrolls, some seven hundred ostraca—potsherds bearing inscriptions—were found. The most intriguing group consists of eleven small pottery fragments, each bearing a different name or nickname and all written by the same hand. One bears the name "Ben Yair"; this may well be the Zealot commander mentioned by Josephus. It is tempting to surmise that these ostraca refer to the ten or so surviving men who drew lots to determine which among them would kill the others before killing themselves, as Josephus records.

Now that the excavations are over, we face the arduous task of studying the thousands of objects found and evaluating all our data from the archaeological and historical viewpoint.

As important as the discoveries are, Masada represents something more—a symbol of courage, a monument to our great national heroes who chose death over a life of spiritual and physical bondage.

The Necropolis
of Beth She'arim

by N. AVIGAD

The hillock known in Arabic as Sheikh Abreik juts out from the southern slopes of the Galilean highlands at a point ten miles from Haifa on the road to Nazareth. It overlooks the valley of Jezreel to the southeast and Mount Carmel to the west. The summit of the hill is occupied by the tomb of the Sheikh and two agricultural farms. Little was known about the history of this site until an accidental find led to systematic excavation in 1936 and raised it from anonymity and oblivion. These excavations, conducted by Professor Mazar on behalf of the Israel Exploration Society, were carried out on the summit of the hill and down the rock slopes. They lasted for four fruitful seasons (1936–1940). In 1953 excavations were resumed by the Society under the direction of the writer.

Six seasons of intensive digging unearthed a wealth of material which enabled the excavators to establish the identity of this historic site, to link archaeological evidence with information provided by literary sources, and to add new data to the history of this important place. It is now established that the hillock is the ancient Jewish city of Beth She'arim, referred to as Besara by the historian Josephus Flavius and frequently mentioned in the Talmudic sources. Beth She'arim was a center of Jewish learning and for some time the seat of the Sanhedrin (Supreme Council of the Jews) at a time when the Jewish community's focus of national and religious life shifted from Judaea to Galilee. The city flourished in the days of the Patriarch Judah Ha-Nasi, the "Prince" (A.D. 135–220), the spiritual head of Jewry at that time and the editor of the Mishnah (code of Judaism's oral law), who took up residence at Beth She'arim and was buried there, according to Talmudic sources. The town, which seems to have been founded in the Hasmonean period (second century B.C.), was apparently destroyed A.D. 352 during the suppression by Gallus of the great Jewish revolt, but it continued to be inhabited on a smaller scale during the Byzantine period.

Excavation on the summit of the hill, the site of the city proper, revealed extensive ruins of buildings, such as a spacious synagogue of the basilical type dating to the third century A.D., a large public building, a glass factory, an olive press, dwelling houses, and the like. Together with artifacts of various kinds—pottery, glass, metal, coins, and inscriptions, they reflect many aspects of the city's cultural and economic conditions.

But it is an extensive and peculiar necropolis which gives Beth She'arim its specific interest. This cemetery, dating from the second to the fourth century A.D., consists of rock-cut catacombs hewn into the slopes of the hill. It seems as if the slopes of the hill were honeycombed with these cavities.

Each catacomb is composed of an open courtyard from which stone doors, still swinging on their hinges, lead into halls and burial chambers. The size of the catacombs and the number of their graves vary considerably. One contains two halls with only twenty burial places, while another is composed of twelve halls with about two hundred graves distributed in three stories. One of the catacombs, which is approached by a long, narrow open corridor, is reported to contain as many as four hundred burial places in several stories. Some of the catacombs are obviously family vaults; others may be regarded as public burial quarters.

The usual burial hall consists of several successive rooms forming an elongated hall with burial chambers branching off on both sides. The vaulted rooms and chambers are connected by arched doorways. The most common plan is the *arcosolium* with one to four cavities sunk in the bottom. Each chamber has three or more of these *arcosolia*. Other types of burial places are the *Kukhim*, or horizontal shafts, hewn in the wall, and rectangular pits sunk in the floor, all covered with heavy stone slabs. Iron nails found in some graves testify to the use of wooden chests. Both permanent burial and the cus-

The central hall of catacomb No. 12. Arched doorways with stepped jambs are typical of Beth She'arim tomb chambers.

Arie Volk

tom of collecting the bones were practiced at Beth She'arim.

One of the catacombs, No. 14, lacks the somewhat stereotyped plan current at the Beth She'arim necropolis. It consists of a spacious main hall and two large rooms with rows of small niches in one wall, which served as receptacles for bones. It has a masonry-built tomb at the end of the twenty-six-meter-long cave, a unique feature at Beth She'arim.

Some of the catacombs are plain; others have decorated interiors. The soft rock made carving and scratching very easy, both for the craftsman and for the occasional visitor. The numerous reliefs, engravings, graffiti, and paintings covering the walls are rather crude, but they represent an interesting style of Jewish popular art of the

Catacomb No. 13, showing two of its three stories. The whole tomb is cut out of rock; only the entrances are constructed of stones. The holes in the right-hand jambs are keyholes.

Arie Volk

Plan of catacomb No. 12.

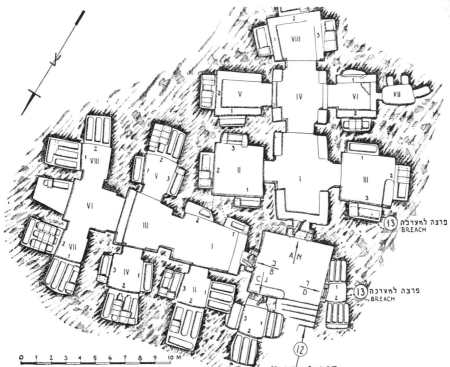

ENTRANCE

Roman period. Jewish symbols are common, especially the *menorah* (seven-branched candlestick), which is executed in all kinds of technique, from bold relief to slight scratching and brush painting. The representation of the Torah shrine (Ark of the Law) is instructive with regard to the architecture of the structure. Other symbols are the *shofar* (ram's horn), *lulab* (palm branch), *ethrog* (citrus fruit), and *mahta* (shovel). All these motifs are well known from the sculptures and mosaics of ancient synagogues. Decorations of secular character include representations of human beings, animals, ships, geometric designs, and other ornaments.

The interior architecture of the catacombs gains its specific character from carved features such as ornamented columns, *aediculae*, and arches. The stone doors, set into frames with moldings, are common to all tombs of Beth She'arim; they are generally decorated in imitation of wooden doors, showing panels, knobs (imitating nail heads), and door knockers. They were locked by bolts operated with keys from the outside.

Arie Volk

Catacomb No. 4. A representation of a Torah shrine carved in bas-relief on the wall of the tomb chamber, showing a tetrastyle front with central arch, standing on a podium to which steps lead.

The "Syrian" burial hall of catacomb No. 12, where people from Antioch, Byblos, Tyre, and Yahmur were buried. A menorah is carved in relief between two arcosolia. Its lower part is destroyed by a breach made by tomb robbers penetrating this hall from a cave behind.

Bas-relief showing a man on horseback, carved on the wall of a tomb chamber.

Arie Volk

A typical door, made of a single heavy block of stone, still moves on its stone hinges. The door is decorated in imitation of wooden doors, showing panels, nailheads, and door knocker.

Catacomb No. 14, where Rabbi Simeon and Rabbi Gamaliel are buried. The triple-arched façade is built of dressed stones against the rock wall. The complete arch at the right is 4.20 m. in height. The hole above the central doorway is the one through which robbers penetrated in search of valuables. The upper part of the façade has collapsed; originally it probably joined the stepped structure above, which terminated in a niched wall. This upper structure was apparently the sepulchral monument of the tomb below.

An Aramaic epitaph which reads: "He who is buried here is Simeon, the son of Yohanan, and on oath, whoever shall open upon him shall die of an evil end."

The people of Beth She'arim did not content themselves with imitating architectural elements in the rock. Genuine structures are found outside some tombs. The rock walls of the courtyard are faced with masonry and the main entrance is adorned by a built arch with fine moldings resting on pilasters with capitals and bases. Above one of the elaborate catacombs, No. 11, which has a paved mosaic courtyard, were found remains of a mausoleum built of dressed stones. The great number of carved and ornamented stones belonging to this building makes possible a reconstruction of its four façades, which were adorned with arches, niches, cornices, and pilasters. Among the decorated friezes, an animal frieze should be mentioned particularly. These architectural features show close relationship to the style of architecture prevailing at contemporary Galilean synagogues (3rd–4th centuries).

Another elaborate façade has lately been discovered in front of catacomb No. 14. It has three monumental arches resting on pillars that have flat pilasters with molded capitals and bases. This arcade, built of fine masonry, points to the importance of this tomb. This is stressed by another structure, the remains of which have been discovered above the arched façade. It consists of monumental steps about thirteen meters in width, leading to a built wall, which has a circular niche six meters wide adorned with pilasters on each side. Only two courses of this wall, which was evidently of a purely decorative character, are preserved. This upper structure is apparently a sepulchral monument intended to adorn the tomb underneath. The entire architectural composition, when complete, was about twenty meters in height. It must have been a striking landmark, worthy to commemorate an important family.

A possible identification of the family is suggested by two Hebrew funerary inscriptions found in this tomb cave; one of them reads simply: "Rabbi Simeon," and the other: "This is (the tomb) of Rabbi Gamaliel." These names are identical with those of the two sons of Rabbi Judah the Prince, who is known to have been buried at Beth She'arim.

The burial inscriptions of Beth She'arim are of great importance. About 250 have so far been found, mostly in Greek, others in Hebrew, Aramaic, and Palmyrene. They are painted in red or incised on the wall of the burial chambers, on lintels or occasionally on marble slabs. They usually include the name of the deceased and his patronymic, his profession, sometimes his place of origin, and often some words of blessing or consolation, for instance: "This is the tomb of Rabbi Itzhak, son of Moqim, Peace"; or: "Be comforted Simeon, no one is immortal." Other inscriptions indicate belief in eternal life and resurrection.

Some of the epitaphs show interesting formulae as, for instance, one in Aramaic: "He who is buried here is Simeon, the son of Yohanan, and on oath, whoever shall open upon him shall die of an evil end." Especially noteworthy are two Graeco-Jewish epigrams engraved on marble slabs in monumental characters. They are composed in Homeric style, which shows that knowledge of Greek literature was prevalent in Beth She'arim. The first of these inscriptions, interesting on account of the occurrence of the town's name, Besara, reads as follows (after M. Schwabe):

I, Justus, the Leonide, son of Sappho, am lying dead, after having picked the fruits (?) of all wisdom; I relinquished the light, the unhappy parents, who will mourn constantly, and the brothers, woe, in my Besara. And after having gone to Hades, I, Justus, the son of Leo [?], am lying here with many of my folk, because such was the wish of powerful Fate. Be confident, Justus, nobody is immortal.

The other slab is decorated with the characteristic assemblage of Jewish symbols: *menorah, shofar, lulab, ethrog,* and *mahta.* The inscription, headed by the caption "Eulogy to the pious woman," tells about Zenobia honoring the memory of her pious mother by erecting the tomb that contains her mortal remains, in immortal remembrance. She praises her famous deeds and prays for new wealth to both of them even after the termination of life.

Another group of burial inscriptions helps us to understand the remarkable expansion of the Beth She'arim necropolis. Such an extensive one could not possibly have been only for a small town like Beth She'arim. We learn from Talmudic sources that Beth She'arim served as a central cemetery for Jews in Eretz Israel and the Diaspora. This is now confirmed by epigraphic evidence. In the first group of catacombs inscriptions were found mentioning towns like Palmyra, Himyar (Southern Arabia), and Mesene (Mesopotamia) as the place of origin of the deceased. Some inscriptions mention cities of the coastal region of Syria and Phoenicia whence the deceased were brought, such as Antioch, Byblos, Tyre, Sidon, and Beirut. Some examples of these Greek inscriptions may be cited:

"Apse (= burial chamber) of Aidesios the Head of the Council of Elders, an Antiochene."

"Be comforted, O Matron Calliope, no one is immortal, she was from Byblos." Other epitaphs mention an "Archisynagogos of Beirut" and a "Priest of Beirut." As we gather from these inscriptions, it was mainly the privilege of Jewish notables to be brought from far away for burial in Beth She'arim. Other catacombs, modest in appearance and

Arie Volk

Assemblage of Jewish emblems representing ritual objects carved on a marble slab bearing a Greek epigram. In the center a seven-branched candlestick. At left a ram's horn and censer shovel. At right a palm branch with citrus fruit.

crowded with burials, apparently belonged to less wealthy persons. There seems to have been a great desire among the Jews to be buried in Beth She'arim, and tomb cutting must have been a prosperous industry.

In the words of Professor Schwabe, the Greek epigraphist of our expedition: "It may be conjectured that the great Jewish cemetery at Beth She'arim was divided according to the communities of the Diaspora, each of which had its own section." It is suggested that Beth She'arim became the favorite burial center for the Jews abroad owing to the fact that the venerated patriarch Judah I and members of his family were buried there. The fact that the Mount of Olives, time-honored cemetery of Jerusalem, was barred to Jewry after the revolt of Bar Kochbah, A.D. 162, may have facilitated the establishment of a new burial center for pious Jews of the Diaspora who wished to be buried in the Holy Land.

The objects found in the catacombs of Beth She'arim were not numerous, since the tombs were rifled many years ago. Still, we have succeeded in collecting pottery vessels, lamps, glass vessels, cosmetic utensils, and some minor pieces of jewelry. Seemingly, not many valuables were put in the graves, since we found some untouched burial places that contained nothing but bones. The objects are helpful in dating these catacombs to the second–fourth centuries A.D.

In 1955, by far the largest catacomb of all was discovered. In many respects it differs greatly from the others. Its plan is distinctly different; Hebrew inscriptions are more numerous, while in the other tombs Greek inscriptions were in the majority; and—last but not least—we find for the first time in Beth She'arim the extensive use of sarcophagi. In the other catacombs the bodies or bones were placed either directly in niches cut into the walls of the rock chamber or in wooden coffins (of which generally only the iron nails remain). Moreover, the new catacomb seems to contain the largest number of sarcophagi—about 130—yet discovered in this type of ancient necropolis.

The façade of the catacomb, about forty feet long, is built of ashlar masonry placed against the natural rock wall. It consists of three arches resting on square pillars, each with an opening leading into the cave. This arcaded façade is largely destroyed, but its molded and decorated blocks, found fallen in front of it, show the style of Roman architecture current in Palestine in the early third century A.D.

The cave itself, cut in the soft rock, comprises a series of vaulted halls and burial chambers. The end of the cave was blocked by a huge heap of collapsed rock, apparently the result of an earthquake. The central hall is about 150 feet long, while another burial hall reaches a length of about 160 feet. The chambers are arched and have small niches cut in their walls, but most of the burials were in sarcophagi. The average size of the

sarcophagi is nine feet in length and five feet in height, including the lid; each weighs three to five tons.

When we entered the cave we found that all the sarcophagi had been forced open and looted by grave robbers. Many clay lamps of the early Arab period, which had been brought by the robbers and left behind, indicated the date of this pillaging. What were the robbers after? Some personal jewelry such as a ring, a pair of earrings, a bronze bracelet, cosmetic utensils, and the like, in addition to a few pottery or glass vessels—these are all one would be likely to find.

Many of the sarcophagi are decorated with carved designs. Garlands suspended from

Glass vessel, pottery lamps, and bronze spatula—the furniture of one of the tomb chambers.

A bearded face on the side of a sarcophagus. It resembles the usual representation of a pagan deity such as Zeus.

A small chamber packed with sarcophagi. Even the doorway is blocked. The coffin at the rear is about nine feet long. The author is looking at a decorated sarcophagus. Gabled lids with undecorated acroteria at the corners are common to all the sarcophagi.

columns, eagles, bulls' heads, *tabulae ansatae*, and other motifs were borrowed from Roman art. Rosettes and other compass-drawn designs, heraldic lions, a seven-branched candlestick, the Torah shrine, etc., all of which occur on the coffins, were current in popular Jewish art of the Roman period. Most of these motifs were taken from the repertory of decorative art of the ancient synagogues. Here for the first time we find them on Jewish sarcophagi of this period.

The most remarkable decoration is carved in relief on one of the narrow sides of a coffin—a bearded face resembling that of a pagan deity. Here it is merely an ornament, but it is startling to see such a carving on a Jewish coffin in a catacomb where, as the inscriptions indicate, families of rabbis lie buried. It is further evidence of the unorthodox attitude of the Jews of that period in matters of art, as proved by representations of human beings in synagogues, where one would certainly expect strict observance of the Mosaic law forbidding the "making of a graven image, the similitude of any figure and the likeness of male and female" (Deuteronomy 4:16). It seems that this law was not taken literally in those days of increased Hellenistic influence. The emphasis was apparently put on the warning not "to worship them and serve them."

These sarcophagi are made of local limestone. The debased style of ornamentation is typical of local craftsmanship and of Jewish popular art of the period. But in this catacomb there were also coffins of quite a different character—imported marble sarcophagi decorated with sculptured figures of men, women, and animals in a developed Roman style. All of them had been broken to bits in the early Arab period, presumably to serve as material for the lime kilns. Heaps of marble splinters and fragments of sculptured figures, which we found strewn about the cave, are the only remnants of these lost art treasures. The small fragments preserved show that these sarcophagi were decorated with scenes from Greek mythology. One can be identified as a combat of Amazons and Greeks. This reminds us of the magnificent Amazon sarcophagus found at Tell Barak near Caesarea, which is thought to have been imported from Athens in the second or third century A.D. During this period sarcophagi with mythological scenes were in vogue in various centers of the eastern Mediterranean. Their importation into Palestine seems to have been more extensive than was previously supposed. The most surprising thing is that they were used in a Jewish cemetery in spite of their pagan decorations. Only one fragment of such a sarcophagus had previously been found in a Jewish tomb, in an earlier excavation at Beth She'arim, and this showed Leda and the swan. Such a find in a Jewish tomb was regarded as so shocking that scholars were inclined to consider it an accidental intrusion. Now, of course, we are convinced that it was not an exception, and that Beth She'arim was apparently a good market for this kind of imported sarcophagus. The mythological scenes must have been meaningless to the Jews, who regarded them simply as of decorative value. Similar pagan motifs had already been found on sarcophagi in the Jewish catacombs of Rome. These, too, were difficult to understand. Now, with the further examples which have come to light in the necropolis of Beth She'arim, it becomes apparent that such representations were commonly used in Jewish tombs of the Roman period.

The excavations at Beth She'arim reveal a City of the Dead unique of its kind in Palestine. Albeit the product of but a limited and peculiar field of activity, this necropolis incorporates instructive material of manifold interest. It contributes to the study of architecture, of the art of stone cutting, of folk art, and of burial customs of the Jews in Roman times. The abundant epigraphic material is an invaluable source for philological and social research and demonstrates the extent of Greek cultural influence among the Jews in Palestine and in the Diaspora during the third and fourth centuries. Subject to some reservation, it may be suggested that we have discovered the vault where the mortal remains of the family of Rabbi Judah the Prince and other notables were laid to rest.

A sarcophagus distinguished by its original ornamental composition and the crudeness of its figure carvings. Here is shown only the left portion of the front, with interlaced circles in relief and a conched aedicula that apparently represents the Torah shrine. A long-legged bird stands at the opening.

Department of Archaeology, The Hebrew University of Jerusalem

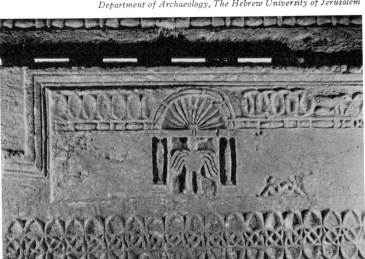

Sbeita: looking north from the house ruins in the center of town toward the comparatively well-preserved church and monastery of St. George. The winding path in the foreground is an ancient street partially blocked by fallen masonry.

Castles in Zin

by HARRIS DUNSCOMBE COLT

Southern Palestine is a land of rolling hills, dry and stony, cut through by shallow valleys and bearing nothing but stunted tamarisk and acacia bushes.

This is the triangle of barren land now known as the Negev, the southern desert, which, commencing at Beersheba, extends westward almost to the Mediterranean coast and southeastward to the Gulf of Aqaba. This is the desert that was named in the Bible (Exodus 16:1) the Wilderness of Zin, through which the Children of Israel wandered after their flight from Egypt. It is not a true sandy desert, but is akin to the scrublands of our own western states.

The desolation is due only to lack of water, and during the short rainy season the present inhabitants find it quite possible to produce a small harvest of crops. The country, moreover, was not always the waste it now is, for in the early part of our era it supported several towns of considerable size, as well as a large settled population that lived scattered throughout the little valleys; but it never could have been a land of plenty, and existence must always have been hard, with the fear of famine lurking in the background.

About the early inhabitants of the Negev nothing is known, as there has been very little archaeological activity in this field. Up to the year 1948, no evidence had been found of any permanent settlements antedating the third century B.C., although the discovery of finely worked neolithic flints indicates the possibility of some Stone Age civilization.

Agriculture came late to the Negev and it was not until the third century A.D. that this district began to develop and flourish. Its prosperity reached a zenith in the middle of the seventh century A.D., after which a steady decline set in; by the tenth century it had returned to its former state of wilderness. The reasons for this are readily apparent. The Negev had always been the grazing area of wandering, marauding tribes, against whom some kind of protection was necessary if settled husbandry was to be initiated and maintained. In the third century B.C., the Nabataean kingdom of Petra rose to power and took control of the caravan routes crossing southern Palestine from the head of the Gulf of Aqaba to Gaza on the Mediterranean coast; and under its aegis a few small towns developed as outposts along

187

these routes. While no large settlements were developed, small groups of people gathered around these military posts and an agricultural life was slowly evolved.

Trajan's conquest of Petra, in A.D. 106, put an end to the Nabataean sway, but, in turn, the Romans left behind them military posts and patrols to repulse the ever-encroaching desert dweller. Under this form of regular protection, agriculture finally was developed on a large scale and a settled population took root in an area that had never before afforded much reward to its inhabitants. This state of peace and plenty lasted until the time of the Arab conquest in A.D. 634, when the defeat of the Byzantine army removed the old controls.

The invading Arab was the brother of the Arab nomad and lacked reasons for maintaining defenses against him. Forts in these southern lands were no longer manned and military precautions were discarded. Slowly the desert reasserted itself against the laboriously won farmlands. Slowly the goat and camel denuded the countryside. City folk and farmers alike abandoned the province and moved northward to seek new fortunes in areas of greater fertility and population. The process of deterioration was a slow one, but within three centuries of the conquest the cycle had been completed; the Negev lay quiescent in the hot sun of the Arabian desert, its fields and orchards gone, its towns in ruins.

The era of prosperity—that is, the five centuries between 106 A.D. and 634 A.D.—saw the development of several good-sized towns containing populations which varied from 6,000 persons in the smaller ones to possibly 20,000 in the largest. Auja el Hafir (then named Nessana), Abda (Eboda), Sbeita (Sobata), Khalasa (Elousa), Kurnub (Mampis), Ruheiba, and three small settlements at Ain el Gudeirat, Bir Birein and Mishrifa all date from this era. The exact history of these desert towns is not yet known, though it may be safe to generalize about them from the results of the archaeological discoveries at Auja el Hafir and Sbeita. The former site unexpectedly produced a great number of

Abda stands dominating its wadi from the crest of a rocky hill. The valley floor, after the spring rains, raises a sparse crop of wild barley that provides thin sustenance for a few Bedouin sheep and goats. During the rest of the year, nothing grows but tamarisk bushes.

papyrus records, a rare find that has thrown considerable light on the daily life of those times.

In appearance the towns generally resembled one another. Each was enclosed by a wall formed merely by conjoining the backs of houses, and presenting no real obstacle to any kind of determined attack. As a defense, however, against the pounce-and-run kind of raid made by the marauding Bedouin it presented an adequate barrier. Large and carefully built forts were found at Auja el Hafir, Kurnub, and Abda, and it is safe to assume that they contained permanent garrisons, as these towns were on the main caravan routes and were probably important stations. But it is doubtful if, at the time when these forts were built (during the later years of the Byzantine occupation), troops were needed for any heavier duty than routine patrolling. The impression that these Byzantine forts were meant to be places of temporary refuge, rather than housings for large garrisons, is strengthened by the absence of elaborate arrangements within the forts, which are very often simply large empty squares into which, conceivably, a crowd of people could be gathered for safekeeping while the armed protectors routed the bandits.

Another aspect common to the appearance of these towns was that all were built of stone cut out of the surrounding countryside, since water in that arid land is much too precious to waste in making mud bricks and wood is practically nonexistent. This local stone is an interesting variety of limestone that turns a deep honey color on exposure to the air. It is found extensively in three qualities, one of which is a hard crystalline type and was used in large rough blocks for the foundations and lower courses of buildings. A finer-grained variety, hard but capable of being carved, was used for doorways, pilasters, and the more ornamental parts of the houses; and a third kind, almost of the consistency of chalk, which though very easily cut hardens on exposure to the air, was used for the upper courses.

The ground plans for these towns were not laid out in the orderly way of the Romans, with provision for wide thoroughfares and colonnaded squares, but followed the haphazard eastern pattern of narrow winding streets with many cul-de-sacs. Houses were built to enclose courtyards and sometimes gardens, but the elevations facing into the streets were left almost blank, any decoration being confined to the doorways, which often had carved lintels and jambs. The windows were mere slits in the walls, serving only as air vents; in a country where there is burning sunlight for the major part of the year, it is best to keep the sun's rays out as much as possible.

Most houses were two stories high and all had flat roofs which provided outdoor sleeping space during the hot, dry summer nights, and collected rainwater for the courtyard cisterns during the cold, wet winter months. In many instances the houses were quite large, some even containing two courtyards. It was customary for several married brothers and sisters to live in one house, each family having its own suite of rooms and all sharing the use of the courts. An interesting example of this custom was found among the papyri of Auja el Hafir, one of which was a long document concerning the apportionment of an estate, by which the house was divided among the heirs, various rooms being assigned to specific individuals with provisions for their joint use of the courtyard.

The method of construction that generally prevailed for houses was dictated by the building material at hand, the limestone of the district. As wood was not available it was necessary to cut stone even for the ceilings and roofs. Vaulting seems never to have been employed and the practice was to

From the middle of the wadi Auja rises a low hill, on whose summit is still another ruined Byzantine fortress, known to the local Arabs as Auja Hafir, but in early Christian times as Nessana. The author's excavations in the sixth-century church of Sts. Sergius and Bacchus, within the fort, yielded the sensational Colt papyri, thanks to which Nessana has become the best-understood ancient site in the region. The ruins in the foreground belong to the period of World War I.

place flat slabs over a series of arches spanning the rooms. The spacing of the arches was governed by the size of the stone slabs, which were generally a little over three feet in length, so that the arches were also about three feet apart. In the Negev corbeling above the arches in order to increase the spaces between them was not resorted to, although it was very common in Syrian houses of the same period. The arches themselves were usually carried on pilasters built against the wall, but occasionally they sprang directly from the wall. Pilasters were ordinarily about three and a half or four feet in height and ended in a simple splayed cap.

The flat slabs forming the ceilings were always rough-cut, so they were plastered on the underside and leveled off on top with a screed of lime cement, to make a waterproof roof or the floor for a room above. The houses were of arches and on abaci of pilasters. Another design is that of a square or oblong divided into segments in a union jack pattern, which is found often on pilaster caps and on the bases of door jambs. Other patterns used were discs with varieties of petal designs and crosses. While the disc patterns and the crosses are found in Byzantine buildings in many other parts of Asia Minor, the union jack pattern seems to be limited to the Negev.

Another interesting variation in ecclesiastical architecture from the general type was the use of wood for ceilings and roofs. Here the spans were of such size that the local stone could not be employed and wood had to be imported. Among the fragments recovered from the ruins of Sbeita and Auja were specimens of Cedars of Lebanon, so that the builders of the Christian churches must have emulated Solomon in importing wood from Syria.

Surrounding the churches, and attached to them, there were often to be found large collections of courtyards and rooms, which were in all probability monasteries. This supposition is strengthened by our knowledge that during the fourth and fifth centuries there was a sudden exodus into the desert of devout churchmen, who wished to practice a purer and more unworldly Christianity than was in existence in the towns. According to records that tell of a monk named Hilarion converting the people of Elousa in about 350 A.D., it would seem that Christianity was introduced into the Negev only in the fourth century.

Sbeita was still pagan in 400, and a story which indicates this exists in a tenth- or eleventh-century manuscript in the library of the Greek Patriarchate in Jerusalem. It concerns the misfortunes of one Theodulus, a disciple of St. Nilus, who was stolen by some raiding Sinaitic Arabs to serve as a sacrifice to the Morning Star. On the day of the sacrifice, however, the kidnapers overslept and the Star had faded before they arose, an accident they took to be an omen against the sacrifice of Theodulus. They kept him for some time in their wanderings and, finally, put him up for sale in Sbeita, announcing that he would be beheaded if he were not quickly sold. Under such incitement, Theodulus himself pleaded before the buyers for a new master saying, "'. . . I prayed with both my hands those who came to the sale to pay what the barbarians asked, and not to be stingy over the price of human blood, assuring them that I would serve with zeal him who should buy me, and that even after I should have repaid what he spent for me.' Touched by his prayers, a townsman did buy him, to resell him later to the Bishop of Elousa . . . who freed him and restored him to S. Nilus."

As we have said, the beginnings of these Negev towns are still shrouded in mystery, but it is fairly certain that Kurnub, Abda, and Auja el Hafir began as Nabataean settlements on arterial caravan routes, and continued as military posts through the Roman period, even though Trajan deflected the main caravan route through Petra to Bostra. Kurnub and Abda became stations in the Roman frontier system, the *limes Palaestinae*, and Auja may well have been kept as a small outpost far to the south of the *limes*. Archaeological finds prove continued occupation there through the second, third, and fourth centuries, although on a small scale. Sbeita is in a different class. It seems to go back no further than about the second century A.D., and it is difficult to account for its beginnings as it was not on any caravan route and never appears to have been forti-

The church of St. George at Sbeita. The foreground is the colonnaded entrance court; in its center stands a drum that once supported a large basin for ablutions. Behind is the narthex, or proch, of the church. Behind that, in turn, lies the basilica proper, dominated by its three apses that have somehow survived the passage of time. To the right of the latter may be seen the apse of a small chapel, and the larger apse of the baptistry.

Basilica of St. George. Reconstruction of the interior.

fied. Furthermore, it has no spring or well; yet it seems to have possessed a large and prosperous population that maintained three public baths. At Sbeita also was found one of the largest and handsomest churches.

Khalasa was the largest city of the Negev and its beginnings possibly antedate Nabataean times. The small amount of exploration done there uncovered tombs that contained remains earlier than any found at the other sites, with the exception of Ain el Gudeirat. Khalasa, however, is in the most northerly end of the Negev, very near Beersheba and quite close to the coastal plain, which has been inhabited from time immemorial. It differs from the other towns under discussion in one respect. It reached its greatest size in the fourth century A.D., and then declined, while the others reached theirs in the sixth and seventh centuries. In many of the papyri found at Auja there are references to the "district of the City of Elousa," which seem to indicate that Khalasa was the capital of the district.

One of the most interesting aspects of the region is the system of water conservation that was developed. Rainfall here measures not more than a few inches a year and is precipitated between the months of October and March. Today it suffices to nourish only the poorest kind of crop and a meager population of 50,000 nomads. As yet we have not enough satisfactory evidence to suppose that during the first centuries of the Christian era the Negev had a much larger rainfall, but we do know that there must have been at least 150,000 people living there in the midst of agricultural abundance.

As far as we know today, this was made possible solely by an intricate and ingenious system of water conservation that involved the most careful terracing of hillsides and valleys. These terraces prevented soil erosion while making possible the fullest utilization of what rainfall there was. On the more barren hillsides, where cultivation was not practicable, channels were cut, through which rainwater was carried to huge cisterns carved out of solid rock. One of these reservoirs in the valley of Gudeirat measures 125 by 125 by 10 feet, but this one was fed also by a perpetual spring about a mile and a half away. Vineyards were plentiful, and there is good cause to believe that pomegranates, peaches, almonds, olives, and figs may have been produced as well.

Within the towns this water conservation system was carefully maintained also. All private houses were equipped with cisterns; there were cisterns in connection with the churches, and in the streets and small squares; and at Sbeita there was an elaborate system of drains in the streets, which conducted water to two large reservoirs in the center of the town. Besides these catchments, there were many wells—Auja had four—the construction of which points to the Byzantine period; and some dams or barrages. At Kurnub, for instance, there is a series of three dams built in the river bed, the lowest of which is of truly great proportions, measuring some 75 feet across and rising to a height of 38 feet and being 20 feet thick.

Some day we shall know much more about the Wilderness of Zin. For the present, we may say that the people were well protected, thrifty, and industrious. The substantial buildings and the evidence of delicacies imported from afar—the clam, mussel, and scallop shells, fishbones, and stamped handles of wine and oil amphoras, found at Auja, for example—even indicate a fairly high level of prosperity. Life in this border country may have been pleasant and full; it could never have been dull.

The Umayyad Palace of Khirbat al-Mafjar

by OLEG GRABAR

Shortly after the armies of Islam under the great Caliph 'Umar had taken over nearly all of the Near East from the Byzantines and the Sasanian Persians, the first Moslem dynasty was established (A.D. 661) with its capital in Damascus. The Umayyad family ruled for nearly a hundred years, increasing the wealth and power of the new Arab empire. The Umayyad rulers, conscious of their newly acquired prestige and imitating their Byzantine and Persian predecessors, built for themselves many palaces. Almost nothing is known of the caliphal residence in the capital, but outside of Damascus, in Syria and Palestine and in the Jordanian desert, have remained many residences which were often built within large "paradises" where the princes hunted game.

In the valley of the Jordan River just north of the Dead Sea, near Jericho, on the plain between the river and the hills to the west, lie the ruins of an unfinished complex of buildings known today as Khirbat al-Mafjar. A graffito inscription dates the complex to the reign of the Caliph Hisham (A.D. 724–743), one of the last rulers of the Umayyad dynasty, but it does not necessarily imply that it was built by and for

Hisham himself. It is also possible that some other member of the ruling family planned it for himself and his followers. Curiously enough, the building, in spite of its magnitude—and insofar as present research indicates—cannot be identified with any place or site known through texts.

The complex of Khirbat al-Mafjar comprises three parts: a palace, a mosque, and a bath. On the east side there was a long forecourt, in the middle of which stood a pool. A glance at the plan shows that the relation between these elements was not entirely worked out in the mind of the architect or architects; the complex was not conceived as a unit. The forecourt was almost certainly an afterthought. Furthermore, the rather awkward relation among the mosque, the bath, and the palace suggests that the three were built at different times, although within a few years of each other.

On the whole the architecture of the palace itself conforms quite closely to the average type of early Islamic castles, except that it is perhaps a little less fortress-like than most of them. The plan is the typical Umayyad square with towers at the corners and on the sides, a central courtyard surrounded by a portico, and rooms along the walls. But a few novelties are worth mention. Instead of the usual round towers, Khirbat al-Mafjar has a square tower at the back of the small mosque (it probably carried a minaret) and a square entrance tower. Furthermore, while most Umayyad palaces have rooms arranged in *bayts*, that is, apartments of two, three, or four intercommunicating rooms on each side of a larger central hall, the arrangement occurs at Khirbat al-Mafjar only in the west wing. The other rooms are generally not connected with each other. Our knowledge of Umayyad palaces is too limited to permit specific identifications, but this rather peculiar arrangement of rooms, their small size and lack of decoration, suggest that the

main official reception halls and living quarters were not on the first floor of the palace but on the second.

The mosque is poorly preserved, and does not seem to present any peculiarity worth attention. The bath, on the other hand, is remarkable. It illustrates quite well the adaptation by the early Islamic artist of the Romano-Byzantine heritage he found in Syria and Palestine. The hot rooms have shrunk in size and importance, occupying less than a tenth of the whole area of the bath. A large hall with a pool on one side (*apodyterium*) is the main feature; its exact function is not clear. This hall was covered by twenty-five domes, the central one a story higher than the others. Each element of the bath architecture can easily find Roman

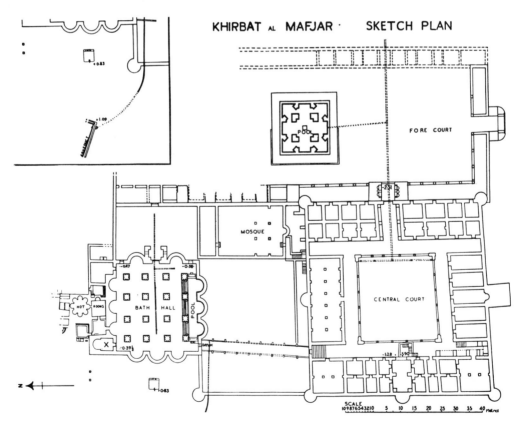

KHIRBAT al MAFJAR · SKETCH PLAN

Plan of the complex of Khirbat al-Mafjar.

Mosaic floor in the apse of the room marked X on the plan. The technique and the motif are classical. The tassels around the central motif suggest that a carpet inspired this mosaic.

prototypes, but the peculiarity of the Umayyad work is the multiplication of the apses, niches, and domes.

The floor of the bath was covered with mosaics in geometric patterns, all of which are preserved, and the walls were decorated with paintings in both fresco and tempera. These consist mostly of repeated and endlessly multiplied motives of triangles, frets, guilloches, imbrications, shells, and so on, all of them brightly, in fact loudly, colored. In the northwestern corner of the *apodyterium* was a small room (X on the plan). It was one of the most highly decorated places in the whole palace, probably a private sitting room for the lord of the palace. The floor was of beautiful mosaic, the walls solidly covered with stucco floral patterns carved in high relief. The domed ceiling also was decorated with carved stucco in a pattern of fruits, leaves, and vines, with six

female heads looking down from the crown of the dome.

Khirbat al-Mafjar provides the most impressive array of early Islamic decorative arts since the discovery of the palace of Mshatta. But at Mshatta were found only ornamental motives of vegetal origin with a few animal themes, while at Khirbat al-Mafjar sculpture and painting have a much wider repertoire. The mosaics, however, although technically excellent, show little originality. All the elements in them doubtless have a Roman derivation. In a few fragments one can observe a tendency to multiplication of patterns in all directions, which is characteristic of Islamic art in general.

The paintings are in a fragmentary state. All the fragments from the bath are ornamental in character. Many motives from the palace are also ornamental, vines, flowers, etc., some resembling textile patterns. One motif of dog-headed dragons within medallions strongly suggests that a textile was the prototype. A few pieces show human figures; the material is so scanty that no scene can be reconstructed, and the figures differ from each other both in scale and style. Two beautiful nearly life-size heads in a classic style, carefully executed, remain; other fragments show parts of roughly painted smaller figures. Some pieces also show parts of painted buildings.

The sculptures of animals and especially of human beings, both male and female, are far more interesting. These are in plaster, and most of them were painted in bright colors. Mountain goats, gazelles, rabbits, partridges, horses, and other animals abound. On the human figures, traces of paint remain on the hair, eyes, and lips; the costumes were completely painted. Human busts project in the round from the high relief of the decoration. Some statues, nude above the waist, may have represented dancers and attendants at the royal court. The statues are all short and stocky, with stumpy legs and heavy rounded figures, prominent eyes, and conventionalized hair and draperies, not unlike some Indian or Central Asian works. Two figures of a standing prince derive from Persian models.

By far the most interesting feature of the sculptures is their iconography. Some thirty years ago it would have been impossible to write about Umayyad iconography. Qusayr 'Amrah, a bath in the Jordanian desert that was decorated with various scenes all including people, was long thought to be the only representative of figurative art, which was supposed not to have flourished in early Islam. But with the discovery of Khirbat al-Mafjar and of Qasr al-Hayr in Syria, these paintings are no longer alone. A comparison, although tentative because of the fragmentary character of the remains, must be attempted.

Palestine Archaeological Museum

Stucco relief set on the ceiling of the room marked X. It was supported by four winged horses, which may indicate an astrological motif. Oriental influences are apparent in the detail (the flower motif within the rinceaux of the border).

This window tracery, found in the palace proper, is an enlargement of a common Roman motif. It illustrates the fashion in which the Umayyads utilized and transformed the motifs they found in the conquered lands.

This group of busts within a motif of interlacing circles is quite original. Each face has individualized features, but this may be due simply to the fact that the stucco was carved, not molded.

These personages, one female and one male, belong to a group of ten that decorated the drum under the dome of the entrance to the bath. In both style and iconography they are related not to classical but to eastern models.

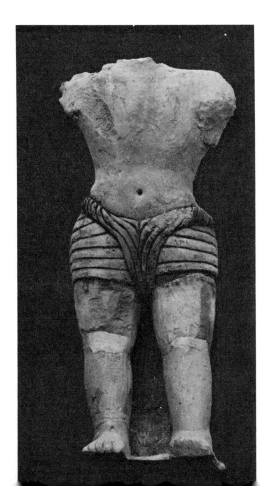

What is the significance of the dancing girls, soldiers, attendants, personages holding baskets of fruit or bouquets of flowers, riders, jugglers, and athletes of Khirbat al-Mafjar? The same—or very similar—figures occur also at Qusayr 'Amrah and Qasr al-Hayr. There seems to be little doubt that we are dealing with a depiction, symbolic or real, of the life of the Umayyad court.

The style of the Khirbat al-Mafjar remains is quite mixed. Many features of the paintings derive from Byzantine, even Roman, origins; and the mosaics are purely of western inspiration. But the style of most of the sculptures comes closer to prototypes found in Central Asia. This raises the question whether Central Asian art directly influenced Umayyad art or whether both reflect a Sasanian art that is now lost. Be this as it may, in the Khirbat al-Mafjar sculptures eastern influence is predominant. And a group of paintings on the walls of the two main rooms of the palace suggests one of the channels through which this influence may have come. Here are themes and motives first developed in the minor arts, especially textiles, and also metalwork. It is possible that the immense booty which, as we know through texts, had been collected by the conquerors throughout the East and sent to the Syrian centers included such textiles and metal work which were imitated on the walls of the palaces. Although this does not solve the whole problem of origins, it does indicate one of the means through which early Islamic art was formed.

Thus from an artistic point of view Khirbat al-Mafjar shows the simultaneous existence in eighth-century Palestine of eastern and western elements. It exemplifies the juxtaposition—rather than blending—of different types as a crucial characteristic of early Islamic art. A curious point about Khirbat al-Mafjar is that eastern influences predominate especially in the depiction of members of the royal court. This suggests that eastern practices were more common in Umayyad times than first suspected.

Another important conclusion to be drawn from Khirbat al-Mafjar affects our interpretation of Umayyad civilization. Older interpretations, in particular those of Lammens, Wellhausen, and Herzfeld, have assumed that the first caliphs were near-Bedouin who went into the desert in order to recapture a type of life they preferred to the official life of their capitals. But Khirbat al-Mafjar is not in the desert. Its art supposes a new, fairly well-developed royal consciousness. A study of the texts dealing with Umayyad life similarly shows that they had a much more developed ceremonial and court organization than is generally realized. A reinterpretation not only of the art but of the whole civilization is therefore necessary, for what we see in Khirbat al-Mafjar is the expression of a way of life that was no longer Bedouin but had already become royal.

The Hospice of the Knights of St. John in Akko

by ZEEV GOLDMANN

The city of Akko, or Acre, situated at the northern end of the Bay of Haifa, was in ancient times the southernmost of the Phoenician towns of the Syrian coast. It has existed almost uninterruptedly from early Canaanite times to the present day. The city rose to fame in four historic periods. First it was the Palestinian terminal of the international caravan road—the Via Maris—connecting Mesopotamia with Egypt. In the time of Alexander the Great it became a kind of bridgehead for his eastern conquests —Egypt and India. In the time of the Crusaders the port was their main harbor and— after the fall of Jerusalem in 1187—the capital of their state for exactly one hundred years (1191 to 1291). And, finally, this was the town which in 1799 successfully resisted the siege of Napoleon and so decided the fate of the Near East and Great Britain as well.

The first written documents mentioning Akko come from Egypt, starting with the "execration texts" of the nineteenth–eighteenth centuries B.C. and continuing with the annals of Thutmose III (around 1479 B.C.), the Tell el-Amarna letters of the fifteenth–fourteenth centuries, the annals of Seti I (around 1314 B.C.), two inscriptions of Ramses II (thirteenth century B.C.), and the Papyrus Anastasi from the end of the thirteenth century. The Bible mentions Akko in connection with the conquest of the country by the twelve tribes. "Asher did not drive out the inhabitants of Acco, or the inhabitants of Sidon, or of Ahlab, or of Achzib, or of Helbah, or of Aphik, or of Rehob . . ." (Judges 1:31–32). As a matter of fact, Akko remained a Phoenician town, not recognized by the Hebrews as belonging to the Holy Land (this situation was changed only with the creation of the Jewish State in 1948).

The original site of Akko is the ancient mound called Tell el-Fukhar or Tell Napoleon, one mile outside the present Old City, south of the Akko-Safad highway. In the third and second millennia B.C. the inhabitants were confined within the walls surrounding this relatively small mound, and it was only in Persian times that they began to spread out and settle on the plain between the mound and the Mediterranean in the west as well as on the peninsula extending toward the south. The town then had a population of more than 100,000. Under

199

Northwest vault of the refectory.

the successors of Alexander the Great, the Ptolemies, the city's name was changed to Ptolemais, and this name was in use until the Arab conquest in the seventh century. In Byzantine and early Arab times the town lost its importance to Caesarea, then the most thriving harbor of Palestine. The chroniclers of the Crusades tell us that when Akko was conquered, in 1104, the town had a population of only some eight thousand souls.

In the twelfth and thirteenth centuries, the time of the Crusades, the city grew again, containing some forty or fifty thousand people, and became one of the foremost medieval towns. After its destruction by the Mamelukes of Egypt in 1291 it was not rebuilt and remained in ruins until the

middle of the eighteenth century, with only a few inhabitants. The walled Old City of today is mainly the construction of the first two Turkish pashas: Daher el Omar (1750–1775) and Ahmed Pasha el Jazzar (1775–1804). This town occupied a much smaller area than the town of the Crusaders; the population never exceeded ten to fifteen thousand. It was now confined to the peninsula and was surrounded by new walls, the northern one being a restoration of the original early Arab wall. The Crusader ruins outside the rebuilt area disappeared altogether, while the Crusader town that still exists beneath the new houses, filled with rubble but still well preserved, is now largely unreachable.

The so-called Crypt of St. John in Akko, situated below the present Government Hospital, is one of many halls from the time of the Crusades that are now underground. Originally these were all above ground level, but when the Mamelukes destroyed Akko, all the streets and alleys were filled by the huge mass of collapsing upper stories, so that the present street level is seven to eight meters higher than at the time of the Crusades. In the second half of the eighteenth century the pashas built their residence on top of these buried buildings. Then, in the time of the Mandatory Government, their residence was converted into the Central Prison of Palestine, where many political prisoners were incarcerated. Since 1948 the prison has become the Government Hospital.

In 1955 the Department of Antiquities supervised the work of clearing the hall, which was carried out for the first two years by the Official Works Department and then continued by the National Parks Authority. Financial support was provided by the American Embassy. In addition, excavations were carried out in 1956 by the writer, and in 1960 by Zeev Yeivin, head of the Survey

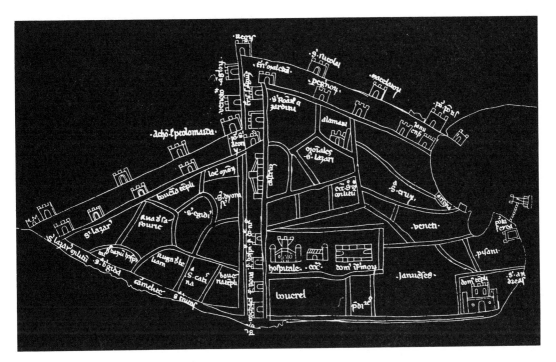

Map of the city of Akko, made by Paulinus de Puteoli in the early fourteenth century.

Department of the Department of Antiquities.

The term "Crypt" is actually a misnomer and can have had no connection whatsoever with the original purpose of the hall. Its form, a two-aisled building with four entrances, indicates a refectory. The hall is distinguished by its early Gothic style—transverse and diagonal ribs below the ceiling, the transverse ribs forming pointed arches. The three round piers, the ribs, and the walls give an extraordinarily massive impression, and it is certain that the hall is a very early example of the Gothic style belonging to the transitional period between Romanesque and Gothic—perhaps as early as the middle of the twelfth century.

What purpose did this remarkable hall originally serve? As we have said, its plan gives a clue: the two-aisled building follows the plan of refectories and assembly halls in the monasteries of the Middle Ages. Three chimneys—two as an addition to the eastern wall, one inside the same wall—probably belonging to a kitchen may be another hint (the kitchen itself has not yet been uncovered). Late thirteenth and early fourteenth century maps of Akko give yet another clue. According to these the whole complex of buildings which today forms the Government Hospital was then the site of the Hospital of the Crusaders. Three main buildings —*hospitale, ecclesia,* and *domus infirmorum* —appear on the map of Paulinus de Puteoli, drawn in the early fourteenth century. The hall is situated in the southern tract of the square northern building marked on the maps as *hospitale*. Its north wall rests on the city wall, as can be seen on another early plan, that of Marin Sanudo.

Hospitale in the Middle Ages meant hospice or inn. The building was therefore a large hostel for pilgrims and knights, where they found their first accommodation on their arrival from Europe. It was also the seat of the Master of the Order of St. John and his Knights, whose special task was the care of pilgrims and particularly the sick.

During the excavation of the hall much pottery was found. The most common type was a simple bowl, of which fragments were found in huge numbers, as well as some complete examples. This kind of bowl—unglazed, with a flat bottom and a narrow rim—certainly was that which pilgrims used at their meals. An important find having a definite bearing on the Order of St. John is a fragment of a glazed bowl with a cross painted on it in light olive color on a buff ground. The bowl is broken at the edges and the points of the cross are missing, but its shape is typical and there can be no doubt that the cross is the emblem of the Order, which is still in use today. This seems to be the earliest cross of the Order yet found, showing the linear style of the twelfth century. This bowl must have formed part of the set of dishes which was in use in the refectory, and it serves as further proof that the hall belonged to the Order of St. John.

Besides the general appearance of the hall—its early Gothic style—is there any other possibility of arriving at an approximate date for it? In the course of excavation two consoles (in the northeast and southeast corners of the hall) were uncovered. Each forms the "starting point" of a vault and each bears in relief the fleur-de-lis, the blazon of the French kings. We know that the fleur-de-lis was introduced as the symbol of French kingship by an *ordonnance* of Louis

Fleur-de-lis carved in relief on a console of the refectory (northeast corner).

VII, the leader of the Second Crusade (1147–1149).

In 1148 a great assembly of all the secular and spiritual leaders of the realm was held in Akko, to decide upon the future political trend of the Kingdom of Jerusalem—"an assembly the like of which has never been seen." It is possible that at this important event Louis VII made a contribution to the building of the premises of the Order, and that in order to honor him his emblem was carved on both consoles.

The fleur-de-lis, which often appears on European coats of arms, was taken over from (or at least influenced by) Oriental heraldry. We find this emblem in slightly different shape above the *mihrab* (niche) of the *madrasah* (school) of Nur ed-Din Mahmud b. Zanki in Damascus (1154–1173) and on the *mimbar* (pulpit) of his mosque in Homs. Not much later it appears on the coins of Saladin and his sons. Although the emblem was taken over by Europeans, it still continued to be used by Moslems. The fleur-de-lis on the consoles of the great hall appears in the European form, that is, with the side leaves attached to the stem, while in all Oriental examples the side leaves are detached from it.

In Europe the fleur-de-lis as the blazon of French kingship makes its first appearance in 1180 on a seal of Philippe Auguste, successor to Louis VII, while from his own lifetime none are known to have remained. If the fleur-de-lis on the consoles of the refectory of the Order of St. John is related to the stay of Louis VII in Akko in 1148, this would be its first known appearance as a royal blazon and it would confirm our approximate dating of the hall by its architectural style.

The stylistic and historical importance of the refectory of St. John in Akko cannot be sufficiently stressed. It is certainly one of the earliest Gothic buildings anywhere in the world. The hall was originally planned in the Romanesque style, that is, only with transverse ribs. The introduction of the Gothic cross-ribbed vaults necessitated certain changes in plan which can be detected in the construction of the walls and ceiling. The Gothic ceiling was placed upon walls which already existed (the western wall is the only one constructed from the outset for a Gothic ceiling).

If the purpose of this hall can thus be established, where should we look for the *domus infirmorum* and the *ecclesia?* South of the refectory now stands the Museum (the former Turkish baths), and east of the Museum is an Arab school. During the years 1959–1962 excavations were carried out under the school, again by the National Parks Authority. Six large parallel halls were cleared of a deep deposit of Turkish remains. These halls, popularly known as "El Bosta," may have served this purpose (post office) in the eighteenth and nineteenth cen-

turies, but certainly not in the time of the Crusades. They open onto a courtyard on the south and have large windows on the street side (north). This plan—parallel halls opening on a court—indicates that the building formed the northern part of a caravanserai, of which the southern and the eastern parts no longer exist. From certain architectural details, for instance a depressed horseshoe arch at the south end of the east wall of the last parallel hall, it can be shown

Refectory, with entrance to underground passage.

View of the refectory, seen from the east.

that the building originated in early Arab times, the tenth or eleventh century, when Akko was under Fatimid rule. These halls (the northern part of the caravanserai) were converted by the Crusaders to their *domus infirmorum*. The six halls are the basement for two upper stories which were built in the eighteenth century as the seat of the local Turkish government and in Mandate times were converted into a school. They contain quite a number of architectural Crusader remains, and their general layout—rooms around a central courtyard—indicates a typical infirmary.

In the middle of the courtyard of the basement remains a single hall: this may well have been an oratory or a small mosque (as is usual in caravanserais), which was made into a chapel in Crusader times. In the course of the excavations a large memorial inscription in honor of the eighth Master of the Order of St. John, Peter de Villebride, was discovered—further proof that the "El Bosta" buildings belonged to the Order. The hall was used in the eighteenth century as a dump for many architectural remains of Crusader, early Arab, and Byzantine times. They were laid down in an orderly way, with many fragments of marble pillars arranged in parallel rows. The pillars were later reused in the Turkish bath. These marbles may have come from the second and third story of the *domus infirmorum* and from the *ecclesia* beside it. At the eastern side of the "El Bosta" buildings exists today the large mosque built by the second pasha of Akko, Ahmed Pasha el Jazzar. The mosque itself was built on top of underground buildings that were converted into large cisterns. Although they are no longer in use, they still contain water, and so they cannot be examined in a satisfactory way. However, they may well be the remains of the Church of St. John, the *ecclesia* on the maps.

A drawing of the year 1686, by D'Orcières,

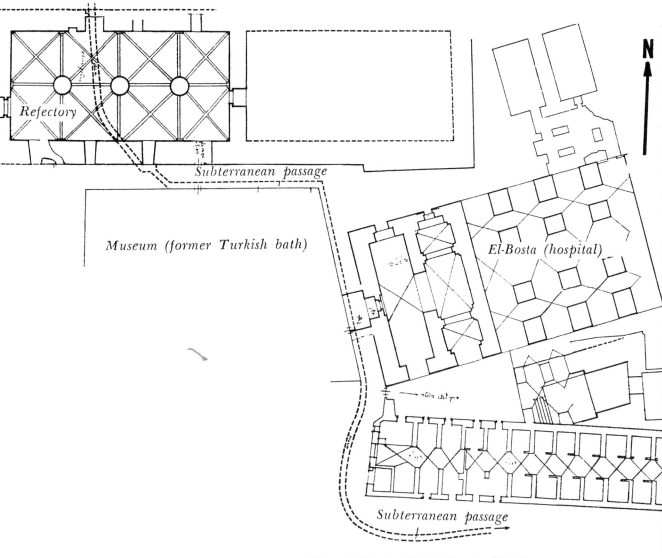

N

Refectory

Subterranean passage

Museum (former Turkish bath)

El-Bosta (hospital)

Subterranean passage

View of Akko in 1686, by Gravier d'Orcières.

palais du grand maitre

Eglise St Jean

reflects the original situation of the buildings much more clearly than can be seen today. The hospice, at the left, called "Palais du grand maître" on the drawing, appears in its characteristic square shape. Beside it the *ecclesia* and the *domus infirmorum* are still in ruins, prior to their restoration in the eighteenth century. It is known that at the beginning of the seventeenth century the famous Druse emir Fakhr ed-Din carried out extensive restoration work at the former hospice, to build himself a residence and fortress; this resulted in the square shape similar to that of the present building. The *domus infirmorum* is less discernible in the drawing, as it is more in the background. The addition of the names "Palais du grand maître" and "Eglise de St. Jean" show that the tradition of the site was still alive in the late seventeenth century.

The excavations of the refectory and "El Bosta" buildings are of great importance for the history of the Order. They have also brought to life one of the earliest caravanserai in the country. The hall of the refectory, moreover, shows by its early Gothic style that the Near East played a rôle in the creation of Gothic architecture, which is usually thought to be purely European. It is true that with the end of the Crusade the local development of the Gothic style ceased, but important features—for example, the pointed arch and the cross-ribbed vault—were known in the Near East long before their appearance in Europe. We find the pointed arch in Syria as early as the sixth century. An important example in Israel is the underground water reservoirs of Ramle, dating from the end of the eighth century, the time of the Caliph Harun al Rashid. The cross-ribbed vault is found in the tenth-century mosque of Cordova, Spain.

The perfection of the Gothic style was achieved on the Île de France, the church of St. Denis being one of its first realizations. But important preconditions for it were created in the Orient. The refectory of the Order of St. John in Akko may be considered as one of the missing links in the development of this new style.

Biographical Notes

YOHANAN AHARONI was born in Frankfurt, Germany, in 1919. In 1954 he received his M.A. in ancient Jewish history from the Hebrew University; in 1955 he received his doctorate from the same institution. Four years later Professor Aharoni became Inspector of Antiquities of the Department of Antiquities, State of Israel. He has been on the faculty of Hebrew University since 1954, where he is now associate professor of archaeology. Beginning his field work in 1950, he started the excavations at Ramat Rahel in 1954. He also directed the first exploration to the Judaean desert caves near Engedi, discovered the Bar Kochbah caves, and participated in the first Masada expedition. In 1955–58 he joined Y. Yadin at Hazor; from 1959 to 1962 he continued excavations at Ramat Rahel under the sponsorship of Hebrew University and the University of Rome. Since 1962 he has worked with Ruth Amiran (q.v.) at Tell Arad. Dr. Aharoni has several book-length publications to his credit in Hebrew and English. Among them are *The Land of the Bible: A Historical Geography* and *Atlas of the Bible*, which he co-authored with M. Avi-Yonah. He has also contributed to many journals and encyclopedias.

RUTH AMIRAN was born in Israel and educated at the Hebrew University of Jerusalem. During the years 1940–46 she assisted Professor E. L. Sukenik in the Department of Archaeology (of Palestine) and worked with him in the field at Tell Jerishe and Afulah. She also was a student member of the staff of Mme. Judith Marquet-Krause at Ai. From 1946 to 1948 she served on the archaeological staff of the Rockefeller Museum, Jerusalem. Her next seven years were spent on the staff of the Department of Antiquities, State of Israel, during which time she made several small excavations. She was at this time Inspector of Antiquities first in Galilee, then in Jerusalem and environs. From 1955 to 1959 she was senior staff member of the Hazor expedition, responsible for Area B. Since 1962 she has been director of the Early Bronze Arad expedition, and in 1962 and 1963 she was field director of the Tell Nagila excavations (see Avraham Eitan), sponsored by the Institute for Mediterranean Studies. She has been field archaeologist of the Israel Museum since 1964.

The Arad archaeological expedition has been working every year since 1962, under the joint sponsorship of the Hebrew University of Jerusalem, the Israel Department of Antiquities, the Israel Exploration Society, and the Israel Museum. Of the many financing bodies special mention should be made of the Arad Development Project, thanks to which the whole enterprise came into being, the Wenner-Gren Foundation for Anthropological Research, and the Haaretz Museum, Tel Aviv. The expedition excavating the fortress mound is directed by Professor Y. Aharoni. The expedition excavating the Early Bronze Age city is directed by Ruth Amiran, with the following staff: U. Paran as architect and surveyor, Y. Shiloh, R. Brown, and Y. Zafrir as area supervisors, and Batsheva Taube as registrar.

EMMANUEL ANATI was born in Florence, Italy, in 1930. He studied archaeology at the Hebrew University of Jerusalem, where he received his B.A. in 1953 and his M.A. in 1955.

A fellowship from the French government enabled his further studies in ethnology at the Musée de l'Homme and in prehistory at the Institut de Paléontologie Humaine, Paris (1956–58). In 1958–59 he studied at Harvard University, obtaining his A.M. in anthropology and social relations. He received the degree of *Docteur ès Lettres* at the Sorbonne in 1960.

From 1951 to 1956 he worked with the Israel Department of Antiquities for which he directed the following projects: excavations of Tell Abu Hawam (1952); excavations of Susita-Hippos (1952–53); archaeological survey of the central Negev desert (1953–55); excavations at Hassorea (1956).

From 1956 to 1958 he was Attaché de Recherches at the Centre National de la Recherche Scientifique, Paris. The major projects he led during this period were: survey of prehistoric art in Andalusia, Spain (1956); two field campaigns at Mount Bego, French Maritime Alps (1956–57); four field campaigns in the Camonica Valley, northern Italy (1956–58); a survey of prehistoric art in Bohuslaan, Sweden (1958).

In 1959 he led the project "Prehistoric art in the French and Italian Alps," supported by the American Philosophical Society, Philadelphia. In 1960 he led the expedition "Prehistoric art in the Negev desert, Israel," supported by the Israel Department of Antiquities, and the Wenner-Gren Foundation for Anthropological Research, New York. From 1961 to 1963 he headed "A Comparative Study of European Post-Palaeolithic Art," supported by the Bollingen Foundation, New York, and the Calouste Gulbenkian Foundation, Lisbon.

In 1962 he led a further campaign at Tell Abu Hawam, Israel. In 1963 he directed the excavations at Dos Dell'Arca, Italy.

In 1964 he was appointed director of the Seminario e Centro Camuno di Studi Preistorici ed Etnologici, Italy, where he spends most of the summer season. In the winters, he teaches at the University of Tel Aviv.

Among his publications are: *La Grande Roche de Naquane*, Paris (1960); *Camonica Valley*, New York (1961); *Palestine Before the Hebrews*, New York (1963). He has written numerous papers on archaeology and prehistoric and primitive art for scientific journals in the United States, in Europe, and in Israel.

N. AVIGAD is Professor of Archaeology at the Hebrew University, Jerusalem, and chairman of its Department of Archaeology. He received his M.A. and Ph.D. at that institution. Since 1930 he has been active in numerous excavations and research projects. In 1953–55 and in 1958 Professor Avigad directed the excavations at Beth She'arim, which is a joint project of the Israel Exploration Society and the Hebrew University. Excavations at this site started as far back as 1936 when they were headed by Professor B. Mazar.

The late Professor M. Schwabe participated as Greek epigrapher, Mr. Moshe Yoffe as permanent supervisor in the field, and Mr. I. Dunayewski as architect. Various assistants and students of the Department of Archaeology took part in the excavation.

PESSAH BAR-ADON was educated at the Rabbinical College and Hebrew University of Jerusalem. He has engaged in extensive field work since 1936, when he took part in the expeditoin at Beth She'arim. In 1944–45 he joined the expedition of Professors Mazar and M. Stekelis at Beth Yerah, and in 1948–49 he was with Professor Mazar at Tell Qasile. At the same time he became a staff member of the Israel Department of Antiquities, and he has headed expeditions on its behalf since 1951, particularly in the Judaean desert. These surveys have revealed much information about the hitherto unknown Chalcolithic period in this area.

The expeditions in the valleys between En-gedi and Masada worked for two seasons, in 1960 and 1961. J. Aviram was co-ordinator of four groups during the operations. N. Avigad was in charge of Group A (southern bank of Nahal Seelim); Y. Aharoni, of Group B (northern bank of Nahal Seelim and Nahal Hardof); P. Bar-Adon, of Group C (Nahal Mishmar, Nahal Asahel, and southern bank of Nahal Hever); Y. Yadin of Group D (northern bank of Nahal Hever· and Nahal Arugot). Professor Bar-Adon's group worked again in 1962. A book on the Cave of the Treasure was published in 1967.

CRYSTAL M. BENNETT, born in England, holds an Honours degree in English Language and Literature and a postgraduate diploma in Education from Bristol University as well as a postgraduate diploma in Archaeology from

London University. She is a Fellow of the Society of Antiquaries of London. Until March 1965 she was assistant director of the British School of Archaeology in Jerusalem. Now she devotes her time to her own researches, particularly in eastern Jordan in the region once inhabited by the Edomites, whose territory the Nabataeans took over. She has recently concluded important excavations at Umm el-Biyara (which some scholars equate with biblical Sela) that have created great interest among biblical archaeologists and scholars. The excavations at Petra are sponsored by the British School of Archaeology in Jerusalem under the leadership of Mr. Peter Parr, lecturer in Palestinian Archaeology at the University of London, who has directed excavations there since 1958.

HARRIS DUNSCOMBE COLT, discoverer of the famous Colt Papyri, was born in New York. He is a trustee of the Archaeological Institute of America and the American Schools of Oriental Research, and is president of the Colt Archaeological Institute. Besides the excavations at Zin, a private expedition conducted under the auspices of the British School of Archaeology, he has excavated in Malta, Syria, Palestine, Egypt, and England. Mr. Colt's assistant director of the expedition at Zin was T. J. Colin Bailey.

FRANK M. CROSS, JR., is Hancock Professor of Hebrew and other Oriental Languages at Harvard University. A native of California, he was educated at Maryville College, Tennessee (B.A. 1942), McCormick Theological Seminary, Chicago (B.D. 1946), and Johns Hopkins University (Ph.D. 1950). He has served as annual professor at the American Schools of Oriental Research in Jerusalem (1953–54), and archaeological director of Hebrew Union College, Jerusalem (1963–64). He is a member of the international staff editing the later finds of the Dead Sea scrolls (1953). In 1955 he was co-director of the archaeological exploration of the Judaea Buqei'ah. Mr. Cross's special interests are palaeography and epigraphy. He is the author (with D. N. Freedman) of *Studies in Yahvistic Poetry* and *Early Hebrew Orthography*. In the area of Dead Sea scroll studies, he has written *The Ancient Library of Qumran*, and edited *Scrolls from the Wilderness of the Dead Sea.*

MOSHE DOTHAN was born in Cracow, Poland, and educated at the Hebrew University of Jerusalem, where he received his M.A. and Ph.D. degrees. Since 1950 he has been a member of the staff of the Israel Department of Antiquities. Since 1957 he has served as director of its division of excavations and archaeological surveys. In the years 1962–65, he lectured on archaeology at the Technion in Haifa. In 1965–66 he was a member of the Institute for Advanced Study in Princeton.

His excavations cover a wide chronological span in Palestinian archaeology—from the Chalcolithic of Beersheba (H. Bittar), to a Byzantine monastery at Sha'ar Ha'aliya. Among his excavations are Meser, Nahariyah, Afulah, Azor, Hamath-Tiberias. The site of Hamath-Tiberias, the first in which the remains of ancient synagogues were excavated stratigraphically, provides most valuable information on this subject. The Ashdod project started with the excavation of Tell Mor, the inland harbor of ancient Ashdod.

The excavation of Tell Ashdod is part of the Ashdod project sponsored by a joint Israeli-American expedition. The participating institutions were represented by Dr. David N. Freedman of the Pittsburgh Theological Seminary (first two sessions), Dr. James L. Swauger of the Carnegie Museum, Pittsburgh, and the writer on behalf of the Israel Department of Antiquities. Each of the three campaigns lasted about six to eight weeks in the summers of 1962, 1963, and 1965. The excavations of Tell Ashdod are a long-range program. Two more seasons are already envisaged. Besides the directors of the expedition, the staff comprised archaeologists both from the United States— mainly from the Pittsburgh Theological Seminary—and from the Israel Department of Antiquities, including graduate and postgraduate students of Hebrew University of Jerusalem.

AVRAHAM EITAN was born in Israel and educated at the Hebrew University, Jerusalem, where he received his degree from the Department of Archaeology. His field experience came as a member of the archaeological expedition at Hazor. Major field work was done at Ramat Rahel (1959–60), in the caves of the Judaean desert, Arad, Masada, Tell Rosh-Ha'ain (Ras el A'in), and at Ramla (early Islamic period) in 1965.

Mr. Eitan was chief assistant at the excavations of Tell Nagila, which was sponsored by the Institute for Mediterranean Studies. Ruth Amiran (q.v.) served as field director. The United States Department of State financed the two seasons, 1962–63, through local counterpart funds. Archaeology students of the Hebrew University and of the Bezalel Art School formed the main professional staff, while students of the Negev Seminar, organized by the Institute for Mediterranean Studies, as well as volunteers from various countries also assisted. U. Paran served as chief surveyor and M. Padan-Piletzki as photographer.

PAUL LESLIE GARBER received his A.B. from the College of Wooster, Ohio, in 1933, his B.D. and Th.M. from Louisville Presbyterian Theological Seminary in 1936 and 1937, the year he was ordained to the Presbyterian ministry. In 1939 he received his Ph.D. from Duke University. He has done post-doctoral work at the University of Chicago, Johns Hopkins, Harvard, Princeton, and the Biblical Seminary, New York City, and at the American School of Classical Studies in Athens, the American Academy, and the Pontifical Biblical Institute in Rome.

Dr. Garber held a fellowship at Duke University, taught at Louisville Presbyterian Theological Seminary, and since 1943 has been Professor of Bible at Agnes Scott College, Decatur, Georgia. From 1939 to 1943 he was pastor of the Trinity Avenue Presbyterian Church in Durham, North Carolina. He is a regional and national officer of the American Academy of Religion, the Society of Biblical Literature and Exegesis, and the Archaeological Institute of America, a member of the American Schools of Oriental Research and the Oriental Institute of the University of Chicago, and the author of articles on Bible history and archaeology.

The late E. G. Howland, professional modelmaker of Troy, Ohio, at his own expense, engineered and constructed the scale representation of Solomon's Temple, for which Dr. Garber did the research.

ZEEV GOLDMANN, born in Thüringen, Germany, studied history of art and archaeology at the universities of Berlin, Vienna, Hamburg, and later Halle, from which he graduated. Forced to emigrate in 1936, he left for Palestine. Since 1953 he has worked with the Israel Department of Antiquities in western Galilee, excavating a number of Byzantine, Roman, and Canaanite sites, including Akko. During the War of Liberation (1948) he collected Arab and Druse folkloric items, which became the nucleus of the Akko Municipal Museum, of which he is the director. Since 1962, Dr. Goldmann has lectured on Islamic art at the University of Tel Aviv, where he also conducts a seminar on Islamic sites in the Holy Land.

OLEG GRABAR was born in Strasbourg, France, and studied at the University of Paris and at Harvard, where he received his B.A. in 1950. After graduate work at Paris (License d'Histoire, 1950) and at Princeton (M.A. 1953, Ph.D. 1955) he became a Fellow of the American School of Oriental Research at Jerusalem and of the American Numismatic Society. He has received a number of other important fellowships and honors, and since 1957 has acted as Near Eastern editor of *Ars Orientalis*. His publications include four books and ten major articles. He joined the faculty of the University of Michigan in 1954 and is now acting chairman of the Department of the History of Art. During 1960–61 he was director of the American School of Oriental Research, Jerusalem.

Excavations were conducted at Khirbat al-Mafjar between 1935 and 1948 by the Department of Antiquities of Palestine, under the direction of R. W. Hamilton and with D. C. Baramki as field director. Preliminary reports have been published in the *Quarterly* of the Department of Antiquities of Palestine, and the final report on the excavations was published by Oxford University Press in 1959. It includes an article by Mr. Grabar.

JACOB KAPLAN, born in Poland in 1908, has lived in Israel since 1914. He is a graduate civil engineer of the Haifa Technical Institute, and has a doctorate in archaeology from the Hebrew University, Jerusalem. He is a member of the Archaeological Advisory Council of the State of Israel.

His first field experience was as a member of the Beth She'arim expedition, 1936–39, which was directed by Professor B. Mazar, of the Hebrew University, Jerusalem. During the 1940s he conducted the archaeological survey of the Yarkon Valley and Nahal Shorek, and in 1948–50 he was a member of the Tel Qasile expedition. Since 1955 he has conducted excavations at sites in the Tel Aviv area, which exposed settlement remains dating to the Neolithic and later periods.

At present his work is concentrated in two fields: research into the Neolithic and Chalcolithic periods in Israel, and the excavations of ancient Jaffa. These have been carried on intermittently since 1955. To date eight seasons of excavations have been conducted, on behalf of the Museum of the Antiquities of Tel Aviv-Jaffa and in collaboration with the Department of Antiquities and Museums of the Ministry of Education and Culture. The excavations were joined by graduate students in archaeology of the universities of Jerusalem and Tel Aviv. Also taking part in the work were epigraphic specialists in ancient Egyptian, Accadian, Greek, and Roman, as well as skilled numismatists.

KATHLEEN M. KENYON was born in London, the daughter of Sir Frederic Kenyon, director of the British Museum from 1911 to 1930. She was educated at St. Paul's Girls' School, London, and at Somerville College, Oxford, where she read Modern History. Her first introduction to archaeology was as an assistant to Miss G. Caton-Thompson on the British Association excavations at Zimbabwe, Southern Rhodesia, in 1929. In 1930 she was an assistant at the excavations of the Romano-British town of Verulamium (St. Albans), and she continued to work there under Dr. R. E. M. (later Sir Mortimer) Wheeler every year until 1935. In 1931 she began a long association with the British School of Archaeology in Jerusalem as an assistant to Mr. J. W. Crowfoot at Samaria, where work continued until 1935.

In 1935, Miss Kenyon became secretary of the newly formed Institute of Archaeology of the University of London. She remained on the staff of the Institute until 1962, as secretary till 1948, and then as lecturer in Palestinian archaeology till 1962, when she became principal of St. Hugh's College, Oxford.

Between 1936 and 1951, she directed excavations at Roman and Iron Age sites in England—at Leicester, Veroconium and the Wrekin, Shropshire, Southwark, London, Breedon-on-the-Hill, Leicestershire, and Sutton Walls, Herefordshire—and in North Africa at Sabratha.

In 1951 she became director of the British School of Archaeology in Jerusalem, and in 1952 resumed excavations in Palestine. From 1952 to 1958, she excavated at Jericho on behalf of the British School, the Palestine Exploration Fund, and the British Academy, in collaboration (in some years) with the American Schools of Oriental Research and the Royal Ontario Museum. The excavations provided evidence for the history of Jericho from its earliest beginnings ca. 8000 B.C., down to its destruction in the fourteenth century B.C., which may be associated with the biblical account in the Book of Joshua. The greatest interest of the results lay in the discovery of two highly developed stages of the earliest Neolithic.

In 1961 Miss Kenyon began excavations, planned to end in 1967, at Jerusalem, on behalf of the same three institutions, with collaboration from the École Biblique et Archéologique de St. Étienne and the Royal Ontario Museum. The major contribution to knowledge of these excavations has been to establish the plans of the successive stages of Jerusalem.

DIANA KIRKBRIDE was born in England and educated at the University of London, where she read Egyptology. She later came to prehistory, specializing in the earliest village settlements, by way of Kathleen M. Kenyon's excavations at Jericho. Since 1953 she has lived in the Hashemite Kingdom of Jordan, where she has taken part in numerous excavations, including five seasons at Jericho. She has directed work for the Jordan Department of Antiquities at both Jerash and Petra and, while at the latter site in 1956, she discovered the early Neolithic village of Beidha. This site was occupied about 9,000 years ago and forms the subject of current excavations. Miss Kirkbride has also worked at el-Jib with James B. Pritchard, at Deir 'Alla with H. J. Franken, and at Diban with A. D. Tushingham. These excavations and those in Turkey and in the Lebanon are in addition to her own work at Beidha and Wadi Rumm in Jordan and in the Beqa'a, Lebanon.

Diana Kirkbride is Gerald Avery Wainwright research fellow in Near Eastern archaeology at the University of Oxford. She holds an excavation fellowship for Beida from the Bollingen Foundation of New York and is a Fellow of the Society of Antiquaries of London. She is the wife of Hans Helbaek, the well-known palaeoethnobotanist.

The Beidha excavations are supported by the Bollingen Foundation of New York, the British Academy, and the Wenner-Gren Foundation for Anthropological Research. Earlier seasons' work was financed by the American Philosophical Society; the Ashmolean Museum, Oxford; the University Museum of Archaeology and Ethnology, Cambridge; the Royal Ontario Museum, Toronto; and the Palestine Exploration Fund.

The following specialists have worked in the field at Beidha: Dr. Hans Helbaek, palaeoethnobotanist; R. L. Raikes, hydrologist; Dr. Dexter Perkins, Jr., zoologist. Peder Mortensen of the National Museum, Copenhagen, is studying the flint material as well as taking part in the excavations. Assistance from the different departments of the Danish National Museum has been provided through Professor P. V. Glob, Director General of Antiquities. Colleagues and students from America, Denmark, Holland, England, and France have worked as assistants during the six seasons that had been undertaken through 1966. The Jordan Department of Antiquities under its director, Dr. Awni Dajani, has also assisted the work.

PAUL W. LAPP has been working in Jordan since 1961 as director of the American School of Oriental Research at Jerusalem where he is Professor of Ancient Near Eastern History and Archaeology. During this time he has conducted excavations at seven widely scattered sites in Jordan, and acted as archaeological adviser to the Jordan Government for the United States Agency for International Development. He holds a Ph.D. in educational administration from the University of California and a Th.D. in Semitic studies from Harvard University.

The excavations at Bab edh-Dhra' have been part of the regular archaeological program of the Jerusalem school. "The Cemetery at Bab edh-Dhra'" reports the results of the first of three campaigns conducted between 1965 and 1967 in the town and cemetery in the vicinity of the still-undiscovered biblical cities of Sodom and Gomorrah.

The staff for these expeditions included Professor E. F. Campbell, Jr., Bruce Dahlberg,

and the author from the American School; Martin Noth and Siegfried Mittmann of the German Evangelical Institute for Archaeology of the Holy Land; and Ronald Douglas of Heidelberg University. Fouad Zoghbi of Bethlehem was draftsman, Muhammed S. Kemal a surveyor, and Miss Renee Lund of Uppsala University aided in registration. Ibrahim Tarawneh of Kerak represented the Jordan Department of Antiquities, whose director, Dr. Awni Dajani, facilitated the work of the expedition in every way.

BENJAMIN MAZAR, born in 1906 in Germany, was educated at the universities of Berlin and Giessen (Ph.D. 1928). On the faculty of the Hebrew University of Jerusalem since 1942, Dr. Mazar was appointed professor there in 1951, later rector (1952–61) and president (1953–61). He was visiting professor at the University of Chicago in 1950–51 and at Brandeis in 1962–63. He is also the chairman of the Archaeological Board of Israel and president of the Israel Exploration Society.

Dr. Mazar has excavated at many Palestinian sites, notably Beth She'arim, Tell Qasile, and Engedi, and has published numerous books and articles on his work. Dr. Trude Dothan, Mr. I. Dunayewski, and graduates and students of the Archaeological Department of Hebrew University joined his expedition to Engedi during the years 1961–1965.

JEAN PERROT was born in France in 1920 and educated at the Sorbonne, at the École Pratique des Hautes Études, and at the École du Louvre. In 1945–46, he stayed at the Ecole Biblique et Archéologique in Jerusalem, on a scholarship granted by the Académie des Inscriptions et Belles-Lettres. In 1964, he was made a corresponding member of that institution. He entered the French Center for Scientific Research (C.N.R.S.) in 1946, where he specializes in the prehistory and protohistory of Southwest Asia. His particular interest is in the transition from food gathering to food production. He is now Maître de Recherche at the C.N.R.S. and Head of the French Center for Prehistoric and Protohistoric Research in Jerusalem.

M. Perrot taught in the United States in 1959 as visiting lecturer at the University of Chicago, Oriental Institute; in 1964 as visiting professor at Harvard; and in 1966 as visiting professor at the University of Michigan. He is author of *Proche-Orient Ancien I*, and numerous articles in scholarly journals.

M. Perrot made principal excavations from 1951 to 1961 in the Negev (Abu Matar, Safadi, W. Chazeh, W. Seita), a pastoral and agricultural culture in a semi-arid zone during the second half of the fourth millennium B.C., and since 1962 at Munhata in the Jordan Valley, a pre-pottery settlement of the seventh millennium B.C. He has also spent several seasons in the Upper Jordan Valley, Turkey, and Iran.

Mme. Thérèse Poulain (Josien), of the Musée de l'Homme of Paris, who studied the human remains, and M. Henri de Contenson, who worked on the pottery, joined the expedition in the Negev for one or more seasons. Mr. M. Negbi, of the Botanical Department of Hebrew University, took charge of the preliminary palaeobotanical study of the material. The mineralogical analyses were carried out by the laboratories of Professor Y. Bentor. Assistants from the Department of Antiquities and students of archaeology at Hebrew University and from abroad took part every season.

JAMES BENNETT PRITCHARD was born in 1909 in Louisville, Kentucky. He graduated from Asbury College (A.B. 1930) and Drew University (B.D. 1935) and received his Ph.D. from the University of Pennsylvania in 1942. He has served on the faculties of Crozer Theological Seminary, the American Schools of Oriental Research, the Church Divinity School of the Pacific, and the University of Pennsylvania, where he has been associated with the University Museum since 1950. Memberships include the American Historical Association, American Oriental Society, and Society of Biblical Literature. He was also the editor of the *Journal of the American Oriental Society*.

Dr. Pritchard began his field work in 1934 in Palestine. He has excavated at Jericho, at el-Jib, and at Tell es-Sa'idiyeh. He is the author of several books on the archaeology of the Near East in relation to the Old Testament and of numerous monographs, articles, and reviews.

The excavations were sponsored by the University Museum of the University of Pennsylvania, with the cooperation of the American School of Oriental Research in Jerusalem. The Department of Antiquities of the Hashemite Kingdom of Jordan not only granted a license for the excavations but helped in many other ways with the arrangements at el-Jib. Mr. G. Lankester Harding, Mr. Said Dura, and Dr. Awni Dajani rendered valuable assistance. In the deciphering and interpretation of the epigraphic materials the author has had the help of a number of scholars, who have examined either the materials or drawings and photographs. Frank M. Cross, Jr., R. de Vaux, J. T. Milik, W. F. Albright, G. L. Della Vida, Emil G. Kraeling, David Diringer, Sabatino Moscati, and the late Robert H. Pfeiffer made many helpful suggestions.

JAMES F. ROSS was born in Omaha, Nebraska, in 1927, and attended Doane College in Crete, Nebraska. He received his B.S. (1952) and Ph.D. (1955) from Union Theological Seminary in New York City and did additional graduate work at the American School of Oriental Research in Jerusalem. After teaching for four years in the Department of Religion at Dartmouth College, he joined the faculty of Drew University where he is now Associate Professor of Old Testament. He is a member of several scholarly societies and in 1965–66 served as archaeological director of the Hebrew Union College Biblical and Archaeological School in Jerusalem. Besides Shechem, his field experience includes a season as director of excavations at Gezer (1966) and several seasons as supervisor of Field VI at Hazor.

LAWRENCE E. TOOMBS was born in Canada and educated at Acadia University, the University of Toronto, and Drew University. In 1956–57 he was Fellow of the American School of Oriental Research in Jerusalem, and in 1961–62 studied at the Institute of Archaeology in London. His first field experience was as a member of Kathleen M. Kenyon's expedition at Jericho in 1957. Since then he has served as staff member of the Drew-McCormick expedition at Shechem in 1957, as assistant director in 1960, and as associate director in 1962 and 1966. He is now assistant director of the College of Wooster expedition at Pella in the Jordan River Valley.

The Drew-McCormick Archaeological Expedition is under the joint sponsorship of Drew University and McCormick Theological Seminary, in association with the American Schools of Oriental Research and with the financial support of the Bollingen Foundation. Dr. G. Ernest Wright is archaeological director, and Dr. Edward F. Campbell, Jr., assistant director. Dr. Toombs was field supervisor in 1957 and associate archaeological director in 1960, 1962, and 1966; Dr. Ross was in charge of excavations in the courtyard temple area in 1960, 1962, and 1964. Both authors are on the faculty of Drew University. Dr. R. J. Bull was field supervisor in 1956, 1957, 1960, and 1962, and directed the excavations on Tell er-Ras in 1964 and 1966.

YIGAEL YADIN was born in Jerusalem in 1917; he received his M.A. (1945) and Ph.D. (1955) from Hebrew University, and is now Professor of Archaeology at that institution. His experience in organization is military as well as archaeological—during 1947–49 and 1949–52 he was Chief of Operations and Chief of Staff of the Israeli Defense Forces. Dr.

Yadin's publications include a book on two of the Dead Sea scrolls, *The War between the Sons of Light and the Sons of Darkness,* and *A Genesis Apocryphon, A Message of the Scrolls, Masada, Warfare in Biblical Lands in the Light of Archaeology,* and *Finds from the Cave of Letters,* as well as numerous articles in scholarly journals. In 1960–61 Professor Yadin led an expedition in the Judaean Desert, where he discovered the Bar Kochbah letters. Through 1963–65 he headed the Masada expedition.

The James A. de Rothschild expedition at Hazor has been operating for four seasons (1955–58) on behalf of the Anglo-Israel Exploration Committee, the Palestine Jewish Colonization Association, and the Government of Israel. The excavations, under Dr. Yadin's direction, have been conducted with a professional staff of about forty-five and as many as two hundred laborers. The principal assistants were Dr. Y. Aharoni, Ruth Amiran, Trude Dothan, M. Dunayewski, C. Epstein, M. Megiddon, J. Perrot, and M. Dothan.

Index